Ten
Greatest
Love
Stories

Leisure Entertainment Service Co., Inc.
(LESCO Distribution Group)
And
Dorchester Media LLC.

For Paul J. Gross,
a man who turned good ideas
into great things. Sorely missed
and deeply loved by family and
friends

Leisure Entertainment Service Co., Inc. (LESCO Distribution Group)
65 Richard Road Ivyland, PA 18974   www.leisureent.com

Published by special arrangement with Dorchester Media, LLC.

Printed in the United States of America.

A Special LESCO Edition

Dorchester Media is
a consumer magazine publisher.

Our Women's Romance Group of
eight titles includes the world's
largest and best selling women's
romance magazine, *True Story*.
True Story has a great history
(1919) and heritage and continues to
touch the heart, mind and soul of
readers by sharing everyday
experiences of romantic life.

In addition to *True Story*, sister
publications include *True Confessions*,
True Romance, and *True Love*.
Special collector magazines from
the substantial archive include
True Story Remember When.

For more information on all of
Dorchester Media publications, write
to Publisher, Dorchester Media,
333 Seventh Avenue, 11th Floor,
New York, N.Y. 10001.

We hope you enjoy the book.

∽ Table Of Contents ∽

This book consists of true stories. Names, characters, places and incidents were changed. Any resemblance to actual events, locales, or persons, living or dead, is entirely coincidental.

An *Original* Publication of Dorchester Media, LLC.

ISBN:
First LESCO Edition Printing: February 2006
1-60016-008-5
Printed in the U.S.A.

Leisure Entertainment Service Co., Inc.
(LESCO Distribution Group)
65 Richard Road Ivyland, PA 18974
www.leisureent.com

TEN
GREATEST
LOVE
STORIES

LOVER'S LEGACY

This is the happy time, I kept telling myself. The happiest time in a woman's life. And some of the time it was. It was so wonderful holding Katy, listening to those little mewing sounds she made as I fed her, feeling my heart stand still when she stared at me as if she already knew that I was her mother.

But then I'd think of Clay, and ache with wishing he could be with us. I wanted him to know what it was like having a child of your own, loving her so hard right from the very beginning. I wanted him to know how it made up for all the hopelessness and the worry and the guilt—the guilt especially. It was always there, nibbling away at our happiness. The first time Clay kissed me, the first time he told me he loved me—those moments were marred because we both knew I'd no right to be there in his arms. He was married and he'd told me he would never leave his wife.

"I can't promise you a thing, Janet," he'd said. "I want you to know that. I can't walk out on a wife who has depended on me for almost seventeen years. I don't mean it's a problem of money. That part would be easy. It's—well, it all boils down to that Nora hasn't a soul in the world to turn to except me. I couldn't leave her. It would be like walking out on a child."

So I knew all that. Only it didn't make a difference. Because by then I needed Clay just as much as he needed me.

I'd certainly needed him that rainy night it all started. I'd dashed out of the utility company building after work, trying to catch a bus that was standing at the corner. Instead, I slipped and fell. It was Clay who picked me up.

He handed me his handkerchief so I could mop myself off. "Don't you remember me?" he asked. "I'm Clay Stevens. Your boss called you in once when there was some difficulty over my bill. Remember? I've just come from his office now."

I remembered him then, and so I didn't have any hesitation about accepting his offer to drive me home. Maybe I wouldn't have hesitated anyway. You only had to look at Clay, and it was right there in his face, the kind of man he was—good and kind and gentle.

"You're drenched," he said as I got in the car beside him. "You need something to warm you up." And though it sounded like one of those usual come-ons it wasn't. If Clay had any wolfish ideas, he would have taken me to a dimly lit bar, not to a big, noisy, bright restaurant. But that was where we went, and we drank coffee and talked, and it was an island of warmth for both of us at the end of a gray day.

It was when we were back in the car again that Clay mentioned his wife. "I should have called her," he said. "She worries when I'm late getting home." And it was silly how I felt that sudden sharp pang. There was no reason on earth why I should feel like that. Only I'd never met a man like Clay before.

It was funny how I kept thinking about him, a man who must have been almost forty, a married man who wasn't at all romantic. Once I even looked him up in the telephone directory, just to see his name. And there, under his home listing, was his business address, the Clay Stevens Electronics Company. It came as a shock to find out he was the owner of the attractive modern building I'd passed so often on my way to lunch.

I felt so self-conscious after that, I couldn't bring myself to walk that way. And I probably would never have seen Clay again if the bus strike hadn't happened a few weeks later. I remember how my heart jumped that first night of the strike when I came out of work and saw him waiting.

"I was worried about you getting home," he said.

No one had worried about me since my mother died, and that was when I was only eight. Afterward, I'd been shunted around from one aunt and uncle to another, and it was plain what a nuisance I was to all of them, an unwanted child whose own father hadn't bothered to keep in touch with her. I'd never thought much about my father until I met Clay. But then it was like I suddenly realized all I had missed, not having one. It was almost as if in finding Clay I had found my father again.

Afterward, Clay told me he had felt that way about me in the beginning. Not fatherly exactly, but as if I were a younger sister who needed looking after. It was just that he was worried about me, he said. A nineteen-year-old girl living alone in a rooming house. He said he didn't even know when his feeling about me started changing.

But I knew when my mine did. It was the day the bus strike ended. I remember how empty I felt when there was no longer any reason for Clay to take me home. And then it was as if something exploded inside of me when I got to the bus stop and saw him waiting for me.

Everything was different after that. I'd wake up in the morning with happiness singing inside me, and I'd keep watching the clock at work, counting the hours until I could see Clay again. And then when I did, when I got to the car and he leaned over to open the door for me, it was as if I could feel my heart coming alive.

There were just those twenty minutes or so together, morning and night. But the minutes began lengthening little by little. Clay started driving more slowly, and then we'd sit in the car talking a while after we got to my rooming house. They didn't seem to mean much at the time, those extra minutes. But they all led up to the evening he pulled me back as I started to get out of the car. His arms went around me, and then he kissed me. It was such a light kiss. It shouldn't have been enough to send my senses reeling like that.

"I'm sorry, Janet," he said then. "I acted like a fool. But it won't happen again. I promise you."

He wasn't waiting for me the next morning. But it was as if I had known he wouldn't be there, so it didn't hit me as hard as if it had come as a real shock. There was just that dull ache that kept growing and growing until I felt I couldn't stand another moment of it.

It was another week before I saw him again. But the ache didn't go even then. Instead, I felt cold fear, seeing the misery in Clay's eyes when he opened the car door for me. A few minutes later I knew why. He told me this was going to be the last time we would be together. I couldn't say a word. It wasn't fair to his wife, he went on. It wasn't fair to me, either.

"That's what I can't live with," he said. "What I'm doing to you."

It was when he said that, when he looked at me, I didn't have to wonder anymore. I knew he loved me. And as his arms went around me and we clung together, I had to tell him that I couldn't let him go.

So instead of resolving never to see each other again, we admitted we could never stop seeing each other, and we kept driving around and talking as if it was all decided that we were going to spend the rest of our lives together. That was when Clay told me he couldn't leave his wife. And it was when I said it didn't make any difference, because I loved him so much there wouldn't be any kind of life for me without him.

It could have been so sordid, having to find ways to be together. But it never was. The first time we went to a motel together, I wore the ring he had given me, his mother's wedding ring. I couldn't feel any fear after that. If I had needed any proof of the way he felt about me, that would have been more than enough to convince me.

It was so wonderful being with him. So wild and

exciting and tender and loving all at the same time. Then suddenly that part of it was over. That first part of being in love, when it's like nobody else exists except the two of you. Then a new dimension was added to our love.

I'll never forget Clay's face when I told him about the baby. He looked so stunned, the way I must have looked when I first knew for sure. Then, even before he took me in his arms, it was like he was going through all the other feelings that had hit me, too. The deep joy that came in spite of our not having a right to feel it, and the excitement and the wonder. He didn't have to tell me how much he had longed for a child of his own. It was all written there on his face.

From then on, though, the guilt kept biting deeper, so much more intense now that there was a child to be considered. And yet it was another bond drawing Clay and me even closer to each other. The first almost unbearable excitement was gone, but another deeper emotion had taken its place. It was the kind of love married people must feel, made up of tenderness and devotion, so they become friends as well as lovers.

The day I gave up my job, I moved into the apartment Clay had found for me. He had been so apologetic about the neighborhood, explaining that it was in an old part of town where there wasn't much chance of his running into people he knew. But I didn't care about anything except having a place where we could be together sometimes. Anyway, I loved the big, old-fashioned rooms, and I worked hard making them into the only home I had ever known.

Of course I missed not having Clay with me when I went shopping for things for the apartment. It would have been so much fun choosing our furniture together. But that was one of the things I wouldn't let myself think about. Like calling myself Mrs. Grant and telling the woman on the floor below that I was a widow.

It was the lying I hated most of all. Especially as the time for the baby's birth kept getting closer. It was as if even before it was born, we were burdening it with our own guilt—giving it a father who had never existed and a name that I'd picked out of a telephone book.

Of course I had known it would have to be that way, that my child could never know Clay as a father. But I had never thought about it as deeply as I did in all those hours alone in the apartment. I came to realize then, too, that the apartment was really only my home. Not Clay's. Just mine until the baby would come to share it with me. For all his love and devotion, Clay never could never really be a husband to me. Even when the baby was born, he wouldn't be with me. It hurt thinking of that, knowing I would have to go to the hospital alone and bring the baby home alone.

But I could never let Clay know how I felt about that. We had so little time to be together, I didn't want to spoil any part of it for him. I never knew when to expect him, except for those times he would call me to let me know he was coming for lunch. Aside from those lunches, we just had to make the most of the times he could get away. Sometimes, and they were the best times of all, he'd manage a few hours in the evening. And then it was like heaven, with the curtains drawn, closing out everything but our own private world.

New Year's Eve was one of those times. It was almost eight o'clock when Clay came, and he had to get back by midnight to the country club and the party he had left. That was the only time he might be missed, he told me. But in the meantime we had more than three hours to be together.

"I thought at least we could have a drink together," he said. "There's a place I went to lunch the other day. A kind of old-fashioned place that isn't likely to be too popular on New Year's Eve. But I have a feeling you'll like it."

"Of course I will," I said. As if I wouldn't like any place just so long as Clay was there!

Clay kept holding my hand under his on the steering wheel as we drove out to the inn in the country, and when we got there everything else was perfect, too. We didn't have to wait for a table. As Clay had said, it wasn't the sort of place people were likely to pick for New Year's Eve. But I loved the quiet of it and the soft lights, and I loved drinking our New Year's toast together. It didn't really make any difference that midnight was still an hour and a half away.

A light snow was falling when we went out to the car again. There wasn't enough of it to make the roads seem dangerous. But Clay's whole attention was fixed on his driving. I felt so relaxed and happy that I didn't feel at all neglected, not having his hand on mine. It was enough just sitting there beside him as we drove along the curving country road.

We had just rounded one of those curves when we saw the flashing red lights ahead of us, indicating there'd been some kind of accident. Clay stopped the car so suddenly to avoid it that I was almost thrown out of my seat. Then the pain came, the sharp, tearing pain that was so intense I couldn't even cry out, and, almost simultaneously, I felt fear. I just sat there numbly, feeling ashamed for worrying about myself or even the baby as I looked at the pile of twisted metal that once had been two cars.

It didn't seem real. Any part of it. The police cars and the ambulance and the blinking red lights. We sat there frozen, as though we were caught in a particularly vivid nightmare, as an ambulance pulled away and a police car followed it. Then a state trooper beckoned us on, and as we passed the wreckage I caught a glimpse of a blanket-covered body lying beside it. So it was almost a relief when the pain came again, so strong it blotted out the horror of that scene.

I knew for sure it was the baby coming, and I caught frantically at Clay's arm. Then, as he stopped the car, I clung to him and I couldn't hold back my fears any longer.

"It's the baby!" I cried. "I know it's the baby. Oh, Clay, I'm sorry, making all this trouble for you. But you'll have to get me to the hospital. I, I—"

"Trouble!" he said, and there was a kind of fury in his voice. "Trouble for me? My God, Janet, what about you? Do you think anything else on earth matters except you?"

He started the car, and this time he took my hand again and held it under his as he drove. I could feel it pressing down on mine as the pains kept coming closer together, so close they frightened me because of the distance we still had to go. Then we swerved into a driveway, and I saw the parked ambulance and police cars outside a small brick building.

"It's the new community hospital," Clay said as he helped me out of the car. "I wasn't sure it had opened yet. But we're in luck, it seems."

His arms began shaking as he held me. "I'm going in with you," he said. "I didn't realize what it would be like. Now nothing can keep me away from you. I don't care—"

"No," I said, and when he tried to argue I put my hand over his lips. "You've got to be reasonable, Clay. Don't you see you're only making it harder?" I pulled away from him and stumbled toward the entrance, and there was nothing he could do but let me go.

There was no one at the desk when I went in. The reception room was empty. I got really frightened then as I almost doubled over with a new wave of pain. But as I stood there holding on to the desk, a nurse rushed over to me. "Oh, no!" she cried. "Not another maternity case on top of everything else!"

I remember how those words kept coming back and how they hurt, as if my having a baby was just a nuisance to everybody. It's the only thing I really remembered that and how I kept wishing the baby would be a boy. For Clay. Everything else was just kind of a blur.

Then, just before midnight, my little girl was born, and I heard her cry. Only, for some reason, it was like two cries coming practically together.

It was funny how vivid that impression was and how I was so sure I'd had twins. I told the nurse that when she brought Katy to me the next morning. "I thought there were two babies," I said.

"There were," she said. "And both of them girls. One of them is Mrs. Harrison's across the corridor. Your babies were born only minutes apart, and we could only spare one doctor and one nurse to look after the two of you. I'd hate to go through another night like that!"

"There was an accident, wasn't there?" I said.

She nodded. "Five people were brought in, and two of them are still on the critical list. And with the hospital opening just the day before yesterday, we weren't prepared to deal with an emergency like that. Actually, the only bright spot yesterday was the babies. They're so adorable. Both of them."

I thought of my Katy and wished Clay was with me to enjoy her, too. I missed him terribly. Of course I'd known it would have to be like this, and I thought I had prepared myself for it. Only I hadn't. I suppose no one is ever really prepared for heartbreak until she goes through it.

During the rest of my stay in the hospital, I couldn't help being jealous of Mrs. Harrison. It seemed as if she was never alone. There were so many relatives and friends visiting her all the time, and in the evenings her husband was always there. Those were the worst times, when I couldn't stop longing for Clay. When I'd know how lonely he must be, too.

I wanted him to share my delight in the baby, but I couldn't even telephone him to talk about her! That was another thing we had decided and that I had to learn to accept. I'd keep telling myself that it had to be that way. That it would probably always have to be that way, and we could never be together when we needed each other the most.

But I forgot all that the day he called me. I knew it was Clay when the nurse told me there was a telephone call for me. I was so excited I couldn't even talk at first when I picked up the phone from her desk. Then my words came out in a rush.

"That baby's so darling!" I said. And I was glad the nurse had left me alone, because I couldn't have managed to sound as though Clay were just a friend. "I can't wait to have you see her. It won't be long now. The day after tomorrow."

"I'll be there," he said. And then his voice got all choked up with emotion, too, as he told me how much he loved me and missed me.

I had to take Katy home in her hospital nightgown and a borrowed blanket. But the minute I got inside the apartment, I dressed her in her own clothes. I smiled as I put on the blue sweater I had knitted for her because I was so sure she was going to be a boy. It seemed so silly suddenly. As if it made any difference, or as if I could have loved her any more!

As if it made any difference to Clay, either! When he saw Katy, his eyes looked the way his voice had sounded over the telephone, so full of pride and emotion he was almost crying.

No father could have loved a baby more. No child could have been more secure in that love than Katy. Even when she wasn't really a baby anymore, when she began talking and paying attention to things, I'd think how foolish I had been, worrying that we could never really be a family. As if calling Clay "Uncle" instead of "Daddy" made any real difference. The love they felt for each other was the important thing, not the name. It was that way with us, too. No husband and wife could have more to offer each other than we did.

Only it did make a difference. I found that out on Katy's second birthday. We had planned for it so long, the first birthday that would really have meaning for her because she could understand what it was all about—the cake and the candles and the presents. It would make up for being alone on Christmas, knowing Clay would be with us then.

I made a casserole for lunch so it wouldn't make any difference if Clay had to be a few minutes late, and Katy was almost as excited as I was as I decorated the table with flowers and favors, making it a real party. She had made up a little song about Uncle Clay coming, and she sang it over and over for me.

When it got to be lunchtime, Katy kept running to the window to watch for Clay. I just smiled at her eagerness at first. Then it was like the smile was pinned on my face, and I stood over by the window, too, looking down at the street and feeling the seconds and the minutes and finally an hour tick away in my heart.

By the time the telephone rang, I was almost sick with tension and disappointment.

"It's the first chance I've had to call you," Clay said. His voice sounded as disappointed as I felt, but I couldn't think of his hurt then. Only my own and Katy's. The fear that something might have happened to him had changed to a kind of outrage. But I made myself bite back the bitter words before I could say them. We had so little time together. I couldn't spoil it by quarreling.

So I listened as he told me his wife had come to

the office just as he was leaving. "She wanted me to look at a new dress for the New Year's Eve party tonight before she bought it," he explained. "There wasn't a thing I could do about it. She's always so unsure of her own judgment, like a child, and—"

I could hear the edge in my voice as I cut him off abruptly. There wasn't anything I could do about that. But I picked my words carefully. "That's all right, Clay," I said. "I know how things are."

But I hadn't really known. Not until then. The anger was still there as I turned away from the phone. A child, he had called her, a woman three years older than he was, a woman of over forty, old enough to be my mother. And her new dress was more important to him than Katy's birthday.

It was as if everything finally went into sharp focus then, as if my mind had finally accepted what I had tried to reason away: No matter how much Clay loved us, we could never really count on him. His wife came first with him. Even the love he felt for me, the love I couldn't doubt even then, couldn't compete with his sense of loyalty to Nora.

There was nothing I could really cling to. For all Clay's devotion and generosity, Katy and I would always have to live in the backwater of his life. We would always have to see him furtively, love him furtively. The leftovers of his time would always have to be enough.

I kept on thinking about it all through the forced gaiety of Katy's party—as she blew out the candles on her cake, three in all because I'd added an extra one "for her to grow on." And I was still thinking about it after I'd finally tucked her in bed for her afternoon nap. I wondered what it would be like really sharing a man's life. Going to sleep in his arms and waking up with him in the morning. Seeing him off to work and welcoming him home at night, and looking forward to weekends when he would always be there. I was missing so much.

But the bitterness didn't last. Even before I saw Clay again, I had buried it along with all the other things that couldn't bear remembering. I'd think of all I had, and how it made up for what I didn't have. I'd remind myself how it was always so wonderful when we were together. And how we had never lost the romantic part of loving each other. I told myself that, in a way, we had even more than some married people.

The next time Clay came, it turned out to be another party for Katy, with new presents and another cake that Clay had ordered for her. So what difference did it really make that her birthday was over—or that when he left, it was like a light going out in the room?

Then, in time, that new philosophy of mine was swept away, too. Katy was almost four when Clay had his first heart attack. I didn't really worry at first when he didn't come to see us. There had been periods before when I hadn't seen him for a few days at a time. But when a week passed, I couldn't reason away the panic that kept crowding in more and more.

I had been reading the papers, so I knew he hadn't been in an accident. Of course if he were ill, I would have no way of knowing. But he'd never had as much as a cold in all the time I'd known him, so I didn't worry about that too much.

When another two weeks went by, another kind

of fear kept crowding into my mind. The pain went so deep the first time I had the thought—the thought that this could be his way of ending an unhappy situation—that I went weak with shock. But once the thought had come, I couldn't tear it out of my heart again.

Afterward, I felt so ashamed for thinking that. As if Clay would ever desert Katy and me! Even if he had stopped loving me, there would still be Katy and his obligation to her. Only I was so torn with worry and fear, I couldn't think clearly anymore.

But I still had to think of Katy and her needs. I had drawn so much out of the savings account Clay had started for me that I'd soon have to find some way of supporting her. But on the very day I decided to call up my old boss at the utility company, a messenger brought me a letter.

At first there was only the relief as I recognized Clay's handwriting on the envelope. Then as I opened it and saw all the money, I was so sure Clay had decided to break off with me that I couldn't bring myself to read the note enclosed with it. But when I finally braced myself, it was the "darling" I saw first, and then I read the rest through tears of guilt and love.

He had been ill, he wrote. I wasn't to worry, because he was getting better and in another week he would be leaving the hospital. But it would be another month at least before he'd be able to see me. He asked me to give Katy a kiss for him, and he said he loved us both. My heart twisted as I read that, and I made a solemn promise I'd never doubt his love again.

It was easier waiting after that. But when I saw

Clay again and saw how thin he was and how the lines around his mouth had deepened and how even his eyes had changed, I knew that worry was another thing I would have to learn to live with. Because Clay had had a heart attack.

"You mustn't worry," he said when he told me. "It wasn't a really bad one. I wouldn't even tell you about it if it weren't for the fact that it made me realize I should make some arrangements for you and Katy.

"I kept thinking about it. And worrying. That's about all you can do in a hospital. I can't take care of you in my will. You understand that, don't you? I couldn't hurt Nora like that. But then I thought of another way, and I had a long talk with Ben Allen. He's a good friend as well as my lawyer, and I can trust him to take care of things without Nora having to know.

"If there's ever an emergency like this again, you just get in touch with Ben and he'll see to everything. If it's nothing serious, he'll give you money to tide you over temporarily. And—and if anything should ever happen to me, he has instructions for taking care of you and Katy financially."

He took me in his arms then, and for a while we just stood there, holding on to each other as if we couldn't bear to let go again.

"Stop looking at me like that," he said then. "As if I were a ghost or something! I'll still be around to dance at Katy's wedding. Heart attacks aren't the death sentence they used to be."

When he smiled, his eyes didn't look so different anymore. And his voice sounded so sure that I could believe him—as long as he was there to reassure me. But it was different when he was gone. Sometimes, no matter how hard I tried to fight it, the worry tortured me. When even a day went by without my seeing or hearing from him, the panic would start again.

Then, little by little, those bad times started dwindling. Clay began to put on weight, and when summer came and he got tanned, he looked so strong and healthy it was hard to believe he had ever been sick at all. Everything seemed so perfect that summer.

Another year went by, and Katy started school in the fall. Like any mother, I guess, I hated to see her go. It meant my baby was taking her first step toward growing up and away from me.

She had always been such a happy, laughing child, so different from both Clay and me. I used to tease Clay about that sometimes. "Your ancestors must have been gypsies," I said once. "Katy has to take after somebody—and with her liveliness and that dark hair of hers, it certainly isn't either you or me."

Remembering my own lonely childhood, I was glad Katy had such a happy personality. She could have been lonely, too, with no other children in the apartment house to play with. At least that was one good thing about her going to school. She'd make friends her own age.

By the time Katy was in first grade, she had plenty of friends. The quiet apartment woke up as soon as school was over for the day. There would always be at least one other child coming home with her, most often a pert little redhead named Donna who lived on the next street.

But one day Katy came home crying, and when I tried to question her she almost pushed me away and ran into her room. It was so unlike Katy to act that way. And she had never closed a door against me before. I was worried, so I followed her.

"I made some cookies this morning," I said to her. "I thought maybe you and one of your friends could have a tea party. Suppose I call Donna's mother and ask if she can come over?"

Katy changed into a small cyclone, flying at me and hitting me with her fists. "Don't call her!" she said as she sobbed. "She said she wouldn't let Donna play with me anymore. She—she says I'm not fit to play with nice little girls! She says you're— Oh, Mommy, you aren't bad, are you?"

I can still feel the shock of it, even now. I suppose I should have expected something like that would be bound to happen. But the people in the apartment had always seemed friendly, and it had never occurred to me that they would gossip about me.

If it was only Clay and me involved, it would have been bad enough. But having it touch Katy was more than I could bear. It was all I could do to answer her over the ache in my throat.

"Do you think I'm bad?" I asked. And when she shook her head furiously and flung herself into my arms, I had to reassure her. "Grownups say things they don't really mean sometimes," I said. "And even though they're sorry afterward, it's best not to listen when they say mean things. Donna will be around again before you know it. And in the meantime, you have plenty of other little girls to play with."

"I know," Katy said. "But I like Donna best."

A child forgets quickly, and that's a blessing. We had our tea party together, and by morning Katy was her own happy self again. I didn't tell Clay about the incident, and when weeks went by and nothing else happened, I was glad I hadn't worried him. I was almost certain the whole thing had been made up of nothing more than Donna's exaggerated imagination. And my own sense of guilt.

That Christmas was such a happy one. Katy and I had just finished opening our presents when suddenly there was a knock on the door. It was Clay, and I remember how exciting and wonderful it was to see him standing there and have his arms reach out to enfold both of us. We were really a family then, having breakfast together and opening the presents he had brought us and looking at the Christmas shows on TV.

Every moment of those two hours stands out so clearly. The way Clay laughed over the Santa Claus suit I had put on to amuse Katy. The way his eyes lighted up when Katy gave him an unexpected hug. But most of all I remember the way he held me so hard when it was time for him to leave, as if—as if he sensed it was the last time he would ever hold me in his arms again.

Christmas had come on a Friday that year, and since Clay could never get away on weekends I hadn't expected to see him again until Monday at the earliest. So I hadn't even worried about him all the time he was dying!

It hurt so terribly afterward, knowing it happened sometime on Saturday afternoon when Katy and I were at the movies, laughing at a silly slapstick comedy. I kept thinking about that when I was really still too stunned to grasp the full extent of what had happened. It was as if that was the most tragic part of it all—that I had been laughing when Clay died.

I found out about his death in the cruelest way possible. I was reading the Sunday paper, and suddenly Clay's picture was staring out at me. From the obituary page! For a second, I thought I would die, too. There was a spasm of pain in my heart that made me gasp, and then all feeling went out of my hands and the paper slipped to the floor.

Fortunately, Katy wasn't in the room. She was out in the kitchen pasting pictures in her scrapbook. So I had time to pull myself together, to feel life creep back into my cold body, before she saw me. And I had time—all the time I needed—before I had to tell her that her Uncle Clay had gone away to be with God.

I told her that afternoon, but even putting it into words didn't make Clay's death seem real to me. I couldn't cry, and, because of Katy, I was glad. I didn't want to upset her any more than was necessary. She understood that I meant he'd never come to see us any more, but I knew it would take weeks and months for her to be convinced in her heart—and to feel the loss.

It was the same with me. An understanding of the stark fact of death doesn't come all at once. It comes gradually—and constantly—with each reminder that breaks your heart.

I went through all that. I lived numbly through the day when I knew Clay was being buried, and then when I knew it was over and that I'd never, never see him again, the first grief struck at me, the overwhelming sorrow that shut out all the lesser things that would hurt in their own way when the time came to meet them.

And then there was the loneliness, like a smothering fog. My tears would start before I was really awake in the morning, and yet my misery didn't keep me from thinking of Clay's wife and how she was going through all the same emotions. I almost felt a kinship with her in the bond of sorrow we shared. But I envied her, too—for not having to hide her loss, for having the comfort of being Clay's widow. All I had was that picture of him from the newspaper—and the letter he'd written me from the hospital. I read it over again before I put it away with his picture, and somehow it had even more meaning than when I had first read it. In it, he called Katy his daughter. "You gave me what every man wants most," he had written. "A child of my own."

Reading the letter made me think of Ben Allen, Clay's friend. I wondered how it would be when I saw him—if he would be my friend, too, and if we would find comfort in remembering Clay together. It might take away some of the loneliness if there was someone I could talk to about Clay.

But when I finally saw Ben Allen a few weeks after Clay's death, I realized he wasn't going to be either sympathetic or friendly. His eyes were so cold when I introduced myself that I wanted to get out of his sight just as fast as I could.

Even if he had been kind and understanding, it would have been difficult to bring up the subject of Clay's providing for Katy and me. I had always felt embarrassed about discussing money, even with Clay. And it was as if Mr. Allen sensed that and was deliberately making it more difficult for me. Even when I mentioned Clay's name, he just kept staring at me coolly, as though he was wondering why I was there.

He wasn't going to help me. That was plain enough. I had to bring up the subject myself, and it was so hard to put into words. I felt so miserable, as if loving Clay and losing him had dwindled down into just a question of money. If only Mr. Allen had acted as if he understood. If only he'd tried to understand what it was like to have the sole responsibility for a child's future suddenly thrust upon you.

"Clay and I loved each other so much," I said, trying to make some sort of contact with this cold-eyed man. "I—well, I guess I don't have to tell you how it was with us, since Clay has already told you."

"Well, yes," Mr. Allen said. "He did go into it. Not deeply, of course. I was very distressed about the situation. But since he never mentioned it again, I assumed it had somehow resolved itself. In fact, I had put it completely out of my mind until this morning when you telephoned for an appointment."

That was when I began to get frightened. For it didn't sound right, what he was saying. There was something wrong that I couldn't quite understand.

"But I don't see how you could think anything like that," I said. "As if it was just a casual affair. Clay wouldn't have made plans with you for Katy if that was all it was."

"Oh, that!" he said. "There was some talk about a trust fund. But it never got beyond the planning stage. So I hope you haven't been counting on anything like that. Clay never brought the subject up again, and it wasn't anything I could question him about."

I felt so frightened then, so heartsick and bewildered. It was like losing Clay all over again. Only worse. It was easier to lose him to death than to know he had deserted me and abandoned Katy. And it was only my desperate concern for her that made me forget my pride and go on pleading with Mr. Allen.

"It's Katy," I said. "Never mind about me. I don't see how he could do this to her. He talked about taking care of her. I just can't understand how he—"

I couldn't go on. I felt so ashamed saying things like that about Clay. Even thinking them. "Maybe he thought he had plenty of time to take care of it," I said. "Do you think maybe that's the way it was? Because it would be easier if I could feel that. I can't bear to think Clay just plain didn't care enough about us to keep his promise."

"That must have been it," Mr. Allen said. "It wasn't like Clay to shirk a responsibility like this. It's natural to keep putting off unpleasant things. Like making a will, for instance. It usually takes a jolt, like Clay's heart attack, before people will face up to such things. Then when the crisis is past, they tell themselves there really isn't any hurry after all. I'm sure that was Clay's attitude, especially since he was making a good recovery. He probably thought he had all the time in the world."

Mr. Allen stood up, and I realized he was indicating that our talk was finished. "I'm sorry," he said. "I wish you would let me help you. In a small way, at least." And he really did look sympathetic as he reached into his pocket and brought out five hundred-dollar bills and pushed it into my hand. "I know Clay would do as much for me if our positions had been reversed," he said.

Even though I was desperate. I hated taking anything from him. I can't explain the feeling I had as I put the money in my bag. I think I would have refused it if I hadn't realized how little it meant to him. Not even keeping it in his wallet! Just pulling it out of his pocket as if it had been a dollar bill!

But it meant so much to me. Security until I found a job. Food for Katy. Medicine if she should need it. Of course I shouldn't have waited until my savings were nearly gone before going to see Mr. Allen. And I should have started job hunting immediately. But I'd been so sure Clay had taken care of us. . . .

Then I found out that it wouldn't have mattered how soon I tried to help myself. I just couldn't find a job! Wherever I went, it always came down to the same thing—I didn't have enough experience. And I'd been out of work too long—eight years. I couldn't even get back in at the utility company.

I finally took a job in the one big department store in town. It meant there would be just that much less time to be with Katy, since I'd have to work Saturdays and one evening a week. But I didn't have any choice. I had to take anything I could get.

I'd have liked the job if it hadn't been for that. I had made arrangements with a woman who lived in the next apartment to look after Katy when I wasn't there. But it worried me, knowing so little about her. I wondered if she'd be good with children, since she didn't have any of her own.

I tried to find out from Katy. "Is it fun being with Mrs. Halsey?" I'd ask. "Does she give you cookies and cocoa when you come home from school? Is she nice? Do you like her?"

But Katy never really answered any of my questions. That was another thing that worried me. The way she was drawing into herself. I had been the same way when I was her age. Secretive and keeping things to myself. I hated to think of her growing up as I had. And sometimes it was more than I could bear, remembering how unhappy I had been with relatives who didn't have any real love for me—no more love than a baby-sitter would have for my child.

I'd think of how it used to be, when Katy and I were so close, the two of us. When we always had so much to talk about and how I never had to question her. It hurt so much, looking back and remembering. It seemed so long ago, as if it had happened in another lifetime.

Remembering Clay hurt, too. He was still as alive in my heart as if he'd held me in his arms only yesterday, and I had to fight the feeling that his death was just a crazy nightmare—that he'd be coming back to me. The feeling was especially strong at night, when I couldn't sleep. He'd seem so close to me then that it would seem I could touch him—just by stretching out my hand. But each time I did, the pillow was always empty. I was just torturing myself. I tried not to think about him.

But he must have been on my mind all the time, even if I didn't know it. Because one day it was as if his name jumped right out of the newspaper I was reading. It was so strange the way I saw it, for I never really read the page with the engagement and wedding notices on it.

But there it was, just as if I had been looking for it. Just as if he was still alive. It was such a shock. I remember how I kept staring at it and how it took me a little time to see that it was really his wife's name that was printed there. Then it was another shock to see Ben Allen's name, too. I felt as if I had been turned into stone as I read the announcement of their marriage the day before.

Then I got mad. This was the woman Clay had been so loyal to! The woman who needed him so desperately! The woman who had robbed me of marriage—and Katy of a father!

I had to push my fist against my mouth so Katy wouldn't know I was crying, crying for all the time and love and happiness and Clay and I had sacrificed to Nora. And Nora couldn't even have loved Clay. If she had felt anything for him at all, she couldn't have married another man scarcely two months after he was dead.

I hated her then, and for weeks afterward I couldn't tear the bitterness out of my heart. Even after it started to go, I couldn't forgive her for what she had done to Katy.

Poor Katy! It was so hard to leave her at school each morning on my way to work. She would hold on to my hand so hard, as if she was trying to stop me, and all day her woebegone little face would haunt me.

Then right before Easter I was sent upstairs to help out in the children's department, and it was harder than ever to be separated from Katy, with so many children around to keep reminding me of her. Especially the little girls. I'd think what fun it would be to go shopping with Katy, to have time to spend with her.

One day a little blond girl came in with her mother, and I couldn't keep my eyes off the child as I waited on them. It wasn't only that she was so well behaved. There was something about her expression as she looked in the mirror at the dress she was trying on that captivated me.

Without thinking, I gave her a quick hug. And then I was so embarrassed, I felt I had to apologize to her mother. "I don't know what got into me," I said. "But she's such a darling. I'm sorry—"

"Don't be," her mother said, smiling. "I love it when people make a fuss about Elsa. She's so quiet, and with three brothers always demanding attention, she sometimes gets pushed into the background."

"I have a little girl who must be just about her age," I said. "She was seven last New Year's Eve."

The woman looked at me, startled. "Why, that's Elsa's birthday, too. And the same age. What a funny coincidence!"

Then she turned back to the little girl, and the two of them discussed the new dress for a few minutes. Finally they decided it would be just right for an Easter party, and the woman had me write up her sale.

There was something so familiar about her name as I wrote it down. But it took a second before it really penetrated. Then I gasped. "There was a Mrs. Harrison in the hospital with me when I had Katy," I said. "It was the community hospital in Midville, and it had just been opened and—"

"Oh, no, it can't be!" the woman said. And then as we stared at each other unbelievingly, she laughed.

"Then you must be Mrs. Grant, the other maternity case that night. Oh, we can't let a thing like this go by! Why, it's almost as though our girls are twins. Katy just has to come to Elsa's Easter party. You will bring her, won't you? Since it's a Sunday, you won't be working. . . ."

I was thrilled with the invitation, and I thought Katy would be, too. But she didn't get excited about it. Nothing seemed to excite her anymore. She wouldn't even try on the new dress I bought her, not until it was actually time to get ready for the party.

Then it was like a miracle, the way Katy changed. Almost from the minute we stepped into the big old-fashioned house in the suburbs, she was a different child. In no time at all she was racing around and shouting with the others, laughing with glee when she found the most Easter eggs and won a prize.

It was such a happy day, and it was only the first of many that were to come after it. Because Connie—she had insisted on first names from the moment she opened the door—said we had to come again just as often as we could. "I feel that I've known you forever," she said. "And Katy is such a charmer. I can't get over the way she just flew into my heart the minute I saw her."

The Harrisons were such a wonderful family. John was just as friendly as Connie. It was as if they had a special happiness all their own. It would have been so easy to envy them if they didn't have the faculty of taking other people into their circle and making them happy, too. As they did Katy and me.

Katy had changed so much since we had known them. She began confiding in me again, and it was so nice to be able to talk to her. Only at the time it never occurred to me that it was always the Harrisons she wanted to talk about. I should have noticed that—just as I should have noticed that she never mentioned Mrs. Halsey or even the children in the neighborhood. I should have known something was wrong.

But I didn't. And I might never have known how wrong things really were if I hadn't come home unexpectedly one night when I was supposed to be working. I had such a terrible headache. It had started during my supper break, and it had kept on getting worse. Finally even the floor manager noticed how sick I looked and sent me home.

I wasn't thinking clearly, so it didn't upset me when Mrs. Halsey didn't answer my knock at her door. I just went into my own apartment to wait. It was only later, after I'd taken a few aspirins and the pain began to ease, that I began worrying about where she might have taken Katy. It was a quarter to nine by then. Almost time for Katy to be in bed. That was one of the things Mrs. Halsey had promised me so faithfully. To be sure to see that Katy got her proper rest.

The throbbing pain started all over again. My worry changed to panic. I was just about to call the police to see if there had been an accident when I heard someone coming up the stairs. I threw the door open, and then I saw them—Katy first, and then the man holding on to Mrs. Halsey's arm, the two of them laughing drunkenly.

I didn't trust myself to say anything then. I just stood there hugging Katy a moment before I took her inside and closed the door. But as I started to question her, she pulled away from me and I saw the terror in her eyes. My own terror was as great as hers then, but I had to hide it. I had to calm Katy down to the point where she could talk to me.

"Tell me where you were," I said finally. "Don't be afraid, darling. You can tell me anything."

Katy looked at me searchingly. "Mrs. Halsey said if I told, you'd get mad and put me away in an orphanage. She said—"

My heart turned over. I could feel the tears rushing into my eyes. "That's silly," I said. "As if I'd ever let you get away from me. Oh, Katy, trust me! Tell me where you went. Was it to the movies? To a restaurant? Where?"

She flung herself into my arms. "It's awful, Mommy," she said. "I hate it when she takes me to that place around the corner. It's so dark and smelly, and once a man tried to kiss me. I wouldn't let him, even if he was a friend of hers. She has so many friends, but I don't like any of them."

That place around the corner—I knew it was a rundown bar, and I could imagine what kind of people went there. But I couldn't let Katy see how horrified I was. Enough harm had been done to her without my adding to it. The less I made of the situation, the quicker she would forget it.

"Well, you won't ever have to go there again!" I told her, and then I heated some milk and made some toast and sat with her until she was finally able to eat.

By the time I had tucked her into bed, she had quieted down enough to sleep. But even then I stayed with her, thinking how wonderful it would be if I could always be there beside her to see that nothing bad ever happened to her.

Only there wasn't any sense in wishing. Wishing never accomplished anything. The only way to straighten out a problem was to unravel all the knots yourself. But it was so hard to figure out what to do about Katy. The only thing I did know was that I never wanted her to go to Mrs. Halsey's again.

The more I thought of that woman, the madder I got. I kept telling myself I shouldn't see her when I was feeling so angry, that it would have been better to wait until morning when I'd calmed down a little. But even as I was thinking that, I suddenly got to my feet and went outside in the hall and knocked at her door.

There was a whispering inside before she opened it. And then she closed it behind her again as she faced me—so I couldn't see inside. She had changed into a negligee, pink satin and lace, and her hair was hanging loose and wild around her shoulders, and I thought that if I'd seen her like that before, I never would have let Katy stay with her. Always before, though, she'd looked clean and decent and respectable, and I had accepted her word that she was a widow who supported herself by taking in sewing.

"I suppose you've come to pay me my money," she said. "Well, let me tell you I won't be taking care of your brat anymore! After the way you acted, and in front of one of my gentleman friends! So just give me my money, and that'll be the end of it."

Her brashness stunned me for a minute. I ran back into my apartment for my purse, then counted out the money I owed her and thrust it in her hand. "Here, take it," I said. "And I hope you know how lucky you are that I'm not going to report you to the police. Doing what you did to a seven-year-old child! Taking her to a bar, getting drunk while you were responsible for her, bringing men to your apartment while she was in your care—"

There just wasn't any shame in her. Every word I said made her laugh harder. "You're a fine one to talk!" she said. "As if anyone could give a worse example to that kid of yours than you've done already. You make me laugh! How high-and-mighty do you think you can get! A woman like you, who let a man keep her—who let him come around any time of the day or night. And that kid calling him her uncle! Who did you think you were fooling?"

I wanted to put my hands over my ears so I wouldn't have to hear her. I turned to go into my apartment, but she thrust herself between me and the door.

"You thought you were getting away with it, didn't you?" she said. "Well, you weren't. The whole neighborhood saw through that 'widow' story. Why, if I wasn't so softhearted, I wouldn't have gone near that kid with a ten-foot pole! No one else around here would, I can tell you!"

I didn't want to hear anymore. I pushed her aside so I could get through the door, and then I locked it beside me. I was so weak with shame and shock, I just stood there leaning against it and crying. *My poor Katy,* I thought. *My poor baby.* And then I realized that no matter what, I'd have to get her away. Get her to a place where no one would know the truth about her mother.

There was no sleep for me that night. I couldn't stop thinking about her. Thinking and wondering. *What will we do, Katy?* I thought. *Where will we turn? How can we get away?*

And then I began whispering to Clay. "Clay," I begged, "if you're anywhere where you can hear me, please tell me what to do." Of course I didn't expect an answer. But it helped pretending he was there to advise me. "Please help Katy and me," I whispered. "If there's any way you can, please help us."

And then all the comfort of thinking about him vanished as I remembered that he hadn't even helped us when he was still alive. Something hard came into my heart then, pushing away all the love so that I didn't want to think about him anymore. Because he couldn't have loved either one of us. It was only his wife he had loved and cherished and taken care of.

The bitterness went so deep it was like a fire destroying everything we had ever had together. If Nora had deserved the way he felt about her, I wouldn't have resented it so terribly. I'd even have felt as guilty as I used to. But all I could think of was how she had married Ben Allen so soon after Clay was gone. It couldn't have been just loneliness that made her do it. You don't go flying in the face of respect and decency and gossip just from loneliness. Especially a woman her age. She wasn't the child Clay thought she was. She wasn't stupid and helpless. She'd proved that by the way she was able to fool Clay.

She must have been crazy about Ben Allen to risk losing everyone's respect that way. It couldn't have been anything new. Maybe he had even told her about me. Maybe they had joked about it. I went cold then, remembering how ashamed he'd made me feel that day in his office—and all the time he was probably laughing inside!

Then a sudden thought came to me. Only it wasn't really a thought. It was more like a voice telling me something. I liked to think it was Clay who was trying to take care of Katy and me, reminding me of something that had meant so little to me at the time that I hadn't thought of it since.

But now the memory was so clear and sharp I could almost feel the smoothness of that new bill Ben Allen had given me. It was as new as if it had just come from the bank, and that was certainly possible. He'd had plenty of time to go to the bank after I telephoned for an appointment to see him. And the way he had the money so handy in his pocket meant something, too! He'd wanted to pay me off as fast as possible and get rid of me. I could see again the confident way he stood up, signaling the end of our interview. I could feel his hand holding my elbow and urging me to the door. He'd handled the whole thing so well that I'd never guessed he was lying to me. Of course Clay had arranged with him to take care of Katy and me. But it had been just a verbal agreement probably, and Ben Allen wanted that money for Nora. For Nora and himself.

At first I didn't think there was anything I could do about it. What could I prove? Nothing at all. Then I thought of Clay's letter, and I got it out and read it again. I kept crying as I read it, because it was so like him, so sweet and tender and full of love. But there was something else there, too. Something maybe Clay had put deliberately in case the time ever came when I would need it—the proof that he was Katy's father.

I made up my mind then that I was going to fight for the security Clay had wanted for me. There wasn't anyone I could hurt now. Not Nora. It made me wince to think that once I would have been foolish enough to try to protect her from knowing about Clay and me. Not Katy. I didn't have to consider what it might mean to her if the whole story came out. That had happened already, so she couldn't be hurt more than she already had been. Realizing all that, it was as if the future was all taken care of. As if all the pressure had been lifted. I could fall asleep at last.

The first thing I did when I woke up the next morning was to call the store and tell them an emergency had come up and I couldn't go to work until Monday. I called Connie then, almost without thinking, as if it had been in my mind all along that I was going to ask her for help.

I felt so lighthearted when I took Katy to school that morning. It was such a wonderful feeling kissing her good-bye and knowing I would be there to meet her that afternoon. Then I got on the bus and went out to Connie's.

She made some coffee and put out some buns, and by that time I had sort of sifted things out in my mind so I could talk to her without getting excited.

"Connie," I said, "first of all I have to tell you I lied to you. I'm not a widow. My name isn't Grant. It's Janet Graham, and there's no 'Mrs.' in front of it."

For a minute I choked up and my heart started racing all over again, but Connie reached out and patted my hand and then suddenly got up and hugged me. We cried a little then, with me sobbing that I was afraid she'd hate me, and Connie begging me to believe that nothing could change her feeling for me. As I felt her sympathy rushing out to me, it was easy to tell her everything—how it began, how it ended, and what was happening to Katy now. She didn't interrupt once. And she didn't cry again until the very end—when I was telling her about Mrs. Halsey and Katy.

"Oh, no!" she said then. "That adorable child! How could anyone hurt her? I'd like to strangle that awful woman—and all the other self-righteous busybodies back there! Oh, Janet, I couldn't hate them more if it was Elsa they'd tortured!"

She looked at me then, so warm and sympathetic. "You can't take any more chances leaving Katy with a sitter. She needs love and understanding. I, I've been thinking, and hoping, too, that maybe she could stay with us while you have to work. It may take time to straighten out your legal claim, and—"

"I was hoping you'd say that," I said. And then I began crying all over again. "I was going to ask you. I was sure you wouldn't refuse me. Only I can't tell you what it means having you offer, so I know you really don't mind and—"

"Mind!" she said. "I'll love it. It'll be like having another daughter. And one who can really stand up to those roughneck boys of ours! It will be good for Elsa, too. She's so shy, but she really opens up with Katy. Why, you're the one who's doing us the favor. I'll hate even having to give her up on your free days!"

Connie made everything so easy. I blessed her for it then, and I'll always keep on blessing her. Connie and John both. For John was the one who found a lawyer for me and went along with me the first time I had to see Mr. Flynn. He was the one, too, who helped me understand all the business about blood tests. He took all of Mr. Flynn's involved explanations and put it in terms I could grasp.

The gist of it was that comparing Katy's blood type with Clay's was necessary as part of the case Mr. Flynn planned to build for proving Clay was Katy's father. The blood test would prove only that he could be Katy's father—not that he definitely was, but it was evidence that, combined with Clay's letter, would be conclusive in proving Katy's claim to some share of her father's estate.

Mr. Flynn pointed out that Clay's blood type would be a matter of record at the hospital where he was taken when he had his heart attack. But he anticipated that Ben Allen would try to keep us from examining those records—and he did. As soon as Mr. Flynn petitioned Nora for the necessary permission, Mr. Allen stepped right in, claiming I was trying to harass and embarrass Clay's widow! Finally we had to get a court order before the hospital would release the records.

By that time, I was almost sorry I'd started the whole thing. I missed Katy so, and, without her, my apartment was like a grim, lonely jail. Yet I comforted myself with the knowledge of how happy Katy was with the Harrison—I could see that for myself every time I went to visit her!—and I told myself I was fighting for something too important to give up simply because I was lonely or tired or scared.

The day after Clay's record came, Katy and I went for our own blood tests. It was much easier than I had thought it would be, and, for Katy's sake, I was glad. She had been so nervous while we had to wait for our turn to go into the pathologist's office in the hospital. There were so many people waiting ahead of us, and we were the last to go in.

The man who took our test looked so young, like a college boy almost, with a string-bean kind of tallness and hair that looked as if it needed a good combing. But he had a relaxed way with children, and he got Katy so relaxed, making a game of it all, that she didn't even flinch when he drew the blood from her finger tip.

"A whole gallon!" he said, nodding down at the drop on the glass slide. "Your mother will have to buy you an ice-cream soda to make up for it!"

Then he did my test, and after that he picked up my record card and kind of slumped back in his chair and relaxed while he looked at it. "So your name's Janet, and you're a widow," he said. Then he grinned. "Well, my name's Pete Anderson, and I'm a bachelor—and, to get the record straight, I'm assistant to the pathologist here. And now that we've got the formalities out of the way, let's go buy that soda for Katy."

What could I say—with Katy jumping up and down with excitement, grinning right back at Pete like they'd known each other forever? So Katy and I waited outside while Pete changed into street clothes, and then the three of us went off for our sodas. And it was fun! It really was, because Pete was as outgoing and warmly friendly as Katy, and the two of them got me laughing harder than I'd laughed in years.

"Thank you very much for the date, ma'am," Pete said to Katy after we'd finished. "I hope we'll see a lot more of each other—like for dinner and a movie tonight." But when he said that last part, it was me he was looking at, not Katy.

"We can't!" I said quickly. "Katy's staying with friends temporarily, and we're both expected there for dinner." Then I added something that surprised me. "I'm sorry," I said—and I actually was.

"I'm sorry, too," Pete said. "But maybe we can make it some other time. How about tomorrow?"

When I told him Katy wouldn't be with me then, he made a great pretense of being disappointed. "I can see you're trying to break up a beautiful romance," he said. "So I'm going to have to insist that you have dinner with me tomorrow—so we can talk this situation over. You've got to give me a chance to prove I'm not such a bad guy when you get to know me. . . ."

So I agreed, and we had our dinner date. From then on, it was like going back in years, being with Pete. I never really knew if he was fooling or being serious. It was like being a teenager again and having the dates I'd missed then. It was all so carefree and happy, and I was so grateful for it, because it gave me so much less time to brood and be lonely.

Then one day I had to break a date with Pete because Connie called me at work to say that something had come up that I had to know. "Come to dinner," she said. "That will give us time to talk later."

She didn't say it as if it was anything really important. But I felt myself getting uneasy before we had scarcely started dinner. There was something so different in the whole atmosphere that evening, something I couldn't figure out. The children were all the same. Katy was as boisterous as the three boys, and Elsa was enjoying it all in her quiet way. That much was the same as it had always been.

Only Connie and John had changed. Not only because they were so quiet. Not even because they weren't really eating. It was the way they kept looking at Elsa and then at Katy and then back to Elsa that bothered me. I knew there was something wrong even before John said he was taking all the children to the movies so Connie and I could have a chance to talk.

The minute Connie and I were alone, I got panicky. I didn't want to hear what she was going to tell me. But I had to, of course, and I'll always be glad she didn't beat around the bush. If there had been a lot of emotion mixed up with it, I'd have fallen to pieces. But because Connie was calm, I managed to be calm, too.

"The report on the blood tests came through," she said. "Last week, as a matter of fact. Mr. Flynn got in touch with us, and John and I decided we wouldn't tell you until we made sure of something. There didn't seem to be any sense in getting you all upset, too."

She gave me a long look then. "The tests proved that Clay couldn't have been Katy's father. I know what a shock this must be to you, Janet, but—"

I couldn't take it in all at once. It was like some crazy dream. Of course Clay was Katy's father! There must have been some mistake in the tests. But no wonder Connie was acting so different with me! She probably thought Clay wasn't the only man in my life.

"There's been a mistake!" I said wildly. "There

49

must have been. I wasn't lying, Connie. There never was anyone but Clay. I know what you must be thinking about me, but it isn't true!"

"I think what I've always thought about you, Janet," Connie said. "That you're fine and sweet and honest. That's what made John and me realize what might have happened—and that's why we had blood tests taken, too. Elsa and John and I."

I still didn't understand. Connie reached for my hand and held it while she tried to understand.

"Don't you remember how it was that night in the hospital?" she asked. "The two of us in the same delivery room? And all the confusion? No wonder they made a mistake. For that's what happened. Either the doctor or the nurse switched our babies. Our blood tests prove that John isn't Elsa's father, but that he could be Katy's. So Elsa is your child. And Katy is mine."

As she said that, her calm left her. "Oh, Janet," she said, "I love Katy, but it will be like tearing out my heart to lose Elsa."

I was still bewildered, but the truth of what Connie had said was already forcing itself into my mind. I was beginning to understand why I had felt that kinship with Elsa right from the start. I was facing the fact of Katy's happy, open personality—so like all of the Harrisons, and so unlike Clay and me. Then I had to face something else: I loved Elsa instinctively, because she was a part of me, but I loved Katy just as much, because she had been my child for nearly eight years. Neither of them could take the place of the other in my heart.

Connie kept biting her lips as she looked at me, but she couldn't control the tears clouding her eyes.

"I know what you're thinking," she said. "There isn't a thing you're going through that John and I haven't been through already."

Suddenly she couldn't hold back her tears any longer. I put my arms around her and tried to comfort her, but I didn't know how. "I know, I know," I kept repeating. Only I really didn't. I just kept thinking it would be Elsa I would be taking home and Katy I would be leaving behind.

It's wrong, I thought. *It would be better if we'd never found out. Maybe Katy will adjust, but it will kill Elsa!*

I kept thinking how quiet she was. And so shy. Elsa could never take what Katy had gone through. She would have broken under a strain like that. She would never have been able to put it behind her as Katy had.

She was made of stern stuff, my Katy. Along with the lightness and love of laughter, there was a toughness in her that Elsa didn't have. No wonder the Harrisons and Katy got along so well. All of them had it—that laughter and strength. But Elsa didn't, despite the fact that she had never known anything but the security of a family's love all her life. What a shock it would be for her to lose it! And if ever there came a time when she found out the truth about Clay and me. . . .

"I hate to think how hard it will be for Elsa to go away from all of you," I said. "And her life will change so in other ways, because I won't be able to give her all the things you've given her. Now that there isn't any hope for the lawsuit—"

The look on Connie's face stopped me. She was staring at me as if she despised me.

"There's still hope for a settlement," she said. "It might be a little bit more difficult. But John has already contacted the hospital, and they've agreed to help. And we'll help, too." Her eyes clouded and her voice sounded so dull as she went on. "The only thing that's changed is that Clay's child is Elsa."

It hadn't occurred to me that the situation hadn't really changed until she said it. Then I knew why she had looked at me with such loathing. "I couldn't do that to Elsa," I said. "Not after what Katy's been through. Oh, Connie, how do you think I'd ever put Elsa through that?"

Connie kept looking at me, trying to smile, and the gratitude in her eyes made me want to cry.

"I'm sorry," she said. "After everything that's happened—well, I guess I just wasn't thinking straight. But I was so scared for poor little Elsa. It would have crushed her. And I was already so frantic over losing her that—oh, Janet, what are we going to do? It's not enough, loving both of them. How can one child ever make up for the other?"

It can't, I thought. *Not any more than one mother can make up for another. No one can take Katy's place. Not even Elsa.*

I felt so empty, so alone, until I looked at Connie. Then I realized that at least I wasn't alone. The two of us were bound together in our common despair. When I heard the car drive up outside, we tried to pull ourselves together. Watching Connie was like looking in a mirror, seeing her force her lips into a smile. I was doing the same thing.

The children were all laughing when they came in. Even John was laughing—until you looked at his eyes. The room was alive again, and I heard my own shrill laughter as Katy came running over to me.

"Oh, Mommy, you're still here!" she cried, hugging me. "Oh, Mommy, I wish you could stay forever."

I held her close. "I wish I could, too," I said, giving her an extra hug. "But that's impossible. And even if it wasn't, who ever heard of a house with two mommies in it? Two mommies to fuss at you and scold. My goodness, wouldn't that be awful?"

"I don't know," Katy said, giggling. "There would be two mommies to love, too. And that part's nice. The love part."

"That's the big part, isn't it?" I said. "But I want to tell you a secret about love, Katy. You don't have to be with someone to love that person. I mean, even when I'm not with you, I love you. Love never goes away. I want you to remember that, Katy, any time when I'm not here and you're missing me. Remember that I love you, maybe even more because I'm away from you. Do you understand, honey?"

She nodded and gave me another hug. But as she turned, she saw Connie staring at us and she ran over to her and gave her a hug, too. "I love you, too," she told Connie. And that would have been all right. That would have been a consolation to me if she hadn't glanced guiltily at me as she said it.

It was wrong for Katy to have to feel like that, as though she were forced to choose between us. She shouldn't be put in the position of having to run from one of us to the other so neither of us would feel slighted. She shouldn't he confused by having two mothers.

I didn't trust myself to say anything more to Katy when I kissed her good night. But when she and the other children had gone upstairs, I turned to Connie. "I—I've made up my mind," I said. "I'm not going to see her again."

"Don't say that!" Connie begged. "She'll miss you. You can visit her whenever you want—"

"No," I said. "It wouldn't be fair to Katy—or to me. What sort of life would it be for her? Having to choose between us, having to pretend and feel guilty for loving one more than the other? Would you put Elsa through that?"

"No," Connie said. "After you take her, I won't ever want to see her again, either—unless she needs me at first when she's scared and lonely—"

I guess I'd known all along that I couldn't take Elsa away from her family, but that was the moment when I admitted it to myself. What could I give her to justify breaking her heart? Not even a name of her own. So my decision was made, but I didn't tell Connie that. Not then. I had to be really sure, I kept telling myself.

I went on turning my heart inside out for the next few days, though I knew how useless it was. For it always came back to the same thing. I had to give up Elsa as well as Katy. There wasn't any choice. There never had been any choice.

Finally I went to tell Connie and John, but I waited to get to their house till I knew the children would be in bed. Of course Connie and John were thrilled and excited by my decision, though for my sake they tried to hide how they felt. But they couldn't do it. Just as I couldn't hide how I felt from them. I couldn't keep my voice or my eyes from betraying that I had nothing to look ahead to any more. Not tomorrow or the next day or ever.

I wanted to get it all over with as fast as possible, but Connie and John kept holding me back, they were both trying so hard to be fair. "Take more time to think it over," they both said. "Wait another week."

"A week won't change anything," I told them. "Everything will be just the same then as it is now. Katy is yours—and I have nothing to give Elsa. Nothing except a chance for happiness here with you."

When they saw I meant it, they didn't try to argue anymore. "What—what are you going to tell Katy?" Connie asked me. "You can't just vanish from her life."

The pain in my chest was almost unbearable. "I don't know," I said. And I honestly didn't. "But if it's all right with you, I'm going to go to her now and try to find the right words."

I went up the stairs slowly, everything in me fighting what I had to do. First I went in Elsa's room. She was sound asleep, curled in a tight little ball. I leaned over and kissed her softly, the child that neither Clay nor I had ever had a chance to love, and then I tiptoed out.

When I stepped in Katy's room, I saw that she was asleep, too, but it was her usual restless, light sleep. Almost before I was in the door, she was stirring, and when I sat down on the side of her bed, she was half awake.

"Mommy!" she said, smiling and yawning all at the same time.

"Hi, honey," I said. "No, don't turn on the light!" She was reaching for the lamp on her night table. "I'm only going to be here a minute or two. Your—

your other mommy will be mad if I stay long enough to get you wide awake. I just want to tell you something, Katy—"

She was still groggy with sleep, and I hoped she wouldn't come fully awake before I was finished. It would make my words less hurting, that cushion of sleep.

"I want to tell you a story, honey," I said softly, stroking the hair back from her face. "It's about a little girl who was the luckiest little girl in the world because she had two mothers. Even when the day came that one of the mothers had to go far away, the little girl had a mother left to love her and take care of her.

"Of course she hated to have her other mother go, but she understood that there would always be an invisible thread of love running between them. So she didn't fuss or cry when her first mother had to say good-bye. She was a brave girl, and she understood about that thread of love."

Maybe it didn't make much sense, my story, but it was the best I could do. Katy had listened to it with her eyes half closed, so I didn't know how much of it she'd taken in. But when I finished, she took my hand and held it terribly tight. "Did the first mother ever come back to the little girl?" she asked softly.

"I, I don't think so," I said. "She wanted to, but there was a special reason why she couldn't. It was because—because she'd found something out. That no little girl can have two mothers—that she's only supposed to have one."

"Then she should have let the little girl choose!" Katy told me, and I thought I heard the beginning of fear in her voice.

"Maybe," I said. "But in the story I'm telling you, the little girl came to understand that the right choice had been made, and—and she lived happily ever after."

Then I knew I had to break through the cloud of fear that was beginning to fill the room, so I gave Katy a quick kiss on the tip of her nose and then I made myself laugh softly. "Don't forget about that secret thread of love!" I said. "If you feel it give one little jerk, you'll know I'm saying, 'Be a good girl, Katy!' And if it jerks twice—"

"Twice means a spanking—and three times means a kiss!" Katy told me, and she was smiling again.

"Right!" I said. "Now you close your eyes tight and see if it's sending any messages. . . ."

She closed her eyes obediently and snuggled down in the covers. I didn't take the chance of kissing her again, for fear it would break the spell of my silly story. But I stood there for just a second more and said a prayer that tomorrow Katy would sort some part of the truth out of my words, and that she'd remember me with love.

When I got downstairs, I said good-bye quickly to Connie, and John drove me home. The last thing he said to me was that they wouldn't hold me to my decision, but I just shook my head numbly. It couldn't be changed, because it was right. But that was small consolation to me then.

From then on, I lived in an empty world. Everything was empty—the apartment, the store where I worked, the streets. The whole world was gray and shadowy.

One evening the phone rang, and when I

answered it, I heard a man's voice saying it was Pete. That was a name from another life—a life I wanted to forget. So I hung up without saying another word. I didn't answer the phone after that. There wasn't anyone I wanted to talk to.

Then one night the doorbell rang and I answered it mechanically. It was Pete standing there, smiling hopefully at me. I couldn't stand to see anyone smile—to know anyone could be happy—so I tried to close the door on him. He wouldn't let me, though. He pushed me aside gently and stepped inside.

"Please go away!" I begged. "I—I'm not in the mood for company tonight. Please, Pete! I just can't stand to have you laugh and crack jokes and try to get me out of this mood—"

He took my hand, and he wouldn't let me pull it away. "I can do other things besides laugh and crack jokes," he said. "I can listen and I can sympathize and I can cry." And then his arms went around me, and he was wiping my tears away with his handkerchief. "Do you want to tell me about it?" he asked.

This was a completely different Pete. I'd never thought anyone so happy and easygoing could be so understanding. I felt as if I'd known him all my life. It was so good to have him there filling up all the emptiness.

I hadn't meant to tell him everything. But once I started, I couldn't stop. I'd never had that feeling with anyone before. I could tell him things I hadn't even told Connie. So there wasn't anything about me Pete didn't know.

He hardly said anything until I was all through.

And even then he didn't say anything for a while. He just took his pipe out of his pocket, filled it with tobacco, lit it, and took a draw on it.

"There's only one thing," he said then. "I want you to call the Harrisons right now and tell them you've changed your mind. That you want one of those girls, whichever one they decide. Even if it's Elsa, that's all right. We can give her a good home. Tell them that."

It didn't penetrate at first—that what he was really doing was proposing to me. "No, it still wouldn't be right," I said. "Connie and John and one of the girls would be suffering for my mistake—for my life with Clay. And I couldn't be happy, knowing that. I couldn't be that selfish, Pete, so don't try to change my mind! Let me at least do this one thing right in my life—one thing I can be proud of."

He didn't try to press me anymore after that. He just sat there holding me, and after a while he kissed me. And it meant so much, that kiss. As if it was easing all the turmoil inside me.

"It's going to be tough on you," Pete said then. "But I'll be around to help."

The warmth kept growing in me, crowding out the emptiness. I wasn't alone—because I had Pete. And it was as if everything had been decided between us long ago, so it wasn't a surprise at all.

"I can't stay in this town," I said, "living so close to them. I might see them, and I don't dare risk that. I couldn't bear it—"

"That's easy to work out," Pete said. "We'll go anywhere you want. California, maybe. That's one thing about working in a hospital. There's never any trouble finding a job. There's one other thing, though. I think I should tell you that I love you!"

"And I love you," I said. And then when he kissed me again, the ache and the love were all mixed up together in my heart. I was realistic enough to know it would always be like that—that I'd never entirely lose that aching sense of loss. It would lessen in time, but it would always be there.

But the love would be there, too. The love Pete and I shared. The love that would teach me to live again.

THE END

HIS FOR
A WEEKEND

I lay sobbing in Tom's arms in the strange, dark motel room.

"Honey, please don't!" he whispered. "Someone will hear you."

But I couldn't stop crying.

"We didn't do anything wrong," he pleaded. "We love each other, and we're getting married in June, right after graduation. . . ."

He went on trying to comfort me, but I hardly heard him. Nothing he said could make me feel less ashamed. All I could think was that it wouldn't have happened this way if he'd married me three years before, when I'd wanted him to. But he'd talked me out of it then—and so had my mother. They were both so reasonable and sensible, explaining how it would be better for us to wait. And so I'd had three lonely years while he was away at college—then this!

I'd saved part of my vacation so I could come up for the big fall weekend on campus. It was a long trip and cost a lot of money, but I wanted to do it because it would be the last time I'd see Tom before June. He had a job counseling freshmen, so he wouldn't be coming home for any of the vacations, and—well, I just had to see him one more time before then. But being with him had made the months we'd been separated seem twice as long, and the desperation I'd felt was at least partially responsible for what had happened that last night of the weekend.

"I can't stand it!" I sobbed. "Let's get married now. I could get a job here—"

Tom went through it all again. He was on scholarship, carrying a heavy load of courses, and had to keep his mind on his classes. Besides, he said, after we'd waited so long, it would be silly not to hold out until June and do it right. That way, I wouldn't miss out on a church wedding, and he could start out supporting me instead of the other way around. All the sensible reasons seemed to be on his side, and nothing I said could convince him.

Finally I said, "Suppose I'm pregnant, Tom? What'll we do then?"

"We'll get married," he said. "But don't worry about it. You won't get pregnant."

He was so sure—so completely sure! For the first time I realized he'd probably planned this from the start. That was why we hadn't gone on to another party after the dance with Marla, the girl I was sharing the motel room with, and her date. That was why Tom hadn't listened to my pleading when our passion started to get out of hand.

"I love you so much, Kathy," he'd moaned. "I want you so."

If he wanted me so much, why was he letting me go home? Why didn't he beg me to stay?

"I have to get out of here," Tom said. "Marla will be back any minute. I wish I could stay with you. I hate to leave you like this, honey. But we'll talk some more in the morning."

He dressed quickly and gave me a light kiss, then he was gone. A little while later Marla came in and undressed in the dark. She fell asleep right away, but I lay awake all night.

I'd never felt so alone and rejected in my life. All the years I'd dreamed of knowing Tom's love, it had been as his wife. Not like this. Not so furtive and hurried, leaving me feeling so alone and so used. My whole dream had exploded. There hadn't been romance; there hadn't been ecstasy. And now there was just shame.

Suddenly it seemed that my love for Tom had turned into hate. The feeling made me shudder. I'd never thought there would be a time when Tom would be anything but perfect to me.

The next morning Marla left before I did. When Tom came, I couldn't look at him. I busied myself closing my suitcase, fussing around checking bureau drawers, pretending to see if I'd left anything.

"Honey," Tom said, "you'll miss your train if you don't get going."

I nodded and picked up my purse while Tom took my suitcase. At the door he suddenly put it down and wheeled me around. "Look at me, Kathy," he insisted. "You haven't looked at me since I came in."

"You, you don't have to marry me, Tom," I

choked. "I won't hold you to an old promise you made so long ago."

He pulled me to him, hurting me. "Are you crazy?" he said. "You're *my* girl. The only girl I'll ever want."

We had no time to talk about it anymore. It was a mad rush to the train, and I just made it. My last memory of Tom was his grim, unsmiling expression as he watched the train pull out.

Mom was waiting for me when the train got in. She looked so young and pretty, with that expectant smile on her face. People who didn't know us thought we were sisters. Mom had married at sixteen. If anyone should have known how it was to be young and so in love that you couldn't stand not being married, it was Mom. But she didn't seem to remember.

She rushed toward me as I came down the steps and hugged me hard. "How was it, darling?" she asked as we made our way to the car. "Was your dress right? What did the other girls wear? Who did you room with? How's Tom?"

Mom had never been to a college weekend, so I tried to answer all her questions and sound like I'd had a wonderful time. I guess I satisfied her, because she kept nodding happily. Then, thank goodness, she changed the subject.

"Honey," she said, "I've got the most exciting news. Your father's been made foreman at the plant!"

"How wonderful!" I said, really smiling for the first time. "I'm so happy for him!"

"And I'm so happy for us!" Mom said. "Now we won't have to have the wedding reception at home. I figured it out. With Dad's raise, we can manage the

Crystal Room."

I gasped. The Crystal Room was where all the girls from the Hill had their weddings. People on our side of town never went there.

"That will cost a fortune, Mom!" I protested.

"Never mind. We'll manage. And I went to see Mildred Frost about your wedding gown."

"Mom, you didn't! We can make it ourselves."

Mom turned to me, her eyes bright. "No, baby, we're going to do it up right. We'll make sure people know Tom picked a wife who knows the right way to do things. Tom's starting in the office, not in the factory. He'll go places. You might as well get used to the idea that you'll be living differently."

Mom made me feel a little sick. She was always thinking about the impression things would make on people, especially people from the Hill. Mom knew how they did things because her mother had been a cook in one of those fine houses. Mom had gotten a job as a maid when she was very young, and that's where she met Dad. Dad had been a gardener, but for years Mom had nagged him about bettering himself, and finally he'd taken a job in the factory.

"Honey," Mom was saying, "I want the best for you. I always have."

She didn't have to tell me. Mom's whole life revolved around me to the extent that sometimes I felt as if she were smothering me.

We drove by the plant to pick up Dad. When I saw him come through the gate, a big man, with that outdoor look to his face that he he'd never quite lost in all his years at the factory, I felt a lump rise in my throat. I ran to him, and then I was enveloped in his arms. I felt so safe for a moment I wanted to cry.

Dad held me at arm's length. "What's the matter, hon?"

"Nothing," I said. "I'm just glad to see you."

He frowned. "That all? You sure?"

Mom hadn't noticed anything, but in one split second Dad knew I was upset.

We went to join Mom, and I congratulated Dad on his promotion. He kissed Mom, looking at her as if they were sweethearts, then he took the wheel.

All during the ride home, Mom chattered away about the Crystal Room and what a gorgeous wedding I would have. She'd figured it all out on paper, and when we got home, she showed it to Dad.

"It's okay with me," he said. "But if we have doctor bills or any other emergency—" He stopped abruptly. "Aren't you flying a little high, Laura?"

"Oh, stop worrying," Mom said. "We'll only be spending money we didn't expect to have. And if we need more, I'll go to work."

"No, you won't!" Dad told her. "Your back has never been right since that fall you had. You know what Dr. Simmons said."

"Don't nag," Mom pleaded, putting her hand on Dad's arm. Usually he let her have her way, he was that crazy about her. Anyway, Dad was so kind, so easygoing, he couldn't bear arguing.

I wanted to remind Mom that Dad had been pretty sick with the flu last winter and that the cough that had settled in his bronchial tubes still hadn't left him. But I knew she wouldn't listen. At last Mom had a chance to show the Hill people she was as good as they were, and nothing Dad or I said would have made any difference.

HIS FOR A WEEKEND

During supper Dad kept giving me curious glances from time to time. Finally he blurted out, "You're upset about something, Kathy. What is it?"

"Nothing, Dad." I bent over my plate. "It's just that—I don't know—the letdown after partying maybe."

"Leave her alone," Mom told him. "She's always depressed when she leaves Tom. It's natural. She'll get over it."

After supper I escaped to my room with the excuse that I had to unpack and get ready for work. I had a job in the office of the country club. Before that, I had clerked at the cosmetics counter in Bartlett's drugstore. But when a friend of mine who worked at the club left to get married, Mom had made me apply for the job.

I'd liked working at the drugstore. I got along fine with Mr. Bartlett and the other clerks. But Mom had insisted there would be more prestige at the country club. I could type, but I didn't know much about office work. However, they hired me, and the job wasn't hard—typing menus, taking phone reservations, filing, and keeping simple records.

While I was unpacking, Mom poked her head in my door. "I forgot to give you the other news," she said. "Mary had her baby while you were away—a girl, seven pounds."

I smiled, feeling a sudden pang of envy. Mary had been one of my best friends in high school, and she was twenty, just like me. This was her second child. I couldn't help comparing the difference between the way things had been for both of us since we graduated. Jim, Mary's husband, had gotten a job at a garage, and they had been married right after school.

All my friends were married, and many of them had children. When we got together, I had nothing to talk about. They were busy with furnishing their apartments and bringing up the babies. Tom was the only one in the crowd who'd gone to college—because he'd won a scholarship—and I realized that when he came home he'd have little in common with his old friends. Mom was probably right when she said we'd be mingling with different people entirely. Only it hurt to know we wouldn't belong with the kids we'd grown up with anymore. We'd had such good times, and they were really a wonderful crowd, completely different from Tom's hard-drinking, reckless college friends.

Mom had the idea that the girls I met when I visited Tom were better than my high-school friends, but she was wrong. I'd tried to tell her that, and it made her mad.

"You're so much like your father, Kathy," she scolded. "Sometimes I don't know what to do with you. You're afraid to aim high. I told you, you have to study those girls and copy them. They are different, I know. I used to be around them before I got married."

Different, yes, but not better. That was what Mom couldn't understand.

I was scared those next few weeks, and so was Tom. I could tell by his letters, the way he kept asking if I was all right. The days seemed to drag while I waited. But I realized that if we'd eloped that night as I'd wanted, Mom never would have forgiven us. I guess it would have just about broken her heart. She was so busy with wedding plans and my trousseau, it made me feel sick.

I started thinking crazy thoughts. Maybe there wouldn't be a wedding after all. Maybe Tom would change his mind. Maybe that night we were together had been just as disappointing for him as it had been for me. Maybe he wanted to get out of the marriage and didn't know how.

I was so mixed up that every time Mom brought me something for my trousseau, I'd get a cold feeling in the pit of my stomach.

"We just ran off and got married, your father and I," Mom told me. "We never had a real wedding. There wasn't any money. Honestly, Kathy, when you walk down that aisle, it'll be me—and when I look at Tom, it'll be your father. He was so handsome, the first time I saw him I nearly fainted!"

I had to laugh. She looked so cute and young when she said it. Dad heard her, and he grinned, but there was something sad in his eyes, and it hurt me. He would have liked to have given her the wedding she wanted, and lots of other things, too, that he'd never made enough money for.

He walked over to Mom and put his arm around her. For a moment, they looked at each other and forgot I was there. It was a beautiful thing to see, and I felt a lump in my throat. But then, Mom pulled away a little impatiently. "I have to work on a dress for Kathy," she said.

I didn't want Mom to do so much for me, but there was no stopping her. Whenever I protested, she'd say, "Honey, I live for you. Don't you know that?"

I knew it, but it didn't make me happy. It wasn't right. I'd rather she lived for Dad. After I was married, it would be lonely for her. I wished there were other children. I knew that after I was born, the doctor told Mom she couldn't have any more children. At first, she said, she'd cried for weeks, but then she decided maybe it was a blessing after all. She remembered the bitter struggle her folks had bringing up six children, and when her father died there was nothing, not even insurance. They used to eat the leftovers her mother brought home from the houses where she worked. Mom said she'd die if she had to bring up a family like that.

So she didn't mind not having more children, but I did. I was lonely, and it was terrible being the only child, knowing that if you failed to measure up to what your folks expected of you, you'd just about break their hearts.

The days passed in slow agony while I waited to see if I was pregnant. Tom's letters became more urgent, and when the month rolled around and nothing happened, I was frantic. *It can't be,* I thought. *It just can't be!* Again and again Mom had warned me about pregnancy. She'd drummed it into me so much, it had become a part of me, like breathing. She and Dad had gotten married almost as soon as they met each other.

Mom kept bubbling over with wedding plans. But the happier she got, the sicker and guiltier I felt. If Tom and I had to marry suddenly, everybody would know why, and I didn't think Mom would ever forgive me.

After two more miserable weeks I knew I was safe, and I wept with relief. I wrote to Tom, but after I sent the letter, I had a strange reaction. There was a resentment gnawing away at me. I looked at the picture of Tom on my bureau and suddenly turned it around so that I couldn't see his face.

I'd already started to wonder if Tom really wanted to marry me, but for the first time I began to wonder if *I* wanted to marry him. Were we both being held to an old promise, afraid of what people would say? Suppose I were to break the engagement—would he be glad or sorry? The awful thing was, I had no way of knowing.

Doubt is a terrible thing. It's a bad seed that grows wild like a weed. It comes between you and reason, crowding out every moment of happiness you might have.

That was the state of mind I was in when I met Bill Jennings. After that, the whole course of my life changed.

Bill breezed into my office at the country club one day. I say "breezed," because Bill didn't just enter a room like ordinary people; he stirred things up. Even the furniture seemed to move a little because Bill was there.

I was alone in the office. He perched on my desk and studied me. His eyes were gray and laughing, as if life was a big joke and he was enjoying it. I remember thinking that he and Tom were probably about the same age, but that was the only resemblance they had to each other.

Bills first words were, "How come they keep you hidden back here instead of on display out front?"

"Can I help you?" I asked, trying to keep my composure.

His eyes studied me, and I felt myself blushing.

"You sure can," he said, and I felt like throwing something at him. But then he grinned, and his eyes were teasing and merry. I knew that I couldn't be angry at him, and the depression that had been with me ever since that last night with Tom suddenly lifted.

He was the new waiter, he informed me, and the manager had told him to ask me where the uniforms were kept. I showed him the closet, and a few moments later he was back. He'd found a pair of pants that fitted perfectly, but the jacket was about three sizes too small for him. I realized we had nothing to fit those wide shoulders of his.

He stood there grinning helplessly, shoulders hunched, arms hanging out of the sleeves, and it set me off. We laughed together, and the tension was broken.

That night Bill offered to drive me home. He said he had a room in town.

"Thanks," I said, "but the bus is only two blocks away."

But, night after night, I'd find Bill waiting outside in his secondhand car, and he'd insist on taking me to the bus.

Then he asked me to go out with him.

"I can't, Bill," I said. "I'm engaged to be married."

His face fell. "I knew it! Some lucky stiff got ahead of me."

He didn't try to ask me out again, but every time I passed through the dining room to give the headwaiter the list of reservations, I'd see Bill dashing around, and he'd grin at me. He gave the fastest service, flashed the brightest smiles, and probably got the biggest tips. Everybody liked him. He was so happy he was like sunshine. Once I caught myself wishing that Tom had a little of that joy of life in him, but then I told myself it was silly to compare

Tom to Bill. After all, Tom was a serious-minded, ambitious person, preparing himself for a fine future.

After a while Bill said it was silly dropping me at the bus when he practically passed my house on his way home. It made sense, so I let him drive me home after that. There was no harm in it, I thought. He knew where he stood with me.

On our rides home, he talked a lot about himself. He'd been born on a farm and joined the Navy when he was seventeen.

"Imagine me, stuck in the wilderness milking cows!" he said. "I wanted to see the rest of the world!"

He'd been to the most fascinating places like India and Japan and Thailand, and he was going back into the Navy after he traveled around this country for a while. He took jobs here and there. When he got restless, he'd move on.

"Don't you ever want to marry and settle down?" I asked him once.

He looked startled, as if I'd suggested he jump off a cliff. "Who, me? Settle down? Sounds like premature old age."

I was just amused at his attitude. After all, it didn't really have anything to do with me.

One snowy night in early December, when Dad was working late and Mom was at the church helping plan the Christmas decorations, Bill suggested we stop for a steak. I just couldn't say "no," his invitation was so warm and enthusiastic.

It was warm and cozy in the restaurant. For the first time, Bill wanted to know all about Tom. I told him how wonderful Tom was, smart, ambitious, reliable. Bill listened, serious for a change, no laughter in his eyes. Then he said, "How could he go off and leave you for four years? He must be out of his mind!"

I defended Tom, explaining how Mom had carried on about wanting us to wait and all, but Bill shook his head.

"You know," he said, "you remind me of a character in those stories I used to read when I was a kid—the fairy tales—about the princess locked in a tower waiting to be rescued. Good thing I came along, just at the right time, too."

I felt a sudden fury. I pushed aside my coffee cup and stood up. "You're the most conceited thing I've ever met," I snapped. "Take me home."

"Hey!" he said. "I was only kidding."

But I didn't talk to him on the way home, and I tried to avoid him after that, even taking the bus home instead of letting him drive me. But the awful thing was that every time I saw him I could feel my heart pounding, and it was hard for me to breathe. I'd go home and write Tom a letter and look at his picture—I'd long since turned it back facing the room—telling myself over and over that he was wonderful and that I loved him.

One night about two weeks later Bill was waiting outside with his car when I got out of work.

"Listen," he said, taking my arm. "Something annoying has happened. I want to talk to you about it."

"Trouble with the job?" I asked.

He opened the door. "Get in. I'll explain."

We drove along a while in silence. He really looked very disturbed. His face was sort of white and set looking.

Finally he turned off in a woody area and parked. He sighed, not looking at me, and we both stared at the stark trees covered with snow, a winter scene in black and white.

"What's annoying you, Bill?" I asked finally.

"You!" he said. "You got me all shook up. I don't like it."

Neither did I! And I didn't like the way my heart was acting. I didn't like the feeling of excitement that seemed to be churning my blood.

I swallowed hard. "There's only one solution, Bill."

He took a deep breath. "What?"

"It's time for you to move on."

He nodded. "Yeah, I figured that, so I just wanted to say good-bye and give you a good laugh."

I didn't understand the part about the good laugh. I looked at him questioningly.

"I'm the guy who's immune, remember? The guy who wouldn't dream of settling down. And here I go falling into the same trap as any ordinary guy."

"I'm sorry," I said, and I was. I would miss not having him around, and yet I knew there was danger in being near him. Especially since Tom was so busy studying, he only had time to drop me brief notes that left me hungry for something I couldn't explain.

The silence lengthened. We just sat there. I wanted to tell Bill to take me home, but I seemed to be hanging on to the moment just as he was.

"Tom will give you the kind of life your mother wants for you," Bill said. "I can't. It's not in the cards for me."

"Bill," I said, "I picked Tom, not Mom. He was my choice."

"Would you have picked him if your mother didn't approve of him?"

I'd never thought about that. "It wouldn't have mattered," I said. "Not one bit!" My voice shook a little, and I didn't understand why.

Bill turned to me, and it happened so fast it took me by surprise. He slid over to my side of the car, pulled me to him, and began to kiss me. Too startled to think, I kissed him back.

For a while there was only his arms tight around me and the thrill of his kisses. But suddenly sanity returned and, with it, the realization of what I was doing. I struggled out of Bill's arms and began to cry.

"I sure make a mess of things, don't I?" Bill said. "I should have packed up and disappeared. Only I couldn't, Kathy. I had to hold you in my arms just once, kiss you, dream that maybe I could change, and settle down. Boy, I'm the world's biggest hypocrite!"

He let me cry, patting my arm awkwardly until I was quiet. Then, without a word, we started for home. We didn't say good-bye when we parted; it would have been too painful for both of us.

The next two days, Monday and Tuesday, I was off. I was glad. I knew I couldn't have done my job anyhow. Mom asked me to help out at church, and it was good to have something to do. But I couldn't concentrate on the decorations or the chatter of the women around me.

All I could think about was that Bill was leaving. I'd never see him again. I remembered the way he made me laugh. I remembered his arms around me, seeming to burn right through my winter coat. And his kisses—exciting, reckless, promising so much.

Tuesday I had a headache, and Mom went off to decorate without me. I felt so sick, I stayed in bed and tried to sleep. But I kept remembering Bill s question. And for the first time I began to wonder— would I have picked Tom if Mom hadn't approved?

I tried to think back, but it was hard. It seemed to me that Tom and I had happened so naturally, Mom had nothing to do with it. Or had she?

I'd never gone steady before I met Tom. Mom wouldn't allow it. She said the boys I knew would never amount to anything, and I'd get tied up with the wrong one before I knew what was happening. I thought they all were nice, and, besides, I didn't think I was anything special. I remember how mad Mom got when I said that. She pulled me over to the mirror and told me to take a good look.

"What do you see there, Kathy? Tell me," she commanded.

I stared uncertainly. "I see me, that's all," I said. I was kind of pretty, I guess. Like Mom, I had dark hair and blue eyes, and because Mom made me diet and kept me off sweets, I was slim and my complexion wasn't spotty like some of my friends'. But I didn't think I was prettier than they were. That really exasperated Mom. She marched me out to the backyard where Dad was working in the garden.

"Look." Mom pointed to the roses that were just starting to open. They were beautiful. Only one was already in full bloom, and Dad cut it and gave it to Mom.

"See, Kathy," she said, "you're like those buds over there, waiting to bloom like this one. When that time comes, you'll be a beauty."

"She's a beauty already," Dad said, "like her mother."

It made me blush and want to cry, and I remember I buried my face against Dad and he held me tightly.

It was true that Tom had been the only boy Mom had ever approved of, but that wasn't why I fell in love with him. In fact, I didn't even know I loved him until the night of the senior prom. I remember, even now, the moment, the exact moment I knew.

We had been dancing, closer than was usual with us. We'd been dating regularly most of that year, but not going steady because Tom had a scholarship to college, and he had no intention of getting serious. We got along well, and I was interested in what he had to say. The other girls who had dated him said he was handsome and a good dancer, but too serious. I liked him because he didn't try to get too friendly or push me for sex. He really talked to me as if I were a person and not just a female to be grabbed at the first opportunity.

That night we'd left the dance and gone out for air. It was a hot night, and there was a moon and stars. Tom was excited about his scholarship and going to college. He talked about how he would have to work for his room and board because the scholarship covered only tuition. I listened eagerly, not daring to tell him how much I was going to miss him.

Suddenly there was a funny silence, and I looked up at Tom. There was an expression on his face I'd never seen before, sort of awed and troubled.

"What's the matter, Tom?" I asked.

He put his arms around me slowly and drew me

to him. Then he kissed me, a strange, sweet, exciting kiss, not like our other kisses. The next moment we were clinging desperately to each other—as if we couldn't bear to let go. When we broke away, we were both breathless and trembling. It came upon us with the suddenness of a cloudburst—one moment talking easily, the next completely overwhelmed by our sudden physical need.

I felt as if the earth were moving under me, and I swayed. Tom caught me and held me.

"I don't want to go," he whispered. "I don't want to leave you, Kathy, I love you!"

We kissed again, and again the kiss left me shaking and frightened.

"I can't go!" Tom said. "I'll stay here, get a job. We'll be married. You do love me, don't you, Kathy?"

I nodded, swallowing hard. "You have to go," I said. "You'd never forgive me if I stood in your way."

We couldn't go back to the dance and face the crowd, so we walked by the lake. Tom put his jacket on the ground under a tree, and I sank down on it. He took me in his arms again, his whole body trembling against mine. I heard him saying over and over again how he hadn't intended to fall in love, he'd tried to avoid it, but now he was lost.

"Will you wait for me, Kathy?" he asked. "I know it's a lot to ask—four years—but, Kathy, I'll make it up to you. I'll work hard. I'll be somebody. You'll he proud of me. I'll never stop loving you—never!"

Never? Never is a long time. Four years to wait. A lifetime. Could I make such a promise? Could I trust myself?

I looked at Tom helplessly. What could I say? If

we could be married right away, it would be different. We were right for each other, and if we didn't have to wait, if we didn't have to suffer the pain of separation. . . .

"Kathy!" Tom said suddenly, as if he had read my mind. "We can be married, and you'll come with me. There are a lot of married couples in college. You'd have to work. I mean, I couldn't earn enough—"

"Of course I'll work," I said. "Oh, Tom, I'm so glad we don't have to wait!"

Tom bent over me then, and our bodies melted against each other. I could feel my senses swimming. I had no control. I seemed to have lost command of my body. But then suddenly I was scared. I cried out frantically for Tom to stop before it was too late.

We had the whole summer to make our plans. But first we had to go home and break the news to our folks. Mom and Dad were having coffee in the kitchen. When we came in, Mom jumped up to get cups for us. We sat down, and I guess we looked sort of funny because Dad raised his eyebrows quizzically.

"Well, kids, how was the prom? Home early, aren't you?"

"We—" I started and then stopped, glancing at Tom for help.

"Kathy and I—" He swallowed hard. "We—we're in love."

There was a dead silence. Mom went white. Dad looked as if he wanted to cry.

"You're babies!" Mom gasped. "Babies!"

Tom shook his head. "We've decided to get married." He gulped out the words in a rush as if they were choking him.

"It's crazy—" Mom started, but then Dad reached for her hand, and she stopped.

"Kids," Dad said, "do you know what you're letting yourselves in for?"

We nodded.

"We won't wait," I said. "We won't."

"You'll ruin your career," Mom said to Tom. "You'll be miserable, both of you."

But then we explained that Tom would still study, and I'd find a job, and somehow we'd manage. They listened carefully, and I could see Dad gradually getting over his shock. But not Mom. Her face was stony, her mouth tight in that way she had when she wanted something badly and Dad didn't give in right away.

"Well," Dad said when we finished, "that makes sense to me."

"No," Mom said, "it doesn't. They don't know what they're talking about. What happens when you get pregnant, Kathy? You couldn't work then, and Tom would have to quit school. You'd both hate it, hate seeing all your dreams go down the drain. I know." She began to sob suddenly. "I know what it's like."

I'd never seen Mom cry like that before. I was frightened. Dad motioned for Tom and me to leave, and we waited out on the porch. We sat scared and close together on the swing till he came out finally.

"She's right," Dad said. "She knows what hardship is. She had a tougher childhood than I had. And you, too, Tom—you know how it is during layoffs and strikes. You know how ends don't meet sometimes in a house where there are five children. You'd never get to college if you had to depend on your father.

"That's what Mom is afraid of, Kathy. We were able to give you things because there was only you. But if there had been more children—" He stopped suddenly and sighed. "Tom, it's a terrible thing not to have enough for your wife and family, to know your wife is disappointed in you. It's a terrible thing. It takes the heart out of a man!"

Mom came out then, calm and sure of herself. "I like you, Tom," she said. "I couldn't wish for a better man for Kathy. She'll wait for you. I know she will. When you're ready, when you're through school, you'll be married. You're young enough to wait. I can't let you both throw away your lives now."

She talked more, but when Tom left, nothing was really decided—or so I thought. But later he said Mom was right. I pleaded with him not to listen to her. Even his folks said it was okay for us to marry, and I knew we could get around Dad. But Mom had convinced Tom, and nothing I said could make him change his mind. That was what nearly killed me.

The night before Tom went away, Dad came into my room and sat on my bed.

"Kathy," he said, "if I could only afford it, I'd support you both and let you get married. But I don't earn enough. That's what Mom's been trying to tell you. I never had a decent education."

"Don't, Dad, please!" I cried, throwing myself into his arms. "There's no better father than you anywhere!"

He sighed, smoothing my hair. "Oh, there's better, all right. There are fathers who can give their children money and see them happy. But I can't, and that's that. You've got to accept that, honey. And don't nag at Tom. His mind's made up. When you lose a battle, take it on the chin, smile. Let him remember you brave and smiling. He'll respect that."

And I had been brave. I finished high school, got a job, spent my spare time helping Mom around the house. While the other girls in my crowd were going steady and getting married, I was alone, left out. I hardly ever had any fun except when Tom was home.

And now that we were closer to marriage than ever before, my mind and heart were tormented by doubts I never thought I would have. I couldn't understand it, and I had nobody to talk to. The girls I knew wouldn't understand. I was ashamed to tell them what had happened to Tom and me on that last night together. And I couldn't tell them about Bill and how exciting his kisses were, either.

Bill s words kept coming hack to haunt me: Would you have picked Tom if your mother didn't approve of him?

Had I really had a choice? Had I ever gotten to know any other boy well enough to love him? Mom had made sure I hadn't, never allowing repeat dates with anyone except Tom. So had she chosen Tom, or had I? I never would have thought about it if it hadn't been for Bill.

He had no right to ask me that. He had no right to come into my life and upset me. I had told him right away that I was engaged. He should have kept his distance.

But he had, I reminded myself, and still the attraction had grown between us without our really doing anything to help it.

"You remind me of a princess locked up in a tower," Bill had said that night in the restaurant. How angry I'd been! Why? Because maybe it was true. Otherwise, wouldn't I have shrugged it off?

But Bill was going out of my life forever, and suddenly I knew I couldn't stand it! Should I ask him to stay? And then what?

The phone rang, and my heart stopped. Something told me it was Bill. Something said, "Don't answer it." But it could be Mom or Dad, I reasoned, and they'd be worried if they couldn't get me. I had to answer it. It was Bill.

"Listen," he said. "I have to see you. Please!"

I knew I should say "no," but I couldn't. I left Mom a note saying my headache was better and I'd gone to the movies. I couldn't remember ever having lied to her before, but I seemed to have become another person.

I was out on the porch before Bill came, afraid Mom might be home early and stop me from going out with him.

He looked awful, as if he hadn't slept all night. He asked if I wanted some lunch. I didn't, but it was something to do, so I nodded. We drove to a kind of isolated place outside of town. I felt, somehow, like an unfaithful wife going off with her lover.

We sat and looked at each other and listened to piped-in music. Neither of us touched our food.

"Listen," Bill said suddenly. "I'm not leaving."

"I wish you would," I said, not looking at him.

"No. I have to stay and fight this thing. Or else I'll do something nutty like coming back and asking you to marry me."

I didn't understand. Wouldn't it be easier if he wasn't around me every day?

"You're not making sense, Bill," I said. "I wish you'd go away."

"Do you?" he asked. "Do you really? Be honest."

"I, I love Tom," I said. "We're getting married. It's all settled."

Bill was silent. Then he sighed. "Okay, that does it!" He picked up my coat, smiling sadly. "How about a last dance? Look, we practically have the whole place to ourselves."

"No," I said, but he put down my coat and took me in his arms.

We danced too long, too close, and I couldn't break away. And later, back in the car, I couldn't turn away from his kisses. It was as if Tom had never existed. It was as if I'd been starved for years—as if it really was the way Bill had said, the princess locked up in the tower, waiting to be rescued.

Finally, with a sob, I made Bill stop. I huddled in my corner, shivering with excitement and fear. Bill didn't touch me again; he just stared ahead.

"We have to see this thing through," he said finally, and I couldn't argue. I felt the same way.

So I became a liar and a cheat. It was easy to fool my parents. The club was very busy during the holidays, and I often had to work late. I was able to go off with Bill freely, without anyone being the wiser. It was so foreign to my nature, and I hated myself. Yet, it was also wonderful. Bill brought out a new side of me—a fun-loving person I had never been with Tom.

Sometimes I was ashamed to even look at Mom and Dad, and I'd feel like a criminal, lying to the people who loved and trusted me. But I was so intoxicated I couldn't think straight. The only thing I was sure of was that I wouldn't let Bill make love to me. There was something—some fear—that wouldn't let me. At the time, I didn't know why.

In March, Mom put a deposit on the Crystal Room and ordered the wedding invitations. I tried to stop her, but it was no use. When I asked her to wait, she stared at me in amazement.

"Wait for what?" she said. "Haven't we waited long enough?"

Dad frowned. "What are you trying to tell us, Kathy?" he asked.

"I-I'm not sure I want to marry Tom," I stammered.

Mom gasped. "See!" she said. "I told you, George, didn't I? And you thought I was crazy!"

I looked at them, a glimmer of hope seeping into my confusion. Maybe they would understand how I felt after all.

"You're not mad at me?" I asked, close to tears. "I thought you would be. I've been so miserable."

"Of course we're not mad, honey," Mom said, stroking my hair. "We understand. Every bride-to-be gets the jitters. I told Dad we could expect a difficult time with you these last months—especially with Tom away." She held me close. "This is a happy time, but a miserable one, too." Her voice broke. "It's hard on us, too. We-we all have to be patient with each other."

"You still love Tom, don't you?" Dad asked.

"I-I don't know," I said. "It's not the same anymore."

"Of course it isn't," Mom said. "You probably have times when you think you even hate him. Why shouldn't you? He's taking you away from us!" She laughed shakily. "Poor Tom, so far away, with nobody to comfort him."

She made me feel so childish and ungrateful. I wanted to tell them about Bill, but what was there to tell? That I'd met this handsome, irresponsible, lovable guy, and I was under his spell? Mom would have explained that away, too. She'd have said I was using Bill as an escape. She'd forbid me to see him and keep close tabs on me. I couldn't have stood that.

After Mom went up to bed that night, Dad said to me, "Honey, your mother's always one step ahead of us. Listen to her. She's smart. She usually knows what's best."

I nodded, hoping he was right.

Mom dragged me to the dressmaker, telling me not to worry about the money. The gown would be worth it, she said. Every time I went for a fitting, I felt like bawling. But Mom and Mildred Frost were so busy with the gown they didn't notice.

"Baby, you're losing too much weight," Dad said one night. "You don't look happy. Maybe we should wait until Tom comes home before we go ahead with the plans."

"Yes," I said with quiet desperation, "that's the way I want it."

But Mom flared up. "That's ridiculous!" she said. "You just don't understand young girls, George." She ran her hand through her hair nervously. "We're all edgy because of the excitement and tension. It doesn't mean anything."

June came all too soon. My gown was ready. Mom was completely taken up with checking lists, keeping a record of the wedding presents that were piling up, and cleaning house for all the company that would be coming. It was impossible even to talk to her. I moved through it all as if I were in a nightmare, wanting to cry, to run, but I couldn't.

I turned to Bill for help, but he was just as miserable as I was. "If I knew what to do," he said, "I'd tell you. I'd give anything to—to have you, but I don't want to get married, and I don't even know if you want to marry me. Do you?"

"I don't know." I sobbed. "Sometimes I think I do, but other times I think I don't. And when I think of Tom, I feel the same way. Maybe I'm losing my mind!"

Again and again we decided that Bill should go away and maybe then our problems would be solved. But he couldn't leave, and I didn't have the strength to stop seeing him.

Just before Tom's graduation, Dad got sick. Naturally, Tom expected me to go up with his folks for the commencement exercises, but I felt I should stay home and help with Dad. They wouldn't hear of it, and Mom nagged until I finally gave in.

When I saw Tom, he looked different to me. He seemed tired, thinner, and it hurt me to look at him. It hurt, too, when he took me in his arms, whispering, "It's been a long time, Kathy. Sometimes I felt as if I'd never see you again."

His kiss was tender, searching. I tried to respond, but I couldn't.

He pulled back. "Guess we have to get used to each other all over again," he said.

I nodded, relieved. Tom wouldn't push me. He

was careful, not impulsive like Bill.

I tried not to think of Bill, tried so hard that there were moments when I succeeded. Especially when I saw Tom in his cap and gown receiving awards and then his diploma. I heard a sob and turned. Tom's mother was watching with tears rolling down her cheeks. I reached out and held her hand.

"He's worked so hard for this," she whispered. "Never had fun like other boys. Just worked, from the time he was a little one. I'm so proud of him!"

I choked up then, seeing it her way for a moment, Tom's way. No, Tom and Bill weren't in the same league. Bill would wander aimlessly all his life, without roots, without responsibilities, unless—unless he married me and I helped him to settle down.

But how could I want Bill? How could any girl in her right mind give up Tom for him?

With all the activities going on, Tom and I hardly had a chance to be alone. We didn't even leave together because he stayed on to clear up some last-minute details. It was such a relief to get away from him, to stop pretending that everything was still the same between us.

Dad seemed a little better when I got home. At least he was allowed downstairs and had no fever. The doctor said he could even sit out in the backyard for a while.

Mom wanted to know every detail of the commencement, and she beamed when I told her Tom had graduated with honors.

"What luck we had the good sense to pick a boy like that," she said.

We? All of a sudden I choked up and ran out of the room.

"Kathy!" Dad called after me.

"Let her alone," Mom said. "She's tired and nervous."

I couldn't stay in my room. I couldn't wait for the next day to be back at work. I told Mom I was going for a walk. When I got out, I ran to the nearest phone and called Bill.

I was shaking when he met me. He bundled me into the car and drove to our favorite parking place. "I nearly went out of my mind," he said, "missing you, jealous as all hell."

I cried then, helpless as he kissed me and held me close.

"I can't go through with it," I said. "I can't marry Tom. He's wonderful, but—"

"You love me, don't you, Kathy?" Bill asked.

I stared at him. "I don't know. That's the awful thing—I don't know."

But I knew one thing: I couldn't go through with the wedding.

"Kathy, if I—if I asked you to elope—" Bill said.

"Don't! Please don't ask me," I cried.

"Maybe it's the only solution."

"Don't!"

Bill shook his head and then drove me home. For the first time I didn't ask him to stop a few blocks away. I hoped Mom would see us. I even thought of bringing Bill in.

When we pulled up in front of the house, Mom was on the porch. As soon as she saw me, she ran down the steps to the car.

"Where've you been?" she demanded. "Tom's been calling all afternoon. He got in sooner than he expected, and he's coming for dinner."

"I, I met Bill," I stammered. "He works at the club." I introduced them. Bill looked guilty as Mom stared at him.

As I got out of the car, Mom looked at me as if she'd like to open up my head and see what was going on. "Come in for coffee, Bill," she said, and it was more an order than an invitation.

Bill glanced uneasily at me and then climbed out. Mom sort of gasped as she looked him over. It was no wonder. I'd seen lots of women at the club react to him like that. He was about as good looking as a man could be.

Over coffee and cake, Mom asked Bill all about himself. Dad joined us, and they both listened to Bill as he told them about the Navy and all the fascinating places he'd been. I noticed Dad kept watching us both, puzzled.

Finally Mom glanced at the kitchen clock. "I don't like to rush you, Bill," she said, "but Kathy's fiancé will be here soon."

Bill rose awkwardly, and it was the first time I'd ever seen him at a loss for words. He swallowed hard.

"I'm sorry I can't ask you to stay and meet him," Mom went on. "He's a wonderful boy, just right for Kathy. So intelligent and ambitious—" She couldn't have been more obvious if she tried.

Bill s eyes met Mom's. "I hope they'll be happy," he said. "If Tom is the one Kathy wants, that is."

"Oh, no question about that!" Mom said quickly. "She's never loved any other boy. She never will. I know my daughter. I know her better than she knows herself."

"Do you?" Bill asked softly, but there was a hard glint in his eyes.

Dad cleared his throat. "Nice meeting you. Maybe you'll drop around sometime again."

Then it happened—the thing I'd hoped for and dreaded. The front door opened, and Tom burst in!

We all stared, and for once Mom's ready tongue failed her. It was Bill who recovered first. "Guess this is the lucky bridegroom," he said.

I introduced them, and they shook hands.

"Bill works over at the club," Mom said. "He was nice enough to bring Kathy home. He's just leaving. Bill, the front door is that way. Tom, why don't you and Dad watch TV while Kathy and I get dinner ready?"

We all heard the words. We all heard the false ring in them. Mom wasn't fooling Tom.

Bill let himself out, and Tom looked at me steadily.

"I-I didn't expect you until tomorrow," I said.

"I rushed," Tom told me. He made no move to go in the living room with Dad. He just stood there watching me. I was so nervous, I kept dropping things as I set the table, and all the time Tom's steady eyes never left my face.

Mom kept up a running chatter, congratulating Tom on his awards, telling him all about the wedding plans and how impressive the wedding would be. Then she suggested we go look at the wedding presents.

"Later," Tom said politely, his eyes still following me.

Nobody ate much dinner. Nobody had anything to say except Mom. And after a while, even she ran out of words. After dinner she suggested we call our minister and arrange with him about the wedding rehearsal.

Nobody moved.

"Go ahead, Kathy," Mom said. "Call Dr. Brent. My goodness, don't you realize all the weddings he has scheduled?"

Tom kept looking at me, his face stern and white, his eyes bleak. "Should I call, Kathy?" he asked. I shook my head.

"Oh, all right, I'll call," Mom said.

She started toward the phone, but Tom put his hand on her arm. "Wait," he said. "Kathy has something to tell us. Something she wanted to tell me a few days ago at commencement."

I stared at him, startled. He had known! I opened my mouth, but no words came. My heart was pounding so hard I felt faint. I could hardly stand up. "What kind of silly talk is that?" Mom cried.

"Kathy, tell me," Tom insisted.

"There's nothing to tell!" Mom said.

I began to tremble. I couldn't look at Tom. I couldn't bear the agony in his face.

"Maybe there isn't anything to tell," he said. "Maybe we all know. We all saw him a little while ago. Kathy, how long have you known Bill?"

"Bill!" Mom exploded. "He's nothing—nobody! He just works at—"

"Do you love him?" Tom forced out the words.

Mom turned on me. "Say something! Where did Tom get this crazy notion?"

"The moment she walked off the train," he said. "The moment she looked at me. The moment I kissed her. I knew she was miles away."

His voice broke, and he turned abruptly and started out.

"Wait," Mom cried. "Kathy, what's the matter with you?"

I couldn't speak. I turned to Dad, and his arms closed around me.

"Listen, Tom," Mom said, "you're imagining things. There's nothing between Kathy and Bill. I'd know if there was."

Tom didn't pay any attention. "I don't want her if she doesn't want me!" he said.

Mom looked wild. "You're crazy," she said, "both of you. You've both got the jitters. Why, when Dad and I eloped, I nearly backed out at the last minute. I was so scared! Remember, George? Remember?"

Suddenly my nerves snapped, and I screamed. "I can't go through with it. I can't!" I broke away from Dad and ran up to my room, wanting to die.

Later Mom came in and sat down beside me. "Kathy, dear," she said, "we talked it over, Tom and I. We decided to postpone the wedding. We'll say Dad's too sick. Everybody will believe that. Meanwhile, you and Tom will have a chance to be together again. This last separation was just too much." She smoothed my hair and kissed me. "Don't worry, darling, everything will be fine."

I felt sick and feverish. I tried to sleep, but all the time I kept hearing Mom's words: *We decided— Tom and I . . .*

As usual, they were making the decisions. That's the way it had been all along.

I couldn't get up for work the next day. Mom fussed over me as if I were a baby. It made me feel stupid, helpless, and the resentment in me kept growing.

In the afternoon Tom came over. He sat on my bed and took my hand.

"I've been thinking," he said. "Four years is a long

time to wait. I-I want you to know I understand. You're free, Kathy. I—" He choked and turned away.

I couldn't breathe. I wanted to reach out to him, to comfort him, to kiss away that awful look on his face. I wanted with all my heart to tell him I loved him. But I couldn't. I had no words for him. All I felt for him was pity, shame, guilt—but no love.

He waited a moment, and when I didn't say anything, he walked slowly out.

A few minutes later Mom came in, her face white with shock.

"What did you do?" she cried. "Tom said it's all over! Kathy, what did you say to him? Last night it was all decided—"

I stared at Mom. Why didn't she try to understand my feelings instead of hurling accusations at me?

Dad came in. "Wait a minute, Laura," he said. "Give her a chance to explain."

Mom turned on him in a fury. "You keep out of this, George! Everything's all set." She turned back to me again. "You can't back out now. It's not right!"

"The right thing is what Kathy and Tom want," Dad said.

"They want each other," Mom answered quickly. "They're just mixed up."

Dad was looking at me. "You like this guy, Bill, don't you, Kathy?"

"Bill!" Mom spat out his name. "Who is he? A nobody!"

"No, he isn't," I said, rushing to his defense. "Bill's got deep feelings for me, and I—I have them for him."

Mom's hands flew to her face. She didn't utter a

sound, just stared at me in disbelief, her eyes wide with fear.

"Do you love him?" Dad asked.

I clenched my fists. "I don't know for sure, but I can't marry Tom. That's the one thing I'm sure about. I just can't do it." It felt good to admit it.

Suddenly Mom found her voice. "You can't!" she sneered. "No, you'll throw away your life on that stupid Bill, lose everything I worked for, planned for. Oh, Kathy, how can you even think of giving up a man like Tom? Look at your friends. Just look at them! What have they got? Tied down with babies and housework and no money. That's all they'll ever have. It's all I ever had, and I know what a miserable life it is!"

"Listen," Dad interrupted, "she can't marry Tom if she doesn't love him. There's got to be love."

"Love!" Mom cried out. "What good is it? It goes, it dies. It's not worth much when you can't live decent and get someplace in the world!"

Dad stared at her, as shocked as I was. Suddenly he looked gray.

"Stop it, Mom," I pleaded. "Stop it!"

But there was no stopping her. She went on and on, all the frustrations of the years flooding out. I jumped out of bed and ran to Dad, but he pushed me away and rushed out of the room.

Mom began to cry. "How can you do this to me, Kathy?" she sobbed. "I always hoped you were going to have a different life, the things I never had. How can you kill me like this?"

It was a terrible thing to realize that part of Mom must always have hated Dad because we were poor. I could hardly bear to be in the same room with her, and I was grateful when she finally left.

I must have lain there for about an hour. Finally I got up and dressed and crept downstairs. I started out the front door without really thinking about where I was going. Dad was on the porch leaning against a pillar, his head bent. I ached so for him I couldn't even cry. How could Mom have hurt him that way?

I went over beside him, but I didn't dare touch him. He seemed so remote—so walled off by his grief and pain.

"It's all my fault," I said, groping for the right words. "I've been seeing Bill on the sly, lying to you and Mom. Oh, Dad, I'm sorry! I shouldn't have. That's what got Mom so upset—"

Dad came to life then. He put an arm around my shoulders. "Don't be sorry," he told me. "If we'd been good parents, you wouldn't have had to lie."

"Dad," I whispered, "what should I do now? I don't want to hurt Mom—"

His answer was so simple that I should have known it myself. "It's your life, Kathy," he said, "not your mother's. Do what's right for you."

When I went back in the house, Mom was lying on the sofa, her eyes closed, her face white. For a moment I felt sorry for her, but then I thought of Dad and my pity went.

"Dad's miserable," I said. "Can't you do something, Mom? Tell him you didn't mean it?"

She sat up and looked at me grimly. "Kathy, I forbid you to see Bill ever again. And I don't want you to go back to your job."

Something snapped in me. "You forbid me?" I said.

"Yes!"

I shook my head. "You can't do that. You can't forbid me to do anything any more. If I'm old enough to get married, I'm old enough to make my own decisions.

She stared at me in horror. Then her eyes filled with tears. "Oh, honey—" she began.

But I didn't stay to listen to what she was going to say. I knew that since she'd found she couldn't order me to do what she wanted, she'd probably try to work on my sympathies—and I didn't want to take the chance that I might give in.

I ran to my room, trembling with rage, telling myself I'd elope with Bill and show Mom she couldn't run my life. Then my wedding gown caught my eye. I stared at it, lace and satin gleaming through its plastic cover. It was so beautiful, and I'd probably never wear it. Mom would have to sell it. I could practically see the ad in the paper: FOR SALE—WEDDING GOWN. NEVER WORN.

I sank down on my bed trembling, trying to think straight. It wouldn't be fair to Bill to run off with him just to get revenge on Mom, not as long as I wasn't sure whether it was love I felt for him or just a crazy infatuation. I looked at Tom's picture, and my heart ached remembering how I'd hurt him. Finally I fell into a fitful sleep.

In the middle of the night I heard it, Dad's strangling cough, worse than before, as if he was choking to death. I jumped out of bed and ran to his room. Mom was trying to give him his medicine, but the spasms kept coming and he couldn't swallow it.

When he saw me, Mom cried out, "He's running a high fever. Call the doctor!"

We waited forever, it seemed, until the doctor

came. After examining Dad and prescribing some new medicine, Dr. Simmons snapped his bag shut.

"George," he said, "I warned you before—you've got to get out of that factory. What are you waiting for?"

Mom gasped and moved closer to Dad. "What do you mean, Dr. Simmons? George never said a word to me about that."

The doctor looked at Dad. "I thought he told you, Laura. God knows, I gave it to him straight. The fumes in the factory have been eating away at his bronchial tubes. It's only a matter of time until his lungs will be affected. I told him last year when he had the flu, and again this spring. But it's like talking to a deaf man!"

When Dr. Simmons had gone, Dad said weakly, "Don't listen to him. He doesn't know what he's talking about."

"Why didn't you tell me?" Mom asked. "George, how could you keep such a thing from me?"

Dad didn't answer at first. "I'll get better. You'll see," he said finally.

But Mom shook her head. "I won't let you go back to that factory," she said. "I don't care what you say."

"But what else can I do?" Dad argued. "Gardening doesn't pay well enough."

"I'll work," Mom said, and as Dad started to protest again, she broke down. "It's my fault," she said as she sobbed. "I know why you didn't tell me. I know. Oh, George, you did it for me. God forgive me, what have I done to you?"

"Stop it!" Dad said, struggling to sit up. Mom knelt beside him, and he reached out to comfort her as she wept.

Maybe Dad had forgiven Mom, but I couldn't, not when he was so sick those next few weeks. Dr. Simmons wanted him to go to the hospital, but he refused. So Mom and I took care of him, taking turns sleeping so he'd never he left alone.

Both Tom and Bill called, offering to help if I needed them. I was grateful to both of them, but all during that time I had only one thought—getting Dad well.

Mom grew thin and haggard, but even that didn't soften my feelings for her. She was doing penance, I thought. Her devotion to Dad came from guilt, not love.

Dad must have realized what was going on between Mom and me. Because one day when I was sitting with him, he took my hand and said, "Your mother meant well. Try to understand that, honey. She meant it for the best."

I nodded, not wanting to upset him. "You should have told her," I said.

He sighed. "I was weak, Kathy. That's why I have no right to blame her, and neither have you."

Yes, he'd been weak, and so had I, but realizing that didn't make me forgive Mom.

The abyss between Mom and me grew wider. We hardly had anything to say to each other anymore, and I couldn't hide my bitterness toward her.

On the day Dad was to come down for supper for the first time, Mom broke down. "Baby," she whispered, "don't do this to me. You're all I have."

"You have Dad," I said. "Or doesn't he count?"

She looked at me with that hurt expression in her eyes that had always made me feel guilty and remorseful. I almost weakened, but then I remembered—that was the way she'd always gotten me to do what she wanted.

"Why have you turned against me?" Mom begged. "It's that Bill! He did it. He's poisoned you against me. I'm trying to help you, keep you from ruining your life."

I looked down at the floor, and the words came out of me so unexpectedly that I was as surprised as Mom was. "Are you?" I asked. "Are you sure it isn't your own life you're thinking about?"

Mom gasped. The silence grew, thick with pain and anger. Supper was ready, but I knew if I took one bite of food I'd choke on it. I grabbed my purse and ran out of the house.

I walked a long time, blindly. Darkness fell, and the lights in the houses went on. I could picture the families together over supper, close, warm. I felt lost, as if I had no home, no place to go. I thought of Bill. He was the only one who would understand. I went into a phone booth, hoping to catch him before he left the club.

He was there. He told me to wait where I was, and he'd come for me. I knew he wouldn't let me down.

And as I waited, a feeling of peace stole into my heart. It seemed that I was about to work my way out of the labyrinth of misery I'd been in for so many months. It seemed that Bill would show me the way—if he still wanted to.

Those first moments together were awkward. So much had happened since the last time we'd been together. Bill hadn't even known my engagement had been broken. I felt such a need to touch him, to be close to him, but I couldn't tell how he felt. He had a closed, guarded expression on his face.

We parked at the lakefront and stared out at the dark water shimmering in the moonlight. At last Bill broke the silence. "I'm sorry I spoke out of turn to your mother," he said. "But it burned me up, her saying she knew you better than you knew yourself."

I sighed. I'd almost forgotten that night, it seemed so far away. "Don't apologize," I said. "You were wonderful. You're the only person who ever stood up to her."

He looked at me in surprise. "I thought you'd be mad at me."

"No," I said, "just grateful. You set me free in a way Tom was never able to."

I clenched my hands tight and choked back the tears. I thought of Dad and his suffering, and then his words came to me: "I was weak, Kathy. That's why I have no right to blame her."

Suddenly I knew I had no right to blame her, or Tom. If I'd been stronger, more decisive—if at any time during the past four years I'd taken a stand and told Tom I couldn't go on waiting—at least I wouldn't have drifted into so much heartbreak. Tom would have seen it my way—or we would have broken up. And I wouldn't have involved so many other people in my mistakes.

"Tom seemed like an okay guy," Bill was saying.

I turned to him suddenly. "You asked me to elope once. Do you still want to?"

Bill opened his mouth, but no words came. He stared at me a long moment and then slowly nodded. With a cry, I went into his arms. Our kisses were wild with hunger, wild with love we were no longer afraid to admit. It seemed like we'd been apart for years. We couldn't get enough of each other.

At last Bill pushed me away. "Not this way, Kathy," he said.

No, not that way, not the way it had been with Tom, hurried and guilty.

"When?" Bill asked in a choked voice. "When, Kathy?"

"Tonight," I told him. "I'll pack a bag and sneak out after they're asleep."

"Oh, honey," Bill said, holding me tight again. "I'm not much, but I'll try to make you happy. We'll travel. We'll see everything. It'll be great, the two of us together. . . ."

It sounded wonderful. It scared me, though, the thought of roaming from one place to another, no roots, no home.

"What about children?" I asked.

"Later," he murmured. "First we'll have fun."

I started to say something more, but I stopped myself. I wouldn't be like Mom and force Bill to do anything he didn't want to. I'd just make up my mind that wherever Bill was, that would be home, even if it was only a furnished room.

We made plans to meet later. Bill had to catch the manager of the club and get his salary. The banks were closed, and we only had a few dollars between us.

Mom and Dad were in the living room watching TV when I got home. I slipped in so quietly they didn't hear me. On my way upstairs I glanced in at them. They sat close on the sofa, holding hands, absorbed in the program. It was strange, after all that had happened, to find them like that. A sudden pain twisted my heart at the thought of leaving them.

I locked my door and began to pack, throwing

things in my suitcase at random. There was a lump in my throat so big I couldn't swallow, and a nagging sense of guilt tugged at me. I knew I was doing the right thing, and yet it seemed such a wrong way to do it, sneaking, stealing away late at night when my parents were asleep.

Mom had never given Bill a chance, never given herself a chance to get to know him, to see how wonderful he was, to understand why I loved him. She'd never forgive me for eloping, I knew, but then I'd never forgive her for being so blind and so stubborn. But it hurt, Mom and I being poles apart, but since I couldn't give in to her anymore, there wasn't any other way. I had to be with Bill.

I sat down on the bed. I had hours to wait until Bill would come for me, hours to think and brood and yearn to be in his arms. If only I could push time forward, make the hours fly.

It was then that I heard the doorbell. I jumped up and ran into the hall. I heard voices in the living room, and one of them sounded like Bill's. What was he doing, coming so early? I strained to hear what was being said, but I couldn't. For a while I was so shocked and frightened I couldn't move. My knees were trembling as I finally got a grip on myself and went slowly down the stairs.

Bill was in the living room facing Mom and Dad. There was a moment of startled silence when I came in, and then Bill said, "When I thought about us sneaking off, I didn't like it." His jaw was set firmly, and his eyes had a determined glint that I loved. "I decided to tell your folks," he went on. "Besides, I didn't want them to worry. Kathy, I, I told them I'm crazy about you, and I'll take good care of you."

"Oh, Bill!" I cried and ran into his arms. I was so proud of him for having the courage to tell my parents.

"Listen," Bill said, "I was telling them, too, that when I went to pick up my pay and quit, the manager offered me a raise and said if I stayed I could assist him in the office."

I clung to him, afraid to say anything, afraid to hope that maybe Bill would decide to put down roots instead of living the gypsy life he'd planned. He lifted my face and said, "I told him I'd have to talk it over with you, Kathy. We could travel on vacations, unless—well, it's up to you."

"No, Bill," I said, "it's up to you."

He frowned slightly. "I could work my way up at the club. Being married and having responsibilities make a difference. I'd like to stay on. Okay?"

I nodded, afraid to trust my voice. Then I turned to Mom and Dad, waiting for the storm. Mom sat as if she were frozen, staring at us. Dad blinked and then stood up and came toward us.

"Looks like you picked yourself a real man, hon." He held out his hand to Bill. "Welcome to the family." They shook hands, their eyes meeting.

Mom just sat, deathly pale and silent.

"Laura," Dad said. "Our daughter is getting married. Give her your blessing."

Mom sighed, conceding defeat. "Yes," she said. "Only you don't have to run away. If you love Bill, then we'll love him, too."

I was stunned. "I thought you said love wasn't enough—" I stopped suddenly, realizing I was hurting Dad. But, to my surprise, he smiled gently and went to Mom, putting his arm around her protectively.

"I was wrong, Kathy," she said. "It was love that held your father and me together through all the hardships, all the disappointments. Only I didn't know it. That's why he could forgive me for all the hateful things I said. When he was sick, I knew that if anything had happened to him, I would have died!"

She buried her face against Dad's shoulder, and I realized it hadn't been guilt that had made her take care of Dad so tirelessly. It had been love.

"I did to you what I did to Dad," Mom said. "But I meant well, Kathy, honestly I did."

I rushed to her, and we wept together, tears of joy and relief.

"This calls for champagne," Dad said cheerfully, "only we don't have any."

"Will coffee do?" Mom asked, jumping up.

We had a wedding after all, a small affair at home with just relatives and close friends. Bill's family came and they got along with my parents as if they'd known each other all their lives.

When Bill and I were alone that night, on the honeymoon I'd dreamed of for so long, it was wonderful to make love without guilt, without haste, without shame. With Bill, I felt all the ecstasy I'd hoped for, and I fell asleep knowing I'd been right to follow my heart.

THE END

MEANT TO BE TOGETHER

"**I** know it's been a long day," I told Willie, "but we'll be home soon, boy."

Beside me in the car, my dog wagged his tail so hard that his whole body quivered. Usually Willie spent his days chasing birds in the fenced-in backyard. Today, my third-grade class at Fairlawn Elementary had had "pet day," and Willie had come to school with me. He'd stolen the show with his antics and tricks, but now he was tired, and so was I.

"See that?" I pointed up ahead to where the overpass crossed the highway. It was a landmark that said home was near. Just a mile more and I could kick off my shoes, mix a tall pitcher of sangria, put steaks on the grill, and fix a salad. Greg loved salads, and he'd said last night that he'd be over right after work today. We'd drink, eat a good meal, and then. . . .

Willie gave a low growl. Watch out, Beth! that growl said clearly.

Watch out for what? I wondered. I noted that a few kids were hanging around on the overpass up ahead, and as I got closer one of them raised an arm as if to wave. Willie growled again.

"What is it, Willie?" I glanced toward him as I spoke, and in that same instant something smashed through the windshield. I heard the glass shattering and simultaneously felt such a shock of pain that my whole head seemed to come apart. I heard my own scream, and then Willie's yelps of pain as there was another shock: grinding, jolting, tearing. And then there was nothing.

After that, the pain came. It was so bad at first that I couldn't think past it, not even to wonder what had happened. The first few times I came awake, I mercifully slid right back into darkness. Then, much later, I opened my eyes and saw Greg sitting near me. I wanted to cry: Greg, what happened? But the words wouldn't come.

He saw me trying to speak, though, and bent his face close to mine. "Beth," he said. I could see he was crying. "Beth, babe, how are you?"

I felt awful. My chest ached. My legs ached. My right hand was okay, but my left hand was all bandaged and so was most of my head and face.

"A rock hit you," Greg was saying. He was near me, but his voice sounded unreal, far away. "A bunch of kids were drinking beer on the overpass and throwing cans down on cars as they passed underneath. One of them got the bright idea to throw that rock at you. The police arrested the lot of them. I hope they—"

"Willie?" I managed to whisper. "Where is—"

"Beth, I'm sorry. After that rock hit your car, it smashed into the side of the bridge. Willie was badly hurt in the crash. His hind legs were paralyzed and he was all cut up." Greg drew a deep breath. "I figured you wouldn't want him to live like that—useless, crippled. It wouldn't be fair."

Willie paralyzed? My Willie put to sleep. My eyes were closing against the blackness and the pain again, but as I slid away I had time to remember Willie the way he'd been. He'd been with me since I was in high school, a mutt with long ears and short legs and beautiful amber-colored eyes that could see into your heart. Willie, who'd met me when I came home from school, and later, when I came home from work. Willie who was so smart he wasn't just a dog but a friend.

"Willie," I whispered and opened my eyes again. I thought that I'd just been asleep for a couple of seconds, that Greg was still with me. But the man who was bending over me wasn't Greg. He wasn't as tall, for one thing, and his hair wasn't fair like Greg's. He was wearing a white uniform, and at first I thought he was the doctor. But then I glanced down at his chest and saw the tag: "Kevin Parks, R.N."

"Hi," he said. "Welcome back to the land of the living. How do you feel?"

"Why do I hurt so much?" I managed to croak.

He looked pleased. "You're better, Beth," he said cheerfully. "Up to now, when you surfaced, you could only babble." He rested his hand against my right cheek for a second and nodded. "Nice and cool. Dr. Taft will be real glad about that."

As he spoke, he put a thermometer under my tongue and, at the same time, took my pulse. His fingers were cool and strong on my wrist. In spite of all the questions in my brain, I watched him curiously. I'd heard of male nurses, of course, but I had never met one.

"Who's Willie?" he asked me as he finished taking

109

my temperature. "You talked about him a lot. I thought it might be your boyfriend, but he doesn't look the type."

I started to tell him about Willie, then remembered he was gone.

"Willie was hurt in the accident," I told Kevin slowly. "Greg said he was cut up and paralyzed, and I guess he—he told the vet to put him to sleep." The tears that filled my eyes hurt. "We'd been together a long time."

"You were friends." Kevin's eyes were quiet with understanding. "I'm sorry, Beth. But you have to look at it this way: You're alive. And you're going to get well."

Now I remembered my first question. "Why do I hurt so much? My legs, my chest, my hand—and my face. Why does my face hurt?"

"Your collarbone is broken," he told me matter-of-factly. "So is your left hand. Your legs were badly bruised."

"And my face?" I repeated.

Kevin's eyes were steady on mine. "The rock hit you in the face, Beth. So, of course it would hurt there, too," he said.

The door opened then, and a gray-haired man walked in. He smiled at me and walked over to my bedside. "So you're awake today!" he exclaimed. "Let's see how the patient looks, shall we?" As he and Kevin worked over me, he told me that he was Dr. Taft. "The hospital called me to come and take care of you after the accident, Beth," he said. "And you're coming along beautifully. You're a lucky young lady. If that rock had struck you a few more inches to the right, you'd be dead."

"I turned my head because Willie growled and warned me," I said. I bit my lip at the memory, then winced with pain as Dr. Taft touched something on my forehead. "Doctor, what happened to my face?" He didn't answer me right away, and suddenly I was scared. "Please tell me!" I cried.

He sighed. "The rock was a big one, and it hit you with a great deal of force." Then he told me what had happened to me. The rock had smashed the bridge of my nose and torn the flesh on the left side of my face.

I begged for a mirror.

"Not yet, Beth," Dr. Taft said. "Not yet. In awhile, when things have had a chance to heal."

But I insisted. Finally, the doctor told Kevin to bring me a mirror before they rebandaged my face. As my eyes focused on my image in the glass, I could only stare in horror. That torn, bruised, damaged face couldn't be mine!

Dr. Taft pulled the mirror away from me. "Beth, calm down," he said. "I'll take care of you. I've already begun reconstructive surgery by taking skin grafts from your neck. All we need is time, Beth."

I don't know what else he said. I was too lost in the horror I'd just seen. I tried to tell myself I was lucky to be alive, but the horrible mask that was now my face kept haunting me. Am I lucky? I kept asking myself.

I'd never been vain about my looks, but at least I'd been pretty enough for my third-grade kids to send me funny valentines in February, and for Greg to love me. A hard knot of pain wedged itself against my throat as I remembered how Greg and I had talked about getting married in the spring.

"Pretty Beth," he'd called me as we held each other close, spinning our dreams. How could he or anyone else call me pretty now?

After the nurse and doctor had gone, I lay in my bed and tried to pull my thoughts together. Just a little while ago, my life had seemed pretty good to me. I had a job I loved. I lived in a good section of town, in a small, rented house with a big backyard for my dog. I didn't have any family living in this state, but I had good neighbors and friends. And most of all, there was the man I loved, the man I was going to marry. But now my whole life had changed.

Greg came by to see me that evening as soon as visiting hours began. He brought me get-well cards from the neighbors, candy from my friends, and a bunch of flowers. "They'll be in to see you soon. They thought you should rest up first and get your strength back," he said. He kissed the unbandaged side of my face, and I wondered whether he'd be able to stand kissing the other side once I had my bandages off.

Maybe he read my mind. "Beth," he said, "it's going to be all right." He held my uninjured hand. "I love you," he said. "We'll get married as soon as you're out of the hospital."

"But my face," I whispered.

Greg held my hand even more tightly. "I know about your face. Dr. Taft told me. Look, corrective surgery can do wonders. And it won't be so bad. You know what you look like doesn't matter to me!"

But it did. The next day, when Greg saw me for the first time without my bandages, when Dr. Taft and Kevin Parks were changing my dressings, I saw the horror in his eyes—horror and pity.

"I'm sorry," he muttered. "I'll come back later."

He didn't come back. All during visiting hours I lay in bed, listening for his footsteps in the hall, waiting to hear his voice calling my name. I told myself that this was the way it had to end—that I'd known this from the second I saw my ruined face—but it didn't help. A ball of misery, a hard, icy ball of pain, seemed to be growing slowly in my chest, till I could hardly breathe. I wanted to cry, but the tears wouldn't come. When the announcement came over the hospital loudspeaker that visiting hours were over, I turned my face toward the wall and wished I could die.

"Beth?" a voice said softly.

The deep, male voice wasn't Greg's. "Go away," I whispered. "Please."

"Is that any way to treat hospital staff?" Kevin Parks asked me. I didn't turn to look at him, but heard the sound of a chair being pulled up close to the bed. "I have a message to deliver," he went on. "Greg Connolly came by. We had a talk. Beth, he really did feel love for you—just not enough. He hates himself for being as weak as he is, and that's why he couldn't face you himself."

The bubble of pain in me had burst open. Tears oozed down my cheeks. The salt hurt, but not as much as I did inside. I felt Kevin stroking my hair, and thought: Greg never could stand to see pain or helplessness. What had he said about Willie? That it was better to die than to be useless, a cripple. To Greg I was a cripple, too.

"Let it out, Beth," Kevin was saying. "Just let it all out." Silent but comforting, he sat beside me as I cried. Then he turned my pillow, straightened up my bed, and gave me a pill to take. "It'll help you sleep," he said.

The trouble was, there wasn't a pill to make me forget. I had plenty of time to remember what my life had been like before, because I had to spend such a long time in the hospital. My hand was operated on twice, and Dr. Taft worked to heal the gaping wounds on my face. During my hospital stay, I had plenty of visitors. Mr. Dunne, the principal from the school where I worked, came to say that the kids missed me.

"We've got a good substitute teacher to fill in for you, but the children all keep asking when you're coming back," he told me. I explained about my face, but he shrugged it off. "The children know you were in an accident, and they know your face was hurt. I'll help prepare them for you," he said. He was kind and supportive but, of course, he hadn't seen me with the bandages off.

In a way, I wished I could keep the bandages on all the time. I couldn't, though. As my wounds began to heal, Dr. Taft ordered the dressings removed. I probably could have left the hospital, but in many ways I was afraid to do so. I didn't want to face the world yet. I kept hoping that if I stayed in the hospital, Dr. Taft could do something to make my face look better.

The doctor was encouraging, and so was Kevin Parks, but I knew that I was asking for a real miracle. I did some reading on plastic surgery and found out how much corrective surgery cost and how much time was needed between the many operations necessary to repair a face as badly damaged as mine. My medical insurance would never cover the costs of such surgery, either. In my darkest moments I wondered if I'd ever be able to look human again.

One day I was walking around the hospital. Since my legs had been badly bruised in the crash, it was part of my therapy to walk as much as possible each day. As I was walking past an elevator, a couple of men got out. They were obviously visiting someone in the hospital, because they were both carrying flowers. As they saw me, they both stopped walking and stared. Then they turned away quickly and scurried down the hall.

My insides tightened like a fist, and my face began to burn. I started to run down the corridor back to my room and nearly collided with Kevin.

"You're in a big hurry, aren't you?" he said. "Don't you look where you're going these days?" Then he looked at me and frowned. "What happened, Beth?"

I wanted to tell him, but shame made me shake my head. "Willie was lucky," I said bitterly. "He's dead. He doesn't have to feel the pain of being crippled—a freak."

Kevin took me by the arm and began walking down the corridor with me. "You're no freak, Beth."

"I'm not?" I turned to face him. "Take a good look at me, Kevin."

"Don't start feeling sorry for yourself," he retorted. "The hospital is full of people worse off than you."

I told him that I didn't want to hear about "other people."

He pulled me close then, his strong arm around my shoulders. "You know what's really wrong with you? Hospitalitis. You've got too much time to think about things. Once you get back home, it'll be better."

The way I felt, I dreaded going home. But at the end of the week I was discharged. Dr. Taft told me to see him in a week. "After I'm satisfied that the work we've done so far has healed, we'll start on additional surgery to pretty you up," he promised.

I thanked him, but I couldn't miss the sad look of pity in his eyes.

Kevin wasn't working the day I left the hospital. I was glad. We'd become close, and good-byes might have been rough. I'd wanted to take a taxi home, but somehow Carol Jacob, one of my neighbors, got wind of it and insisted on driving me home. On the way she scolded me for not telling her of my homecoming. "I could have gotten your key, stocked your refrigerator, helped you out," she said. "If you need anything—"

She glanced at me quickly, then looked away. She was a good friend—the best—but she pitied me, too. My face had made me a stranger to her, and I wanted to be alone.

But after I got home and Carol had left, things got worse. Everything was so quiet! There was no Willie waiting in the yard, barking his joyous welcome. Inside the house was no better. Food had spoiled in the refrigerator and dust was everywhere. Dead flowers stood in a vase in the living room, next to a framed photo of Greg and me.

There was a knock on the door. Other neighbors welcoming me home? I went to see and gasped when I saw Kevin on the front steps. His arms were full of grocery bags, and he had a wilting rose in his teeth. In spite of myself, I burst out laughing.

"Thanks a lot," he said, talking around the rose. "Take this weed out of my mouth before . . . Hey, is that all the thanks I get for running around town gathering up food and flowers?"

"What a flower!" But I dumped the dead flowers out of the vase to make room for the rose. Meanwhile, Kevin took the spoiled food out of the refrigerator.

"You didn't have to do all this," I told him.

"That's debatable. The Board of Health would condemn this place." On his hands and knees, Kevin was rearranging groceries in the refrigerator. "I should have done this earlier, but I had an errand to run." He stopped talking and gave me a strange look. "Meanwhile, I bet you've been sitting around feeling sorry for yourself."

I felt indignant! I was ready to laugh, but at the same time I was angry. "I have not! I just came home now and—"

"And what? Sat around? Where are your housekeeping instincts? Get a dust cloth." Kevin winked at me. "If you play your cards right, I might even cook us up the steaks I bought."

So we cleaned. Then I cooked the steaks, while Kevin tossed a salad and teased me for not having wine in the house for special guests. By the time we sat down to eat, the house felt different—not cold, sad, and neglected, but full of life. As we ate, we talked—not hospital talk, but about ourselves. I asked Kevin what I'd wanted to ask him for a long time—why he'd decided to go into nursing.

He grinned. "Money," he replied.

"Nurses make a lot of money?" I asked.

"Nope. I mean the lack of money. I wanted to be

a doctor, but I didn't have the cash. Anyway, I wasn't quite smart enough. Lab work didn't appeal to me, so nursing seemed to be the answer. I like what I do. The hours are terrible, but I feel I do valuable work."

I nodded. "Yes," I said. "I'd say you do valuable work. If it hadn't been for you, I'd never have made it. I mean, when Greg—"

"Greg was a shortsighted idiot." Kevin pointed a fork at me. "What about you? Why did you go into teaching?"

I talked about myself a little, and then a lot. I told Kevin how much I liked kids, and how I felt good about being with them, teaching them. He listened, watching me, and I thought: I can talk to Kevin so easily, it's as if I've known him for a hundred years. There was a warmth about him, an acceptance of me that I'd never felt before with anyone else, not even with Greg. But that was, I knew, because Kevin was a nurse. He was trained in the ways of people and of their pain. I was sorry when he said he had to go.

He had the midnight shift and had to get to the hospital in time to settle into the evening's routine. As we said good night, I thanked him. "I'm glad you came by, Kevin," I said. "I can't think of how to thank you."

He smiled and reached out to touch the rose that I'd put in the vase. "See?" he said. "It's perked up." It was true! The rose was alive and fresh again. "Just needed a bit of tender loving care," he said. "Like all of us."

For a second, that strange look was back in his eyes. Then he smiled and it went away. "I'll be seeing you, Beth," he said, and bent and kissed my cheek. Then he left.

He's being kind, I told myself. *He's just being a friend.* I touched the place where Kevin had kissed me, and turned to look at the rose again. As I did, I saw the photo of Greg and me on an end table— saw my face as it had been. If only Kevin had known me then. . . .

Suddenly, I couldn't stand the thought of how I'd once been! I grabbed the picture from the table, then ran through the house collecting everything that reminded me of my "old" self. There were snap-shots of Willie, too, and as I gathered these up, I began to cry. *Why?* I thought. *Why Willie? Why me?* I put all the photos in a box and shoved the box away in a corner of my closet. Then I went to the big mirror over my dressing table and looked at the reflection there—at the gaping scars, the new me. The me I had to learn to live with.

The doctors at the hospital had told me to take things easy for a while after returning home. I took their advice literally. Carol and my other neighbors wanted me to visit them, to go shopping with them, to go to their homes for dinner—but I refused. I also refused Carol's offer of her car—my own car had been totaled in the accident. "Until you get another car, use mine," Carol had said, but I told her it was-n't necessary. I wasn't going anywhere. I had enough food, and in any case, I wasn't hungry. I didn't want to shop, or see anyone or talk to any-one.

Then, a couple of days after my return home, Kevin came by again. He breezed in one evening before suppertime, saying he wanted to take me out to eat, and that he wouldn't take no for an answer.

"Look," he told me, "you can't hide out here forever. One of these days you'll have to go back to work, go out to shop, and do all the everyday things that have to be done. You might as well start now." He pulled a pair of very large, dark glasses out of his pocket. "Maybe these'll make you feel a little better."

The glasses covered some of my face—or at least gave me a sense of being partially protected from stares. Kevin hustled me out of the house and we walked for some time. It was dark, and not many people were out. As we walked, I began to relax. Later, we went to a small pizza place, sat in a back booth, and had pizza and beer. Kevin got me laughing over hospital jokes.

"You're too much," I told him. "Like my third-graders." I stopped. They hadn't been "my" third-graders for quite a while. Kevin seemed to read my mind.

"Maybe it's time you went back to work," he said gently. "The first day will be hard, but all first times are hard."

We talked of other things then, but my mind kept going back to his words. Kevin was right. First times were hard, but I had to get back on my feet. For one thing, I had to have a paycheck. And the school had been calling me to find out how I was and when I'd be back. Maybe I could start next week.

I told that to Kevin as we were walking home. "Good girl," he said approvingly, "but don't wait till next week. Do it tomorrow."

"Tomorrow! That's impossible! I haven't called Mr. Dunne yet, and I don't have any lesson plans prepared."

"So prepare. Go to the school tomorrow, talk to the substitute, and get your plans together," Kevin said. "You're feeling gutsy right now, Beth. Keep it up."

We were standing in front of my house. The night was dark, but a crescent moon hung in the sky. "You order me around a lot, you know that?" I said.

He grinned. "It's part of my charm. I know what's good for you."

"Do you?" I asked. I'd meant to make it sound like a joke, like part of our teasing, but the words came out sad and forlorn and hung in the air between us. "Do you, Kevin?" I whispered, and I saw his face change.

"Beth," he said softly, and then his arms were around me. Strong and warm and holding me close, so close that I could feel the thud of his heart against my chest. "Oh, Beth," he said. And then he kissed me.

Not on the cheek, but on the mouth. His lips were warm and loving, seeking, sharing. I felt a rush of desire run through me, so strong that it left me shaking. "No, Kevin," I whispered. He didn't pay any attention to me, just kissed me again. And then gently he pushed me aside a little to unlock the door so we could go in.

Our lovemaking was something wonderful— almost incredible. There was passion, but tenderness, too, and moments of intense feeling enlivened by just a trace of humor. It was like we were meant to be together, locked in each other's arms. It seemed as if we were part of one another.

When I could speak again, I murmured, "Kevin, you do know what's good for me."

121

"What's good for me, too," he said, kissing me again. "You remember that, Beth. Remind me whenever you want to. Every hour or so would be just fine."

I couldn't help chuckling. I nuzzled down against Kevin's warmth, and thought: *I'm happy. So happy!* Then I was afraid. How could this joy last?

As if sensing my fear, Kevin said, "You know I love you, don't you? I've been in love with you for a long time—ever since that night when Greg left you and you lay there crying. I wanted to hold you and kiss you and comfort you."

"I love you too, Kevin," I said, but my voice had a hollow ring. The fear was still there. Why had Kevin used the word "comfort" when he spoke of his love for me? Did he pity me, and was he mistaking pity for love?

Kevin fell asleep beside me, but I couldn't sleep. *He loves me now—tonight,* I thought. *When he sees me in the morning, how will he feel? When he looks at me and sees my face. . . .*

I pushed the thoughts away and put my arms around Kevin. Please, God, I prayed, let him keep on loving me. Please!

I was up early next morning, but Kevin was awake even earlier. When I awoke, he was sitting on the bed getting dressed. "I have to get going," he said. "I have the morning shift." He turned and put his arms around me, kissing my forehead, my nose, my lips. "It's too bad I have to work. I can think of better ways to spend the time."

I searched his eyes. There was nothing there but love. My heart lifted with joy. *He loves me . . . he really does!* I thought. As I got up to cook his breakfast, I felt like I could carry the world around on my fingertips.

Before Kevin left for work, he reminded me to go to school. "Don't chicken out, Beth," he said. Then he frowned. "How will you get there? I need my car to go to work, but—"

I said there was no problem. I'd borrow Carol Jacob's car. I hadn't driven since the accident, and it was time I started again. "I'll call Mr. Dunne at school and then ask Carol," I said.

But once I got onto the highway, I found I had a problem. I didn't even want to see the overpass where the accident had occurred, much less pass under it! In order to avoid the bridge, I had to swing several miles out of my way, so I arrived at school around noon.

I'd worn my dark glasses, so Mr. Dunne didn't get a really good view of my injuries. What he saw, however, made him look shocked, then determined not to show his shock. He shook my hand in an overly friendly way and said that he was glad to see me back on my feet.

"The substitute teacher, Mrs. Warner, has gone to lunch and so has your class. However, she'll be glad to see you," he said. He added that if I'd like to go down to my classroom, he'd ask Mrs. Warner to meet me there when she was finished eating.

The corridor seemed familiar, and so did the noises and smells of the school. I was humming as I got to my classroom. *Mrs. Warner certainly did a fine job with the kids,* I thought as I looked over the artwork on the bulletin board and the neatly written paragraphs tacked up on the walls. On the desk lay her plan book, and I went over to take a look at it.

123

But I couldn't see very well with the dark glasses on, so I slipped them off and bent over the book.

Suddenly I heard footsteps, and the door opened. Without thinking, I looked up and saw that one of my pupils, Jenny Clark, had walked into the room. I started to smile and say hello just as she screamed.

"A monster!" she shrilled. "There's a monster in the classroom!"

"Jenny!" I cried. "It's me! Miss Shafer."

But she'd whirled and had run out of the classroom. I heard her footsteps clattering down the corridor, her shrill cries about the monster at Mrs. Warner's desk. And then there were other footsteps, and Mr. Dunne's incredulous face poking through the doorway. For a second, his eyes filled with horror. Then he cleared his throat and shook his head.

"Kids!" he exclaimed in a loud voice. "Always joking around. I'll have a talk with Jenny, Beth. And, uh, Mrs. Warner's on her way here to talk with you."

With shaking fingers I picked up the sunglasses and put them on. I couldn't see too well with them on, but I could see well enough to see the relief in Mr. Dunne's face. "A monster," Jenny had called me, and that was what I looked like. Last night in Kevin's arms I'd forgotten that, for just a little while. But I couldn't forget for long. There was no way I could forget. As Mr. Dunne left the classroom, I knew that there was no way I could come back here to teach, no way I could resume a normal life. I wasn't normal. I was a freak!

I hurried out of the room, wanting to be gone before Mrs. Warner arrived. As I hurried down the corridor, I could hear voices. Mr. Dunne was in his office speaking to some of the teachers.

"It was—awful. I never dreamed—remember how pretty she used to be? She looks—she looks—"

"Plastic surgery can do wonders," someone said.

"Yes, but that'll take awhile. In the meantime, she's going to be teaching here at this school. There's nothing I can do to prevent her. She's got tenure and she hasn't done anything wrong. But I know I'll have problems. Jenny'll probably have screaming nightmares, and I know her parents will complain."

I wished I had the guts to walk into Mr. Dunne's office to tell him I was quitting, but I didn't. I told myself I'd phone him instead. I hurried out of the school, got into Carol's car, and started it up. My mind and heart churned with hurt. Well, I told myself, Kevin said the first time would be rough. . . .

Suddenly I wanted to be with Kevin in the worst way. With him, the hurt would recede. He'd make me forget the way Jenny Clark had looked at me and called me a monster. Instead of heading for home, I drove toward the hospital.

The parking lot was crowded, and it took me some time to find a space to park. When I finally did, I practically ran inside. I hurried up to the floor where Kevin worked. He wasn't in the nurses' station, but since I had come to know most of the nurses on the floor, I soon found one I knew. When I asked her where Kevin was, she looked surprised.

"Kevin? That's funny, Beth, I thought he was off today," she said. "Let me check. Maybe he came in to cover for someone else."

She checked, then told me that Kevin was definitely not at work. "You can call him at home if it's important," she added. "Here's his number."

I took the slip of paper from her and felt a sourness in my mouth. Kevin had deliberately lied to me about going to work. Why? I walked toward a pay phone, then stopped and looked at the phone number in my hand again. Did I really want to find out why Kevin had lied to me?

It took me a long time to dial his number. At first, all I heard was whirring and clicking. Then a woman's voice said, "Hello?"

Could I have the wrong number? My voice came out in a croak. "Can I speak to—to Kevin? Kevin Parks?"

"Kevin?" she answered. "You just missed him— he left a second ago. This is Sarah. If you want to leave a message—"

I hung up the phone, cutting her off in midsentence. I felt as if my legs had suddenly turned to jelly. A woman was in Kevin's apartment—and he had lied about working today! Who was she? Would he go home tonight to make love to her?

Somehow, I stumbled out of the hospital and got into Carol's car again. As I pulled mindlessly into traffic, the tears came. *Stupid fool,* I told myself. *Stupid!* I believed him last night when he said he loved me!

I had believed Kevin—and loved him, too. I loved him now. Why had he lied to me, made me feel alive again?

How could he have made me believe, even for a few moments, that I was lovable and not the freak, the cripple, the monster that I was?

Suddenly, up ahead, I saw the overpass. Through my tears I saw men leaning against the railing. My mind leaped back to the afternoon when it had happened—the drunken teenagers, the rock that had killed Willie and taken away the life that I once knew. Were those men going to throw something at me, too? Well, I didn't care! What did it matter if I lived or died? I couldn't work; I was incapable of loving or being loved. Why bother to live at all?

I was crying so hard I could scarcely see the road. "I don't care, do you hear?" I yelled to no one. "I want to die! I want to die like Willie did!" I gunned the motor and drove the car under the bridge.

There was a blast of sound. A horn! Suddenly I was aware of something huge barreling down on me from the other side of the road. In a split second, I realized that I'd been driving down the middle of the road. Any second, I was going to collide with the huge truck that was coming from the opposite direction.

I jerked my wheel to the right. It wasn't a second too soon. There was a whoosh of sound as the truck passed me, and a grating sound as it sideswiped me. Then I was pulling up on the shoulder of the road, shaking all over. I'd nearly been in another accident; I'd nearly crashed. This time, I'd been asking for it. I'd wanted to die. But instead of dying, I'd saved myself at the last second!

"Lady, are you okay?" a voice was asking. A guy with a hard hat tilted back on his head was staring in the car window. "Are you hurt?" he demanded.

I shook my head. "I'm fine."

"Hey, you had us worried. We all saw you from up there." He pointed to the overpass. "We're installing a high screen. That way, nobody can throw stuff down from the bridge to the highway. Seems some poor young woman got hurt that way awhile back." He peered more closely at me. "You sure you're okay?"

Finally he went away. After I stopped shaking, I slowly began to drive home. So they were erecting a high barrier on the bridge! No one would be hurt again the way I'd been hurt. I should have felt pleased about that, but all I felt was numb. I wanted to die. So why had I pulled away at the last moment? I couldn't think of a good answer.

Still feeling that same strange numbness, I returned the car to Carol, telling her how it got dented and that I would pay to have it fixed. She wanted me to come in, but all I wanted to do was go home, lie down, and be alone. But as I drew near my house, I saw Kevin's car parked in my driveway.

I stopped and stared. What was he doing here? Why wasn't he with her, with Sarah? I didn't want to see him. I didn't.

And then my dark thoughts faded away as I heard the faint, but familiar, bark. It came from inside the house. It was the same bark I'd heard during my high school days, and later, welcoming me home from work.

"Willie?" I gasped. I started to hurry toward the house, and then stopped again. A long, wooden ramp had been built next to the front steps. As I stared at it, the front door opened and Willie burst out.

His eyes were the same, and his bark, and the way he scrambled to reach me. But he came down the ramp—not the stairs—and he was only using his two front legs. His hind legs were resting on a weird wooden contraption on wheels that was attached to his neck by a kind of yoke.

"Willie?" I screamed.

He came running toward me, nearly knocking me down with the force of his greeting. I dropped to my knees and he started licking my face. His lapping pink tongue, and his warm amber eyes said, "Beth, where have you been? I've missed you!"

I tried to hug him, but he was out of my arms and trundling down the yard, intent on chasing a bird. His bark was full of glee. Hey, world, look! I'm back where I belong!

"He doesn't know he's crippled, Beth," Kevin's voice said. I looked up and saw him standing on the top step, watching me. "His hind legs are paralyzed, but he doesn't care. It doesn't matter. He can do everything he could do before the accident."

"How—" I shook my head to clear it. It didn't help. "But Willie was put to sleep! Greg said—"

"Greg did tell the vet to put Willie to sleep, but when the doctor saw how hard Willie was fighting to live, he just couldn't do it. The doctor waited, wanting to talk to you first. Greg told me all this the night he came to say good-bye to you. I went to see Willie myself, and I talked to the vet. He said Willie could be trained to use that contraption. It takes the place of his hind legs."

"But why didn't you tell me?" I cried.

He came down the steps and stood next to me, looking down into my face. "I wanted to, Beth, but you were too upset. You were convinced you were a freak. I thought that seeing Willie helpless would upset you—depress you even more. I wanted you to see him completely able to function like he used to. So I took him home to live with me for a while."

He nodded to where Willie was running in circles, chasing a butterfly. "It wasn't easy. I had to train Willie to use the contraption, and keep reassuring him when things got rough. I couldn't have done it without my next-door neighbors in the apartment building. You'll meet them—Ted and Sarah Michaels. As a matter of fact, Sarah helped me fix Willie up before we came over here."

Sarah—the woman who'd answered the telephone! And I'd thought she was Kevin's girlfriend! I hadn't stopped to question her, or ask Kevin about her. I'd just assumed that because my face was scarred, Kevin couldn't possibly love me, that he'd been lying to me. "Kevin," I whispered. "Kevin, I'm sorry."

He didn't ask me what I was sorry about; he just pulled me close to him. I leaned my head against his shoulder, thinking that Willie certainly had a lot more guts than I did. My conviction that I was a freak, a monster, had made me want to run from the slightest problem. Sure, people stared at me. But if I accepted myself, people would get used to me, the same way I was already getting used to the "new" Willie!

I moved closer to Kevin. "I didn't expect you home so early," he said. "I wanted to get Willie all settled in before you came home. Was it that bad at school, Beth?"

I thought of Jenny and winced. "Yes, it was pretty bad."

"Well," he said, "we figured it would be—right? Tomorrow will be easier. In a week or so, the kids'll be eating out of your hand again. By the time we get married in a couple of months, they'll think you're the prettiest bride in the world."

Pretty? I balked at the word, and then felt a sudden rush of joy that made me feel like dancing and singing—like throwing my arms around Kevin and hugging him tight. And I did.

"I love you," I told him. "You're something else! You know that, Kevin Parks? You're beautiful!"

He grinned and kissed me. Then he kissed me again. "So are you, Beth," he said. "So are you!"

THE END

MY DREAM MAN

It's funny, but when that telephone rang a strange shiver raced down my back. It was almost as if I knew it would bring me the happiest, yet most terrifying adventure of my life.

It was Uncle Jack, Dad's oldest brother, calling from his farm to boast they'd just had a baby boy, but Aunt Maria needed help for a couple of months. Would I come?

Would I? Nothing could stop me. I loved Aunt Maria. She was so young that she was more like a sister. Besides, summer out in Texas was as hot as the devil, even to a native like me.

I flew out a week later and found I loved summer—and I looked forward to going to Pennsylvania. But there was more to it than that. After the sun set, I would slip out of the farmhouse into a twilight world of secret adventure.

My last chore of the night was the supper dishes. Then I'd hurry in to where Aunt Maria rocked the baby in the front room and tell her I was going for a walk. After a month, it became a routine for my walk in the cool evening air.

I tried to keep the excitement out of my voice as I spoke. "I'll take my walk now. I won't be too late."

Uncle Jack looked up from the TV set. "I don't know what a young girl like you finds to do out in those fields at this time of night. If we hadn't needed you so badly, I never would have dragged you way out to a quiet farm like this for the summer."

"Uncle Jack, you know I love it here." I leaned over and kissed him quickly, hoping he wouldn't sense the excitement pounding through me. I had rushed the chores so I'd be free to get out, and now I couldn't stand to wait another minute. Outside in the darkness, waiting for me, were all my dreams come true.

I hurried from the house and down the lane. It all seemed the same—the cool fragrance of the bushes, blurring into shadow as the twilight deepened, and the freshness of the air, now that the summer sun had finally set. The only difference was in me, because I had decided I was going to share my secret with my family, starting this very night.

I was so excited I could hardly keep from breaking into a run, and when I could make him out, a blurred shadow waiting in the first nook of the old fence, I did run. And a moment later, I flung myself into his strong arms.

He gathered me in and held me tightly. He was tall—my head barely came to his shoulder—and his arms were long. I felt warm and loved and safe, cradled there.

"Oh, Kevin. It's been such a long day. I've missed you so," I whispered.

MY DREAM MAN

With one hand he gently smoothed my hair. "I thought evening would never come," he murmured. I could feel his breath warm on my face. "The day seems like an eternity while I'm away from you."

I felt a sudden thrill of hope. He'd missed me as much as I missed him! Maybe this would be the night when I finally could convince him to meet my family. I wanted so badly to take him home to Uncle Jack and Aunt Maria, then to write my parents about this wonderful man I had met. It had been hard to keep our meetings secret all summer long, and I hated to deceive my family.

"Please, Kevin, let's not wait any longer then." I was so full of hope, I was sure Kevin could hear it in my voice. "Let's go right now, tonight, and tell my aunt and uncle. When they know how much we love each other, they won't keep us apart."

I could feel Kevin stiffen, and his arms around me became like iron bars. "No! No! It's much too soon. You're still too young. They'll keep us apart. I couldn't stand to be separated from you, Jenny. We'll keep our love a secret until you're older. No one can come between us then."

I pulled away from him and gazed up into the shadows that blurred his face. "Kevin, this is foolish. My family is going to like you. They'll be happy that I've fallen in love with you. Please, please, let me tell them tonight!"

I felt torn in two. On one hand I loved Kevin and didn't want to do anything to make him unhappy, but on the other hand there was my family and I loved them. I wasn't that kind of girl who enjoyed this game of meeting a boy behind my family's back. I had a feeling of shame every time I thought about it.

Oh, it had begun innocently enough. About a week after I arrived, Aunt Maria suggested I take a walk down the lane and into the woods in the cool of the evening. As she said, the day was scorching, and what with cleaning and cooking and helping care for the baby I needed to get out and relax. The little farmhouse held the heat until long into the night, even with all the doors and windows open wide. I was glad to get out, because now I could explore the land where my dad grew up.

I met Kevin that first night. I wandered way down the lane, and when I came to the strange old zigzag fence, its heavy logs covered by the rampant growth of a climbing rose vine, a tall figure, some- where between man and boy, rose to meet me. He was nineteen or twenty, but his face made him look older. He was wearing tight jeans. He walked straight toward me, holding his hands out and smil- ing a warmly personal smile.

"At last. I've been waiting for you to come." He took my hand in both of his and pulled me over to a comfortable seat on the fence. "What took you so long?"

"You . . . you mean, you knew I was at my uncle's farm, and you've been waiting for me?" I stammered in surprise. "Oh, I'm Jenny Morgan."

He smiled, and his whole face lit up. "With hair like that you have to be called Jenny." He took one hand and ran it through my hair, but somehow I did- n't mind. He was so gentle.

Still holding my hand, he sat beside me on the fence and talked, telling me he'd been watching me from a distance as I went about my work at the farmhouse, and he knew it wouldn't be long before I found my way to the old fence near his cabin.

I tried then to bring him home to meet Uncle Jack and Aunt Maria, but he wouldn't come. Looking down at his work jeans, he explained he farmed his land differently from the other farmers in the area—natural farming he called it—and until he could prove he was successful, he was too shy to meet and talk to the others. "They won't approve of my ways," he said simply.

He'd never changed his decision, but now it had become important that he meet my family. Besides, there was a new reason. My dad had sent my plane tickets—my visit was over.

"Please, Kevin," I begged. "I'm going home in two weeks. We've got to tell them before I leave. Let's do it now."

"No," Kevin shouted. He gathered me so tight in his arms, pain raced through me. "No! They're not going to take you from me. I've waited too long for you to chance losing you now."

He was so upset I let the subject drop, but I knew I had to try again. For the moment we just shared the joy of being together. We strolled with our arms laced together, and Kevin talked of our future . . . the two of us together stretched out in our cabin before the blazing fireplace. Or at Christmastime when snow frosted the windows and we would hang pine boughs over the doors and across the mantel. We'd bring my family up from Texas, he promised, because he knew how close we were. We'd all be together, a happy, laughing family.

They were beautiful dreams we whispered to each other as we walked slowly down the lanes.

MY DREAM MAN

Though I had grown up near a big city and was used to the bustling excitement of the area, I was willing to exchange it all for this quiet little farming community, as long as Kevin was there.

I don't know why I felt so jumpy that night, but my head seemed to be swimming and I felt so hot I could hardly stand to have Kevin's loving arm around me. When he talked, as he usually did, of what a wonderful future we'd have as he raised crops behind the cabin while I tended our family, I could hardly follow him. My mind seemed to wander, and I just saw hazy pictures.

I know we were just like all other couples in love, but our love seemed so different, so strange, and Kevin's next words frightened me.

"Jenny, I love you so much," he whispered. "I couldn't stand to lose you now. I've waited so long. Just one more year, until you're eighteen, then you'll be my wife, and no one will be able to keep us apart."

I could hear his voice, but the world seemed to be swimming and the woods around us tilted and whirled. It all seemed mixed up, with the idea that I had to hide my love from Mom and Dad for a full year while I lived at home and went to business college as I planned. None of my old dreams of studying merchandising and then working in a boutique, maybe even working up to buyer, seemed to mean anything to me anymore. I was ready, now, to marry Kevin and take my place in the world as his wife and the mother of his children.

"No, no, Kevin," I said in a hushed voice. "It's all wrong. We can't make a good marriage by deceiving people. We've got to tell them. I'm going to tell them I love you, tonight!"

"No!" Kevin's voice was stern, and I felt that he was terrified of something.

"It's all right," I said reassuringly. "I'm seventeen years old. My parents know I'm old enough to decide what I want to do with my life. Besides, they'll like you, Kevin, and my dad loves Pennsylvania. He grew up right on this farm that Uncle Jack owns now. Why, Dad must have walked down this very lane and stopped at this very fence. I'll bet he remembers your cabin. Maybe he even has a friend who lived in it when he was a boy."

In my spinning head, visions swirled mistily. I could see my dad as a little boy running through the lanes with his dog. I could see other figures, another boy tumbling with him. Behind them the misty image of a young man in short pants, and a girl whose long skirt swept the weeds of the lane. I didn't want to see more. I was terrified, and I felt so peculiar. I had to make everything seem right and normal again.

"Kevin, Kevin, we've got to tell them this very night. We can't hide anymore from the world. Our love is good and honest, and hiding it like this is making me ill. We'll go right now and tell them together."

In this strange, dreamlike world I could find only one thought. If everyone knew we planned to be married, then our love would be solid and real. No one could take it away from us then, and all these swirling visions would have to go away.

"Jenny!" Kevin's voice startled me. It was stern and deep, not like the loving voice I was used to. "You will not say a word. Not one word! When spring comes we will be married, then it will be safe. They cannot take you from me when you are eighteen. Until then, no one is to know of our love. Do you understand me?"

Trembling, I looked up at him and he stared down at me forbiddingly. His eyes were dark in the shadow of his jutting eyebrows, but I could still see the flash of fire in them. It was hard to believe this was the tender, romantic man I'd fallen in love with. A shudder of fear went through me, but even as I drew back from his overpowering anger, I sensed that behind it lay terror and a deep gulf of sorrow.

A wave of heat washed over me and I felt my body slump in weakness. Something was horribly wrong! Suddenly I wanted my mom's reassuring arms around me. She would know what to do! Mom would make everything right again. I had to tell her.

"I'm telling them tonight, Kevin," I said as bravely as I could. "I must. I'm leaving in two weeks."

"Jenny, I forbid it!" Kevin loomed above me, powerful and angry.

Trembling before him, I hid my face in my hands. "I've got to tell them, Kevin," I whispered.

"Don't," he thundered. "If you tell them, we will never see each other again." He took my shoulders in his powerful hands and started to draw me close to him.

"No!" I jerked back from him. In my whirling mind, it was all mixed together—the stern shadowed face of the man I loved, the misty visions crowding out from every dark corner, an ominous, distant roll of thunder, and an overwhelming feeling that only home in my mother's arms would I find sanity again.

"I must tell them, I must!" I cried, and turning from

him I plunged into the lane and ran as fast as my legs could carry me.

The ground floor of the house was dark. The only light shone from Uncle Jack and Aunt Maria's bedroom. It was too late to tell them tonight, and I was glad. I felt so strange and weak and confused, I didn't know if I could tell them a sensible story, or if I'd babble of girls whose long dresses dragged on the stones of the lane. All I wanted at that moment was to lay my head on my cool pillow.

Quietly I crept into bed and pulled the covers about me. Now I seemed to be shivering, and the soft warmth of the blankets was comforting. The moment I lay down I felt better, and my shaking body relaxed. In a few minutes I had drifted into a troubled sleep.

I must have dozed an hour or two. The rumbling of thunder wakened me and I lay there with a feeling of foreboding, but not remembering what caused it. Slowly the memories came back. I'd had a fight with Kevin! I had run off, crying that I. was going to tell everyone of our love.

I sat up as the realization came to me. Kevin had said if I told them we would never see each other again! I'd never asked him why I couldn't tell. Perhaps there was some deep family feud between our people. I groaned in anguish as I thought of his face just before I broke away from him and ran home. Behind the sternness there had been fear of something unknown to me, and a deep sorrow.

"Kevin," I whispered in the darkness. "Kevin, what have I done?" I had fought with the man I loved and run away from him. I had left him, his face shadowed with sorrow, and run home. The way I had felt, with the dizzy feeling in my head and the visions, was no excuse. I knew I had to go back to Kevin and tell him I loved him, and we would work out our problems together.

Slowly I pulled myself from my bed. My legs still trembled, but they were better. I could stand and walk, and I didn't feel as weak. I still had on the light cotton dress I'd worn to meet Kevin, and now it was wrinkled, but I didn't have the time to change. As quietly as I could, I tiptoed down the stairs and out across the porch. Soon I was flying down the lane. The air felt heavy and still, as if it were waiting for something, but in my rush I didn't notice it.

I was afraid Kevin would be asleep. Surely he wouldn't have been waiting all these hours for me to come back. I thought I would have to go to the little cabin and knock on the door to wake him up. I had never been in Kevin's cabin. Some old-fashioned sense of propriety had made him meet me out in the open lane, and never once had he asked me to come in. I only knew about the inside of the cabin from his stories of the happy life we'd share after we were married.

The lane was dark and frightening at this hour, but finally I reached the worn fence and saw the cabin in the distance, the light in the windows glowing with a warm welcome.

"Jenny!" A figure rose from the corner of the worn fence and Kevin engulfed me in his arms. "I've gone half mad with worry, waiting for you," he murmured as he kissed me tenderly. "Never run off and leave me again, dearest. You're all there is in my life."

"I'm sorry. I'll never do it again. After this, we'll work things out together," I promised.

Kevin cuddled me warmly in his arms. I could see his loving smile in the patches of light as the flying clouds scudded across the face of the moon.

"You'll come back in the springtime, Jenny, when the daffodils are blooming, and I'll be waiting here in our cabin. We'll never be separated again."

I snuggled against him and the rough material of his jeans felt scratchy through my thin cotton dress. "I'll come back to you, Kevin, and we'll spend a lifetime together," I promised.

He leaned over and broke off a flower from the single rose vine that twined along the old fence, then twisted it into my hair. Just as he leaned and kissed me, a terrific clap of thunder sounded directly above us, almost beating us to the ground with its power, and a blinding flash of lightning threw the woods into stark relief.

The darkness and quiet that followed were impenetrable, but in a moment gusts of wind began to eddy around us, and the heavy air I had noticed before seemed to lighten and grow cooler.

"It's going to storm. Quick, run for home," Kevin said. There was just time for a quick kiss and a promise to meet in the evening, then I turned and raced down the lane.

I was only halfway home when the storm overtook me, and, drenched to the skin, I sloshed on through the deepening puddles.

When I reached the house, exhausted and chilled, I could just about climb up the stairs and crawl into my bed, covered with mud and still in my soaking cotton dress. I didn't know another thing until I felt rough hands shaking me in the morning.

"Jack, Jack!" It was Aunt Maria. "Call the doctor,

quickly. Jenny's sick. She's burning up with fever and I can't wake her up."

I opened my eyes groggily. "Aunt Maria," I moaned. "Water."

In a moment she was back with a glass and a cool damp cloth, which she put on my forehead.

I dozed off again, and it seemed a moment later that I heard the doctor's voice. "It's a little virus that's going around. She'll run a high fever and be dizzy for a couple of days. I'll give her a shot and send out some medicine, and you give her lots of liquids and keep her in bed. What did you do, go to the fair last week? That's where most people picked it up." He patted me on the shoulder and left.

I dozed off and on all morning, while my aunt and uncle tiptoed in and out. Now I understood what the dizzy spells had been the night before. It was the approaching fever that made me feel so strange and see those weird visions in the lane. I wanted to go to Kevin and tell him, but I was too weak to sit up.

In the afternoon I was a little better, and Uncle Jack came in to talk to me. "Jenny, what happened?" he asked. "I heard you come in just as we went to bed, long before the storm struck, but we found you this morning, soaking wet and covered with mud. Have you been out walking through the woods alone at night?"

"Not alone, Uncle Jack," I murmured. I didn't mean to tell him about Kevin just then, but I was still weak and sick and the story spilled out.

"Jenny, you're dreaming," Uncle Jack told me sharply. "Or are you making, it all up just to worry me?"

'It's true, Uncle Jack," I insisted. Again I

described the old fence and the cabin.

He shook his head and stepped to the door to call Aunt Maria, and when she came he had me repeat my story. Aunt Maria listened carefully as I told her about Kevin and how much I loved him. Then she turned to my uncle. "It's very simple," she told him. "She's heard all the old stories of your descendant, Aunt Jenny, and her tragic love story, and last night in her delirium she relived them." She put her cool hand on my hot forehead. "Jenny, you just dreamed all those things up in your fevered mind," she said. "There's nothing to worry about. Maybe you used to dream you really were that aunt when you were a little girl. After all, you are her namesake."

I struggled to sit up. "But I never heard about Aunt Jenny. Everything I've told you was true. It all happened to me."

Uncle Jack shook his head. "Your dad must have told you about Jenny. She died before you were born. I guess she looked a lot like you, slim and proud, with hair like yours. She had your eyes and nose, too. At least it looked that way from the old family albums. Those black and white photos looked a lot like you do now. She grew up right here on the old farm and used to walk the same lanes you've walked."

He stopped for a moment and looked me questioningly. "Are you sure your dad never told you this?"

I shook my head. "He always said he'd tell me something about my great-great-great-aunt someday, but he hasn't told me yet."

Jack seemed reluctant to go on. "Well, one time, Jenny, she must have been sixteen, seventeen then, met a boy. No, I don't know his name," he said in answer to my unspoken question, "but she fell in love with him. I guess he was a good man, I don't know, but his family had been on the wrong side of the war. People cared about those things around here at that time. It was over, but that Civil War lived in everybody's heart. My grandfather refused to let her see this boy again, so she used to slip out secretly and meet him down the lane. When my grandfather found out, he sent her away to his brother's home to stay. She caught typhoid there and died."

Uncle Jack sat silently thinking for a moment. "You see, Jenny, you've heard this story before, and when you got caught in the storm and came down with the fever, you dreamed in your delirium that it happened to you."

"No, no," I argued. "It's true. Kevin is real!"

"No, Jenny, it's all been over for almost one hundred years," he said gently.

Even Aunt Maria tried to convince me. "It's an old story, dear. Everybody here about knows it all. It was just the fever and sickness that made you dream it."

I tried desperately to sit up, but fell back in my weakness. "No, it's true. I know it is. The cabin and the fence, I've seen them. Last night the lights were glowing in the cabin. You see, Uncle Jack? There couldn't be lights in the cabin unless someone was living them, could there?" I was so anxious to convince him my voice trembled as I spoke.

Uncle Jack shook his head slowly. "That cabin's been in ruin since I was a boy."

Aunt Maria looked at me with sad eyes, and she

shook her head, too.

"It's true," I argued, but Aunt Maria and Uncle Jack tucked the blankets around me, saying I needed sleep to get well, and tiptoed from the room. I tried to stay awake so I could find some way to prove that Kevin was real, but my eyes kept closing. Just before I dozed off, I put my hand to my head and there was a wilted little rose still tangled in my hair.

Happiness flowed through me. I knew that Kevin himself had put that flower in my hair, and there it was in my hand, a real flower. Kevin was no dream! He belonged to me, forever.

It was two days before I opened my eyes again, Aunt Maria told me about it. I guess I was pretty sick. When finally I opened my eyes and knew where I was, I found my dad had come to get me and take me home. No one had any idea what had happened to my little rose. I guess it had fallen from my hand and been swept up.

I couldn't get anyone to talk about Kevin. Aunt Maria was so busy taking care of me and packing my things I didn't blame her, and Uncle Jack just shook his head and walked away if I mentioned the subject to him.

Finally I got my dad alone. He sat on the side of my bed and listened to the whole story, then took my hand in his and patted it gently.

"The doctor says to let you talk about it. It will get it out of your system, and you'll get over it sooner. You can talk about it with me any time you want, honey."

"But it's true! Kevin's real!" I cried.

Dad shook his head. "I must have told you about

your great-great-great-aunt when you were a little girl. I don't remember," he mused. "You were such a sweet, quiet little girl, and that's such a sad story. I meant to wait until you were grown."

I cried and argued. I couldn't make my dad believe it was true.

The next morning Aunt Maria packed all my clothes, and Dad carried me to the car in his arms and we went to the airport. I tried to make someone walk down the lane and find Kevin, but they all said there wouldn't be anything there but the ruins of a cabin. The lane was still filled with mud, and I could understand why they didn't want to slosh through that muck when they were convinced I was dreaming.

I cried half the way home. Then I looked at my dad's tired, drawn face. It wasn't his fault. The doctor and my uncle had convinced him I was delirious from my sickness. It was so easy for them to blame the old family story. I knew I couldn't worry my dad and mom all winter until I could prove I was right in the springtime when I returned to Kevin.

By the time we reached Texas, I was composed, and I acted just the way I always had. I enrolled in business school, and I'm making good grades now, too. I still see all my friends, and I'm very busy with them. In fact, I'm on the go so much I don't think my parents have noticed that I don't date. I'm making my life as full and rich and happy as I can, and soon I'll be eighteen.

When spring comes and the daffodils are in bloom in Pennsylvania, I'm going back to Kevin. I won't have to say a word. I know he'll be waiting for me. I'll meet him in the lane, and we'll go together to the little old church where so many of my ancestors were married and buried. Then, we'll walk down the aisle, where the minister will say the words that make me Kevin's wife. Then we'll go to face my family, and neither family feuds nor ancient stories will ever separate us again.   THE END

THE MAN
I WAS BORN
TO MARRY

He was already twenty-one when I was born, so there are many things I don't know about him. I do know that by the time I fell in love with Brian Stone, he'd been married, divorced, and had very little to do with women.

My parents were close friends of Brian's sister and her husband—Sue and Craig. They lived next door to us all my growing-up years, and I spent many hours in their home. It was not unusual for me to be included in family gatherings or activities since Craig and Sue didn't have any children of their own. Brian was around all the time, but he never was anything special to me until the summer I was thirteen.

I started maturing early, and at thirteen, I was five-feet eight inches tall and looked like a woman. I wasn't pretty, but I wasn't ugly, either.

Like all teenagers, I was interested in getting money to buy CDs and makeup. In a small town like Brooksville, it's not unheard of for kids to start work very young doing odd jobs. Baby-sitting was an easy way to earn some money if the kids weren't too active. My favorite was a little sweetheart named Trisha.

I was ten when Trisha became "mine" if her parents wanted an evening out or whenever her mother wanted to get rid of her for an afternoon. She wasn't much trouble, especially after she was potty trained.

The summer I was thirteen, her mother was pregnant and felt really lousy. But before the summer was over, I was the one who was miserable.

Trisha and I spent lots of time playing in the park, swimming, and taking walks just to give her mother some time to rest. Trisha's dad, Gus, was a schoolteacher who worked on a farm during the summer. I never liked Gus. It seemed as if he was always watching me. I never let him drive me home when I'd been sitting with Trisha. Even in the dead of winter I'd walk, saying that I liked the cold weather.

The day Gus took Anna to the hospital, Trisha's grandparents came and took her home with them. I was glad to see Anna's time come, but I was sad to see Trisha go away. My vacation from work was welcome, but all too brief. Just three days later Gus called to see if I could clean the house before Anna came home. Forty dollars was too good to turn down even when it came from Gus.

The next day I let myself in and immediately got to work. The radio was blasting some good rock music when Gus came home. I said "hello" and went on working. He went to the bedroom and was changing his clothes when he yelled over the music, "Hey, Pam, hope you like Daphne for a name, because that's what we're going to call the new baby."

"Daphne—that's pretty. Trisha and Daphne. They sound good together. Too bad she wasn't a he. I know

Anna wanted a boy," I said as I walked to the door.

"Well, there's always next time," Gus said with a laugh and a wink.

Trying to ignore his meaning, I walked back to the kitchen to attack the stack of dirty dishes Gus had forgotten to scrape before putting into the sink. With a sigh, I began to get the job organized, and was thinking what a loser Gus was when I felt his hand on my arm.

"Pam, how old are you?" he asked, turning me around.

"Thirteen," I answered, trying to ease away from his hand.

"You sure are all grown up, though, aren't you, honey?" He was looking at my legs sticking out of a pair of shorts as he spoke. His eyes traveled up to my skimpy T-shirt. I was wishing that I was home, or swimming, or anyplace but between the sink and Gus.

His hand slid up my arm to my shoulder. I tried to move, but he was quicker than I thought he would be. He grabbed both wrists and twisted my arms up behind me. He had me up next to him so close I could hardly breathe.

"What's the matter, Pam? Haven't you ever been this close to a man before?" he asked.

"Let me go now and I won't tell anyone. Please, let me go," I begged.

"You aren't going to tell anyone anyway. It'll be your word against mine. Besides, you're going to love being with me. I'm the best there is," Gus bragged.

"Please, Gus, let me go—you're hurting me." I was crying and struggling against him.

"Don't fight me. Don't cry. Let me kiss you," he said. He lowered his head and I felt his lips on my cheek, then on the corner of my mouth.

"Gus, you're scaring me. Stop!" I was yelling at the top of my voice.

Savagely, he jerked me to him and his mouth crushed mine so hard I could feel the outline of my teeth against my lips. Remembering what I'd been told to do by my mother if this ever happened, I pretended to faint. Suddenly, I just sagged. Startled, Gus's eyes opened as he tried to support me by getting a different hold on my arm. Grabbing my opportunity, I pushed against him with all my strength and began to run.

My hands were on the front doorknob when he grabbed my shoulders and spun me around. He'd ripped my shirt and my bare skin showed red marks where his fingers had raked me. Frantically, I kicked at him. He lunged for me, forcing me against the door. I was sick with fright as he began kissing my neck. As he deliberately moved his lips to my bare shoulder, one hand was working at the zipper on my shorts. Then, just as I was about to scream, his other hand moved to cover my mouth. I screamed through his hand, concerned only with trying to get away. As the scream died in my throat, I brought my teeth down sharply on his fingers. He jerked back in surprise. I pushed him hard, opened the door, and ran.

The day was hot and still as I crossed the vacant lot to get home, but I was shaking as if it were freezing. I couldn't seem to stop crying. Just as I was cutting through Craig and Sue's backyard, the screen door opened and Brian stepped out. "Hey, Pam," he hollered, "how goes it? I haven't seen you all summer."

I didn't want him to get a good look at me or I'd have a lot of explaining to do. "I've been busy," I said. "See you around." I kept walking, hoping he wouldn't stop me.

"Wait a minute," Brian said, coming closer. "What's happened to you?" His eyes took in the torn shirt, the tear-streaked face, and the reddened marks on my arms.

I was crying hard again and just wanted to get home, but I thought he might tell my parents and I didn't want that to happen. Somewhere in the back of my mind, I guess I thought I was partly to blame. "I fell down," I lied, not looking him in the eye.

"Oh, come on!" he said. "You expect me to believe that?"

I tried to walk away, but Brian grabbed me by the arm and turned me around. "Pam, those are the marks of somebody's fingers on your arms. Who did this? Please tell me. I'll take care of it."

Stuttering and sobbing that I couldn't tell him, I again tried to go home. He stepped in front of me and very gently wrapped both of his arms around me, telling me not to cry or be afraid. He held me close and patted my back as if I were a baby. He let me cry for a while, then told me to get into the pickup and he'd take me home with him. I said that my mom would be looking for me, but he argued that he'd let her know that I was with him. We walked to the truck, and he put me inside and closed the door. Telling me he'd be right back after he called my mother, he went back into the house.

After a few minutes I calmed down, and by the time he got into the pickup I had stopped crying. He started the motor and looked at me. "It was Gus, wasn't it?" he asked. I didn't say anything. I couldn't look at him. He backed out and drove over to Gus's. Telling me to wait in the truck, he jumped out and ran into the house.

Just being back at Gus's made me start crying and trembling again. After what seemed an eternity, Brian appeared at the door and walked back to the truck. He told me that I didn't have to be afraid, because Gus would never bother me again.

When we got to Brian's farm, he helped me out of the truck and took me inside. He suggested that I wash my face and while I was doing that, he'd see if he could fix the T-shirt. As I put cold water on my eyes, I began to plan a story in case my parents questioned me.

"Pam, I can't fix your shirt, but here's an old one that Sue left here," Brian said as. I heard the door open and shut quickly.

Brian was in the kitchen when I came out. Two glasses of iced tea were on the table. I sat down and Brian began to tell me his idea. He thought that my parents would believe that while I was cleaning Gus's house, he'd needed some help on a combine. In helping him, I'd torn my T-shirt beyond repair. As for my arms, I could explain the bruises away by saying I got them when I slipped and fell inside the bin. I agreed with Brian when he said that he thought that since he'd taken care of Gus, my parents really didn't need to know the truth.

We sat there in silence for a while, then Brian asked me if I didn't want to tell him what really happened. I looked at him and knew that I could trust him. Starting at the time when I first watched Trisha, I told him all about Gus. When I finished, he looked at me and said that he'd figured out most of what I'd said, even though Gus had denied everything.

"What did you say to Gus?" I asked.

"Not much," Brian replied. "Just to keep away from

you. Anyway, don't worry about it. He won't bother you again."

Now, I realize that a thirteen-year-old girl is too young to fall in love, but believe me, as I sat there with Brian Stone, I felt as if my heart would burst with happiness. I told myself that someday he would belong to me—that we were born to love each other.

Time has a way of making things more tolerable, and so as the summer passed, I found myself thinking less and less of the afternoon when I was nearly raped. I never sat for Trisha again. I always had an excuse when Anna called. So Gus never had an opportunity to bother me again. The one thing I couldn't forget was standing in the circle of Brian's arms.

Over the next several years, Brian and I saw each other as much as we had before. He treated me the same as always, and I did well at covering the feelings I had for him. I started dating when I was fifteen, and I enjoyed the boys I went out with. I tried not to measure each one against Brian, but it was inevitable. Not one compared favorably with him.

As my seventeenth birthday neared, I suspected that Steve, a guy I was going with, was planning some sort of surprise party. I pumped him for information, but he was not about to give me a hint. The night before my birthday, I did my hair, my nails, my eyebrows—everything I could think of to make the time pass. I jumped into bed at ten-thirty, determined to get right to sleep. Mistake! The more I tried to sleep, the wider awake I was.

About an hour or so later, I heard a noise outside. With my heart thumping loudly, I got up and peeked out the window. There was Steve crawling on the ground toward the house.

"What are you doing?" I whispered loudly.

"Watching you," Steve whispered back.

I started giggling and went to shut my bedroom door so we wouldn't wake my parents.

"Pam? Pam?"

"I'm right here, Steve," I answered.

"Why don't you come out, and we'll see your birthday in?" Steve asked.

I thought about it for a minute. It seemed like a fun thing to do. "All right, you're on," I said, unhooking the screen. I climbed out the window with Steve's help and was rewarded with a very nice kiss. When the kiss ended, Steve's hands were against my bare skin. It felt so wonderful that I didn't want him to stop.

"Happy birthday, Pam," Steve said as he began kissing me with more assurance. He pulled me close to him and whispered that he loved me, and all the time his hands and kisses were making a buzzing sound in my head.

As we started toward his car, Steve would stop every few feet and kiss me again. I was feeling more desire than I'd ever felt before. I knew that I didn't love him, but the feelings I was experiencing were too much to ignore.

We got to the side of the yard, just a few feet from Steve's car, when I heard a voice say, "Good night, Sue. Call me before you leave tomorrow." Brian Stone's lanky frame was outlined clearly in the glare of the porch light. Shame washed over me as I realized that if he saw me, I'd have to explain what I was doing out of the house in my pajamas with a boy!

Brian walked quickly to his car and started it. There Steve and I were, frozen in the headlights. As Brian pulled up, Steve opened his car door and tried to get me inside. I wanted to die, but no such luck! Brian stopped and got out of his car. As he approached Steve, I could feel his anger. "What's going on here?" he demanded.

"What business is it of yours?" Steve shot back.

"Pam, get out of that car. Now!" Brian said through clenched teeth.

"Brian, please, don't start anything," I pleaded.

"Then get out right now and I'll forget this, punk!"

Slowly I got out and faced a furious pair. Steve was ready to fight and Brian was glaring at me.

"Get back in the house," Brian said in measured staccato.

"Oh, come on, Brian," I begged. "We were just having some fun. It's my birthday."

I could see that he wasn't going to buy it, so I said that I'd go back in if Steve left right now. Brian agreed, but Steve wasn't going to be pushed around. After convincing Steve that any more noise would wake my parents, I told him I'd see him tomorrow. Reluctantly he got into his car and drove down the street.

"Now, young lady, let's get you back into the house," Brian said.

"What makes you think you have a right to run my life?" I asked.

"Pam, I'm not trying to run your life. I just don't want you to be sorry for doing something stupid."

"But I want to make my own decisions. I don't need another father," I snapped.

"I'm not trying to be your father! I'm trying to keep you from getting grounded for the rest of your life. You know how mad your dad would be if he caught you out here." I was starting to see the sense of it, but didn't want to give in so quickly. "Honestly," Brian said, "I only want to help you. I care about you and don't want you to get into trouble."

Turning around, I started back to the house. I got to the window, but the screen wouldn't lift. I tried a second time. It wouldn't budge.

"Now I suppose you need help getting back inside," Brian said.

"I think the screen hooked itself shut," I whispered.

"This is all I need tonight!" Brian muttered. He took out his pocketknife and gingerly worked the hook loose. He grabbed my arm and told me to hurry up and get inside before my dad found us and had him shot. Thinking of my dad shooting Brian, I started giggling. Brian put both hands on my shoulders and shook me.

"This isn't funny, Pam!" he snarled.

He let go of me very quickly and I stumbled against him. Suddenly I was looking into deep, gorgeous eyes that weren't angry, or amused, or fatherly. His arms were around me again, just holding me. He looked at my lips and bent his head. I raised my lips to meet his—and nothing!

He stepped back and said, "Good night, Pamela. Stay out of trouble for the rest of the night, would you?"

He walked across the yard, and I climbed back into my bedroom. As I drifted off to sleep, I was wondering what it would be like to be kissed by Brian Stone. Sometime in the night, I woke up trying to remember something important. Finally it hit me! Brian said he cared about me. Granted, he didn't say love, but caring was a start.

The next morning Mom yelled a "happy birthday" as she left for work. I jumped out of bed, put on the shortest shorts I could find, and a haltertop. Later I called

THE MAN I WAS BORN TO MARRY

Mom to tell her I was taking the car. She wanted to know where I was going, but I groaned and told her since it was my birthday that surely I could be allowed a little freedom. She agreed, but told me to take it easy.

I drove to Brian's, praying that he would be there. When I pulled into the yard, he was coming out of the house. He walked out to the car as I was getting out.

"What's got you up and around so early?" he asked.

I was scared and nervous, but I tried to sound very confident. "I came after my birthday present." I started toward the house, not looking at Brian, but hoping desperately he would follow.

I got to the door when Brian demanded, "Pam, will you please tell me what you think you're doing?"

He followed me into the house and watched me as I turned to him. I walked to him, put my hands behind his head, and pulled his face toward me. "I want you to give me a birthday kiss, Brian," I said, standing on tip-toes and closing my eyes.

Brian said nothing, but at least he kissed the top of my head. I moved closer to him and put my arms around him. He kissed my cheek and I turned to meet his lips. His touch was soft and light.

"Happy birthday, Pam," he said.

He smiled and started to move away, but then suddenly, like it was almost against his will, he pulled me to him and really kissed me. His lips were moving over mine, forcing them apart. His arms held me so tightly I was nearly lifted off the floor. My pulse raced as he trailed kisses down my neck to the top of my halter.

"Pam—Pam," he whispered in a voice I'd never heard before. His lips found mine again, and I knew that this was what I had really wanted for the last four years. I loved him. Plain and simple. I loved him! I

161

kissed him back with all my heart.

Somehow my halter was gone and the buttons on Brian's shirt were digging into my skin. Wonderful new sensations swept over me. I couldn't get close enough to Brian, and it seemed to be the same for him. He picked me up and carried me to the bedroom.

We lay on the bed as Brian began to teach me how to love. He helped me when I became shy and guided me when my instincts failed. My heart beat faster and faster until I felt fulfillment. Tears of happiness streaked down my face as Brian held me close.

He saw my tears but misunderstood. "I'm sorry. I didn't plan for this to happen."

"Brian, I—"

"I just lost control. Why didn't you stop me? Why didn't I stop myself! I'm sorry. It won't happen again—"

"Shut up, Brian! I'm trying to tell you that I'm happy." I went on to explain that although I hadn't intended this to happen, I had planned on letting him know how I felt about him. I told him how very special he was to me and how he had been since he'd helped me the summer I was thirteen.

He let me tell him all my secret feelings, and then he shook his head. "Pam, you know that I was married before," he said. "What you probably don't know is that she was miserable living with me. I made up my mind years ago never to get involved in a serious relationship again. You're too young to know what commitment is all about, and I'm too old to adjust to looking out for someone else, especially a kid."

"You can't be that selfish!" I cried. "I know you must feel something for me. Age has nothing to do with feelings!"

THE MAN I WAS BORN TO MARRY

"I'm telling you it wouldn't work, no matter how much you want it to," he insisted. "Any two people can get it on in bed, but there is so much more than that to what you call love."

I couldn't stop the hurt that was flooding over me. I had given my all to him and it wasn't enough. Tears of rejection slid down my face. How naive I was! What a fool I'd been. I'd believed that because I loved him, he would love me. Because I wanted to marry him, he would want me. I'd never thought he could turn away from me.

"You'd better get dressed and get back to town," Brian said without emotion. He didn't seem to notice the tears or the dejection I was feeling. He was only concerned with getting rid of me.

By the time I got home, my head was aching so badly that it wasn't a lie when I told my mom I was too sick to be bothered with a birthday celebration. After a restless night, the one thing that terrified me was the thought that I might be pregnant, but I was determined never again to let a man hurt me, no matter who he was.

As the days passed, my worry over being pregnant proved to have no foundation in fact, but my depression over Brian's treatment of me still hung on. My parents noticed and assumed that something very serious was wrong. When questioning me didn't bring satisfactory answers, they secretly enlisted the aid of Craig and Sue.

The first time Sue came over to "visit" with me, I thought maybe Brian had told her what had happened. As she talked, though, it was apparent that she knew nothing about it. Even Craig tried in his awkward way to help find out what was bothering me.

THE MAN I WAS BORN TO MARRY

One evening while I was over at Sue's for supper, Brian opened the back door and yelled, "Sis, I made it back. What's for supper?" I had to give him credit, because even when he looked me in the face, no one else in the room would have guessed that he was my problem.

I volunteered to do the dishes while they talked, and I heard Sue telling Brian that maybe he could help find out what was bothering me. She was far from subtle when she suggested that Brian take me to the store to bring her some ice cream. There was just no way out of it, so he agreed.

We left her house and drove in silence to the store. I ran in, got the ice cream, and got back in the pickup without looking at Brian. Several blocks from Sue's, Brian pulled to the curb and stopped. "Is everything all right, Pam?" he asked. "I've been thinking that it's possible you could be pregnant."

"Well, I'm not!" I told him. "Evidently you're not man enough for that!"

Without another word, or even a look, he drove back to his sister's.

Senior year in high school had a way of dragging, then rushing to an end. Soon I found myself packing for college and looking forward to a change in my life.

I was resolute in my determination to let no man make a fool of me again, so I always stayed in control of every relationship I entered. Truthfully, as I look back, the men I dated were nice, but I was really too much on guard to notice their good qualities. My parents teased me about being an old maid, and by the time I finished college, with a degree in Special Education, I believed that I would be.

My teaching job kept me in a fairly large city about

four hundred miles from Brooksville, and I rarely went home. My job was in the classroom and my contentment was my apartment.

Then, one very hot day in July, my mother called and asked me to come home for a visit. It was so unlike her to ask me that I said yes immediately. By evening I was on my way.

The closer I got to home, the more beautiful the country night became. I remembered similar nights from a long, dead past. Brian's face was clear in my mind, just as the stars were in the heavens. The hurt had lessened over the years, and I couldn't keep the good memories from coming.

Sometime after one in the morning, I got to Brooksville. Glad to be home at last, I drove to my parents' street and was surprised to see Craig and Sue's lights on as well as my parents'. I barely had gotten out of the car when Mom came out of the house to meet me. "Oh, Pam, I'm glad you came right away," she said. "Come in the house. I need to talk to you."

"What's wrong?" I asked, thinking it might be Dad. "It's Sue," Mom replied. "She's in the hospital. I don't know if she'll make it till morning."

"Mom, why didn't you tell me this on the phone?" I asked.

"I'm sorry, but I didn't know if you'd have come if I'd have told you. You see, although I don't know what was wrong with you and Craig and Sue, I do know that something happened, because you stopped going over there and wouldn't have anything to do with them. Sue always was concerned for you—always asked how you were, and I couldn't bring myself to ask her what had caused things to change. I went to see her this morning. She asked me if I would tell you she wanted to talk to you as soon as she could. I came right home and called you."

"I assure you that neither Craig nor Sue caused me any problems," I told Mom. "I'm going to go to the hospital right now."

I drove to the town where the hospital was, trying to blank out the image of Sue dying. I concentrated on my driving, knowing that weariness causes accidents. As I turned into the hospital parking lot, I thanked God for a safe journey and asked for His help to guide me through the next few hours.

The nurse on duty was an old classmate of mine from high school, and as she recognized me she said, "I'm glad you're here. Sue asked me just a while ago if you'd tried to call her while she was asleep. I have instructions to wake her no matter what time it is. She'll be even more pleased to see you than to get a call." She led me down a short hall to a room with a dim light.

"Sue?" I asked as I approached the bed. "It's Pam. Are you awake?"

A voice much stronger than I expected answered, "Yes, I'm awake. I've been waiting to talk to you. I'm glad you came." I picked up her hand and held it between my own. "I feel that something is undone between us, and I'm restless about it. Please just let me talk, and then maybe I'll get it straightened out." She took a deep breath and smiled at me. "I've made my apologies to those I've wronged. You're the last one I've wanted to see. Now I don't owe you an apology, so don't think you're going to get one. I feel that you were the daughter I never had, and I wanted you to know that I love you. You've given me a taste of motherhood. But, Pam, why didn't you love me enough to tell me what caused such a change between us? If it was something Craig or I did, tell me. I want to know.

"I've been puzzling over this for a long time, and for a while I thought maybe it had something to do with Brian. I know that there was something very special between you two, but suddenly that changed, too. I thought maybe Brian caught you with a boyfriend and got you into trouble with your parents, but that wasn't it. I figured that you were avoiding us for some reason, but Brian says that you just grew up and no longer needed a second family. Whatever it was, I need to know—because it's really bothered me."

Confusing thoughts jumbled through my head. Mom had said she was dying, but she sounded strong enough to battle death and win. I felt that she would see through any lie I made up, so only the truth would do. I didn't want her to think less of Brian, but I had to set her mind at ease.

I took a deep breath and told her what had happened, omitting only the fact that he had made love to me.

"I'm glad it wasn't something I'd done," Sue said when I'd finished. "But why didn't you tell me this before? You knew I would have understood. Maybe it's not over for you yet, because you and Brian haven't talked it out. You see, Brian was really hurt by his first wife. She ran around on him, tormented him with her affairs, and made him feel worthless as a person.

"He loved her so much he took her abuse for longer than he should have. She left him one day, taking everything she could with her. He never trusted any woman again. For a while he used women as much as he had been used, but he felt that was a sordid, ugly life to live. That's when he stopped seeing anyone at all. So you see, Pam, you may have loved him, but you didn't really know him. There's so much more I need to tell—"

The nurse poked her head in the room, interrupting our conversation. "You'd better leave for tonight," she told me. "You can come back tomorrow afternoon, but Sue needs some rest now."

I said my good nights and walked out of the hospital into the fresh night air. I drove home feeling drained and sad. I slept dreamlessly for the rest of the night and woke up when Mom called me for breakfast. I asked how Sue was, but she hadn't heard.

As quickly as we could, we got ready and drove to the hospital. A "No Visitors" sign greeted us at the door of Sue's room. A nurse explained that only the family could be at her bedside, and that she seemed a little less strong that day. The next day, Craig came to our house to tell us she was gone.

The day of the funeral was a typical summer day, one like Sue always enjoyed. My parents and I went to the church together, and I sat next to the aisle so Dad could be with Mom. In Brooksville, it was the custom for the casket to be carried to the front of the church, with the family following the casket and sitting in the first few seats.

As the organ played a familiar hymn, Sue's casket was carried to the altar. Craig and Brian walked slowly behind it. As the body of my friend passed, I turned my head toward her and said a silent prayer. Without warning, Brian's hand closed around my elbow, pulling me gently.

"Come with me," he whispered.

Quickly, I stepped to his side and moved to a seat

up front.

When the service was over, we followed the casket to the waiting hearse. Craig's car was directly behind the hearse, and Brian guided me there. He opened the driver's door and I slid to the middle as Brian and Craig took their places on either side of me. Brian started the car and began the slow drive to the cemetery.

"Thank you, Brian," Craig said, "for having Pam sit with us. I can't think of anyone who was more like family to Sue than you were, Pam." Unashamed, he cried as I held his hand.

"We'll miss her very much," I said, crying, too.

The drive to the cemetery was short, and after the minister spoke a few simple words, Sue was lowered to her final place of rest. We returned to Craig's home where people were already gathering. As I helped serve coffee to many people I hadn't seen for years, I realized how long seven years had been.

When everyone had something to drink, I slipped out of the living room and went upstairs to Sue's sewing room. I walked around the room, touching familiar thing, the dressmaker form, the box for quilt pieces, her thimble. So many memories.

"I thought I might find you here."

I knew without turning around that it was Brian. "She asked me to give you something," he said as he walked to the sewing machine and opened a drawer. He took out a small jewelry box and handed it to me. I opened it to find a wide, gleaming gold band. I was puzzled, because I'd never seen Sue wear it. She always wore diamonds on her left hand.

"Put it on, Pam," Brian said. Not moving, I just looked at him. "Here, let me," he said, stepping in front of me and taking the ring from the box. He slipped it on the fourth finger of my right hand.

"This was Sue's first wedding ring, the one Craig gave her when she was just sixteen. He always had promised her diamonds, and when he could afford them, he gave her the set she wore for the rest of her life. Craig doesn't know it, but she always loved this ring best. She never told him, because it was so important to him that he give her diamonds. She wanted you to have this because she loved you, too."

"Brian, I don't think I should take this. Craig may want it," I said, shaking my head.

"No. You see, Craig thinks she gave the ring away a long time ago. I don't think he'd understand why she kept it. Finding out might hurt him," Brian explained.

"Thank you," I said, starting to cry.

Brian wrapped his arms around me and held me. It felt so good—just like coming home.

"We need to talk, Pam, but right now we have to get back downstairs," he said.

The day passed without another opportunity to talk, and I went back to my parents' house. The next day came and went without hearing from Brian. By the third day, I had convinced myself that Brian had only carried out Sue's wishes and really didn't want to see me again. I packed in preparation for my return to the city. I was placing the first suitcase in my car when Mom called me to the phone.

"Hello," I said.

"Hello," a voice answered. "This is Brian."

"How are you today?" I asked, trying to keep my voice light.

"Fine, fine. Could we get together this evening? I'd like to talk to you."

"I'm sorry," I said. "I'm going back to the city just as

soon as I've finished packing."

The silence was deafening. It lasted so long I thought he might have hung up on me. "Brian? Are you still there?"

"Yes," he answered. "Pam, I realize I've no right to ask a favor of you, but would you please stop by on your way? It's just a few minutes out of your way. Please."

I couldn't say no, even though I wanted to. I told him that I'd see him within the hour. I quickly finished loading the car and headed toward the highway. Before I was ready mentally, I was in Brian's driveway.

"Thank you for coming out," he said as he opened my door.

"I can't stay long. I have to get going before it gets too late," I said, looking at a face the years had been kind to. "What is it you wanted?"

"Come in." He held the door as I passed him. The house was much the same as it had been years before. "Sit down, please." He indicated a chair and I sat on the edge of it. I could feel his tenseness as he began to talk.

"I've been thinking how to explain this for so long that now that the time is here, I don't know if it's going to come out right." He was looking at his hands as if they could give him the right words. "First of all, I have to tell you that I love you. I have since you were a kid. In fact, you were so young that for a while I thought I must be sick in the head to feel that way. Secondly, I'm sorry I had to hurt you that day by telling you that I didn't care about you." He looked at me, got up, and walked to the kitchen.

Disbelief surged through me. I couldn't make sense out of all this. Brian returned with a beer. With big gulps, he drained the can.

"What are you saying, Brian?" I asked. "Are you telling me that you sent me away from here because you loved me? If you are—well, you sure had me fooled!" The old bitterness welled up in me, and I picked up my purse and started for the door.

"Pamela, don't go!" he begged. "Let me explain this as best I can. If I can just make you understand . . ." Then he began to tell me about his first marriage—how he'd loved her, but how unhappy he'd made her. He explained how that experience had left him bitter and distrustful. No woman would ever get the chance to hurt him again, or so he vowed, but then I'd changed his feelings.

"You made me feel ten feet tall every time you looked at me," he said. "I used to dream of us being together. I knew it was impossible, but that never stopped me. Remember how mad I was when I saw you with that boy? It wasn't just anger. I was jealous. Then the next day when you came out here—oh, Pam, it was so good!

"But then you started talking about how much I meant to you, how happy we could be, even marriage. It sounded like the way I used to talk to my wife! That really shook me up, because I was afraid that I'd end up hating you like she hated me. And, in honesty, I also didn't want to give you the chance to hurt me. You were so young that I thought you probably didn't know what you were feeling and that you'd get over it, which you obviously have."

I stood at the door sorting things out. What Sue said had been true. His ex-wife had really done a number on Brian's ego. He was unsure of himself when it came to dealing with feelings. Brian, self-assured, self-sufficient, was as vulnerable as a baby. What it must have cost him to tell me this after so many years! *No wonder he needs a drink,* I thought. I figured I could use one myself. I went to the refrigerator and got two beers.

Handing one to Brian, I asked, "Why are you telling me all this now?"

"I guess losing Sue made me want to square things with you," he answered. "You never know when your number's up."

"Brian, do you really think it's settled?"

"It has to be. You're leaving soon and our lives will go on as before. I just wanted you to know how sorry I am about everything, and I need for you to understand that it wasn't your fault—it was mine."

I sat down without saying anything. I watched him as he sat there drinking his beer, and I realized that even after all the years of trying to get over him, I hadn't. I cared more for him than I wanted to admit even to myself. I decided that I'd better tell him good-bye and get home where I could think things out slowly.

I stood up, saying, "I don't think it was anybody's fault, and I am beginning to understand why things happened the way they did. Now I'd better be on my way."

On impulse, I leaned down to kiss Brian's cheek. He smelled just like I remembered and had a hint of stubble on his chin. "You haven't changed a bit," I said softly. "You still make me want you."

He pulled me down on his lap and kissed me hungrily. I felt him draw a ragged breath, and then he said, "Stay with me tonight. Don't go back till tomorrow. I need you, Pam."

I kissed him again to let him know my answer. Time stopped as he pulled me down beside him on the floor.

"Pam," he said softly, "I've wanted you for so long."

"I know," I whispered, surrendering myself to him.

Later, we lay quietly, each enjoying the other. Brian picked up my right hand and looked at Sue's gold band. Silently he slipped it off my finger and put it on my left hand. "Consider this your first ring, too," he said softly, "because for tonight, we're married."

We went to the bedroom where we made love again, this time with more sharing, more feeling. We didn't talk, we only touched. Then we slept, and some time in the night we made love again.

As the sun sliced through my drowsiness, I awoke to see Brian standing at the window looking out over a field that just a few weeks ago had rippled with uncut wheat. I walked to his side and he put his arm around me.

"How long have you been up?" I asked.

"For a while. I like to watch the sun rise and a new day beginning," he said.

"And I like the sunsets. And the night," I commented. "Opposites, you and I."

"We need to consider this 'you and I' thing, Pam," Brian said, still not looking at me. "I'll start breakfast."

I got dressed slowly, trying to make myself stop imagining what Brian would say. Surely he would want to see me again as soon as I could come back to Brooksville. I refused to let myself think of him telling me good-bye forever.

I went to the kitchen to offer my help, but was too late. Everything was ready. As I sat down, Brian looked at me and smiled. "Do you always take this long to get ready in the mornings?"

"Well, I have to put my makeup on, do my hair—you know, all that takes time."

"It's worth it, too. You're beautiful. But I refuse to cook breakfast every morning for us," he replied.

"Every morning? Brian, I have to go back—"

"There's only one thing you haven't said that I need to hear," Brian interrupted.

I got up, walked to him, and knelt down by him. I looked up at him and said slowly, "I love you, Brian. I have for so long that I can't remember when I didn't. And I'll love you forever."

"I love you, too, Pam, and I can't go on without you by my side," he told me. "We can be married in three days if you'll say yes."

My mind tumbled from one thought to another as I got up and went back to my chair. I had always hoped that Brian and I would be married, but never believed it was possible because of what had happened. Both he and I had been single a long time, and it would be difficult for us to adjust to one another. My work was important to me, and I realized that marriage to a farmer would change my whole way of life. Also, our age difference was a fact that couldn't be dismissed. Most of all, I was afraid. What if I couldn't be the wife Brian wanted me to be? We really didn't know each other. How could we survive emotionally if it didn't work out?

Brian was waiting for an answer, and I didn't have one. "I do love you," I said sadly, "but I'm so afraid of that kind of commitment."

"It won't be easy, but we can work at it. I know we can," he argued.

"Give me some time. Let me stay with you for a while to see if things work out," I said.

He thought it over for a minute, then asked, "Is there someone else?"

THE MAN I WAS BORN TO MARRY

"No," I answered. "You're the only one." I hesitated, then said, "Truthfully, I'm scared! I'm unsure of what the future holds for us."

"Nobody knows what's going to happen. Love doesn't come with a written guarantee! Neither of us are kids. We should know what we want. I want you. Do you love me enough to trust me?"

As I started to answer, Brian reached across the table and put his fingers on my lips. "Don't say anything. Come with me," he said, getting up and walking toward the door. I followed him as he quickly walked to the wheatfield that bordered his yard. He bent over and picked up a handful of dirt.

"See this?" he asked intensely. "Every fall I plant seed in this earth. Then I worry that it will freeze too early, or that the snow won't come, or that too much will come. I wonder if spring rains will last too long and wash out the young plants, or if a summer storm will come up and I'll be bailed out. I worry and wonder about all that and a hundred other things, and I don't have any guarantees that they won't happen. I'm just a plain dirt farmer who believes that success comes from hard work, luck, and the good God Almighty. And because of that, I believe that I will have a crop.

"I love this earth," he said, putting the handful of dirt in my hands. "And I love you. Trust me as I trust this. . . ."

We've been married for almost a year now, and as we'd expected, it hasn't been easy. The gossip has all but stopped, and my parents have accepted my decision. Brian promised me that if the wheat is good this year, he'll buy me diamonds for our anniversary, but he knows I'll never part with the plain band he gave me first.   **THE END**

WAITING FOR LOVE

I don't know exactly when I became dissatisfied with my life, but it isn't hard to feel that way when you're eighteen and the town wallflower.

My Aunt Adessa, who I've lived with since I was a baby after my parents were killed in an auto accident, says I'm a late bloomer, like my mother. Ordinarily, that's a consolation to me. I have a photograph of my mother on my nightstand, and she was a very pretty woman. But lately it hasn't helped because of what I can see in my mirror.

What I see is a girl with drab hair and a nothing kind of face. The only dates I've had so far, including my senior prom last month, were with awkward boys I've known all my life. And that's as exciting as going out with a brother or cousin. In fact, boys are just now waking up to the fact that I am female, though the discovery doesn't seem to be lighting a fire under any of them.

I like living with my aunt and helping her with the day-to-day routine of running her rooming house, and my friends envy the good relationship I have with her. She has never laid down a lot of heavy rules and encourages me to make my own decisions. Of course, I know she'll be right there if I fall flat on my face, but so far I haven't disappointed her.

Everybody in Tyler Springs makes their living off the tourists who migrate from the snowbelt every winter. They come to enjoy the fishing and boating facilities or just lay around on the beach getting a suntan. Just up the coast, in the next town, there is a modern motel for people who want luxurious accommodations and some sort of nightlife, but we attract a more family-type guest in our comfortable, old rooming house.

The tourist season starts in the fall, peaks in the winter, and dwindles off by the spring. Then, for a few months, we make minor repairs and improvements as we were doing now, until it starts all over again.

The winter people who take over our town during the season think Tyler Springs is a little paradise. I suppose it is pretty—in a picture-postcard kind of way—with its stretch of white sands dotted with palms and quaint little beach cottages. You can look out of any window on a nice day and see brightly colored sails dipping in and out of the waves against a clear blue sky. The effect can take your breath away if you haven't seen it every day of your life.

Every once in a while someone passing through gets excited about the possibility of building a resort hotel here and putting Tyler Springs on the map. But no one here encourages the idea. People like things the way they are.

And that's exactly what's wrong with the place. Nothing ever changes. One day follows the next. It's as predictable as the pattern of figures on our kitchen wallpaper. I know all the people in town so well that I almost know what they're going to say before they say it. My friends are all kids I've grown up with. Although I complain about my wallflower status, there's really no one around I could get interested in.

I think the restlessness began soon after I graduated from high school. Until then, I'd always helped my aunt after school and during vacation, but now it was a full-time job, and I was beginning to wonder if that's all I had in store for me for the rest of my life. To make matters worse, there were no jobs in town, so I felt I was stuck in one place permanently.

However, the picture changed abruptly when I least expected it. It was a bright, sunny morning, and I was up on a ladder painting the trim of our front porch when I heard the sound of a motorcycle approaching. It stopped in front of me, and I found myself looking down into a face that almost toppled me from the ladder, it was so unexpected.

I was never at ease with strangers, especially young men, so when the rider removed his helmet, and I caught a look at a quick smile on a handsome face topped off with untidy hair, I froze in my tracks. I barely managed a weak, "Oh" as a greeting.

Luckily, my aunt picked that moment to appear. I could feel my face getting red as she looked from me to him, sizing up my embarrassment as I grappled for words.

"Bryan Fortson," he said as he introduced himself

with a polite nod of his head in her direction, flashing that same quick smile. "I'm looking for a place to stay a few days."

"Just passing through?" she asked looking him over with careful skepticism.

"Yes, ma'am, I'm stopping to have some work done on my bike down the street, so I'll be needing a room till it's ready," he said.

"Well, since this is the only rooming house in town, you might as well come in. Meals included, too, if you like." She was already rattling off rates and house rules. I escaped behind the paintbrush again, my ears straining to pick up information she expertly drew from him.

He'd been traveling around the country for almost a year following a hitch in the Army, he said, stopping in different places to take a job whenever he ran out of money. His bike had started sounding strange just outside of town, so he thought he should get it repaired before continuing.

"How do your folks feel about your traipsing around the country?" My aunt pried without shame when it came to interviewing strangers, but he talked freely without seeming to take offense.

"They're waiting for me to outgrow it," he said with a laugh. "My dad makes boats and wants me to go into the business with him, but I'm not sure that's what I want."

They stood around talking and I continued painting, enjoying the deep warmth of his voice. Suddenly my aunt said, "Goodness, it's lunchtime, Michele. Young man, would you care to share some seafood chowder with us?"

"I sure would!" he answered. Then he jumped off

his bike and followed us up the stairs, two at a time. We settled down at the big kitchen table over steaming bowls of chowder.

Between appreciative mouthfuls, it was his turn to draw my aunt into conversation about Tyler Springs. When she got up from the table to get pie and coffee, he turned directly to me for the first time.

"It's a beautiful town. What do you do evenings and weekends?"

I managed to tell him about the beach and our boating and fishing facilities. When I got to the part about church picnics, the annual county fair, and the one movie theater, I just knew I was describing a nowhere town. We didn't even have a bar or a place to dance.

While my aunt showed him his room, I cleared away the dishes and wished I had something pretty to wear for dinner. I practically lived in jeans, T-shirts, and sandals so worn they were practically falling off my feet, but they would have to do.

He showed up for dinner freshened up and looking so handsome my tongue tied itself into knots again. The meal passed pleasantly with Bryan entertaining us with stories of his travels.

I almost choked on my coffee when he asked me to give him a tour of the town. ". . . that is, if you're free. I know it's short notice. . . ." He apologized as if expecting me to have previous plans.

Heads turned curiously as I walked him around, and people made a point of calling out a greeting as we passed by. *How typical,* I thought. During the tourist season when we were knee-deep in strangers, we hardly gave them a second glance, but now one new face caused a buzz.

Out of the corner of my eye, I saw two girls go into a huddle, eyes sparkling as they looked Bryan over. Wouldn't you know, the prettiest girls in town had already spotted him! But there was an unexpected dividend—some of the boys who passed actually looked at me with new interest, as if I had come alive in their eyes just by being seen in public with a good-looking stranger.

I've never been good at holding up my end of a conversation, but he was so easy to talk to that before long I was completely at ease.

The next day, when he heard that his bike needed a part that had to be sent away for, he took the news cheerfully and asked me to introduce him around town. Within a week, he was on a first-name basis with everyone he had met. He had the kind of personality that made you feel good just being in his company. He had a special way of listening and a gift for storytelling that made him welcome wherever he went. People naturally gravitated toward him, and when he began to pick up odd jobs around town, I suspected it was their way of keeping him around.

"The last time I met a charmer like him," my aunt said with a twinkle in her eye, "he ran off with the church-building fund." Then she started baking his favorite pie.

He didn't talk much about his family or his life, and occasionally he would lapse into a thoughtful silence as if he had gone away somewhere. I hated those moments because they reminded me that he would soon be leaving us in a very real sense.

We were sitting on the beach one day, looking out

across the water, when he turned to me and said, "It's beyond me how you can look at all this and find it dull."

"I just think it must seem awfully slow to you after all the places you've been," I said.

"Relaxed, but not slow." He smiled at me. "People here seem to know who they are, and I like that." He was looking off into space again.

If it's so great, I thought, *why are you leaving?*

Two weeks flew by magically. While Bryan waited for the new part, I was falling in love and struggling with a whole new set of sensations just being near him. What had started out as a simple girlish crush on a handsome stranger had developed into an emotional rollercoaster ride, slowly climbing to new heights only to plunge down again, leaving me dizzily afraid and excited at the same time. I wasn't even sure if it was love or infatuation. I only knew I was miserable wondering why he didn't love me back, and even more miserable at the thought of his leaving me before I had a chance to find out. I longed to confide in someone, but it was somehow too private to share and too important not to work out for myself.

One day as the three of us were having lunch, my aunt broached the subject I'd been trying not to think about.

"I hear your motorcycle is ready," she said to Bryan. "I suppose you'll be moving on soon."

"Aunt Adessa, it's been ready for three days, but I just couldn't tear myself away from your cooking," he teased. "I've decided to stay on, that is, if you can put up with me on a permanent basis."

She gasped. "Why, nothing would please me

more, but how on earth will you support yourself?"

"I've been keeping this as a surprise. This morning, I bought Heath Tyson's trailer and beachfront property, and I'm turning it into a snack stand. Mr. Watson at the bank thinks I'm a good prospect." His dancing eyes sobered as he went on.

"I haven't been exactly honest with you. You're the best friends I have, and I want you to know the truth. I lied when I said I'd been in the Army . . . it was a drug-rehabilitation center. I got involved with a wild crowd in my first year of college. At first, it was a few beers and a little pot, but before I knew it, I was heavily into drugs. There was a girl . . . I was driving one night, half-stoned. A trailer truck hit us, and we went over an embankment. I only had a few scratches, but she died."

His voice dropped so low we had to strain to hear it, but neither one of us said a word until he had finished.

"I couldn't face anyone after that. I dropped out of school and just bummed around until I realized I was destroying myself, that I had to get professional help. I admitted myself into the hospital and was there for four months. When I was discharged, I wasn't ready to face my family, so I decided to travel around until I got my head back on straight.

"I had a small trust fund back home that my grandmother left me, but I would have had to contact the family attorney to get my hands on it, and that would have alerted my family as to my whereabouts. So, I started taking jobs along the way instead. It was the best thing that could have happened to me because it got me in touch with the real world again . . . and it brought me here. This is where I want to settle down. I just hope what I told you hasn't changed how you feel about me."

"You're a fine young man, Bryan," my aunt said, reaching out to put a hand over his. "We're proud to have you stay on. After what you've been through, you'll be able to do anything you set your mind to do."

I didn't know what to say to him, or how to tell him that my heart ached over what he had experienced, or how happy I felt that he wouldn't be leaving. All I could think to say was: "Your parents must be worried about you."

He smiled. "I contacted our attorney today, then I called my mother."

The next day, Bryan began working on the trailer. He left every morning whistling, with a picnic basket we made for him over his arm, and returned after dark, tired but happy.

He named the stand Hot Dog Heaven, and when it opened for business, the whole town turned out. At first glance, you would think the carnival was in town; it was that flashy, but it was done tastefully.

I sat on a stool at the end of the counter watching as he waited on customers and stopping to talk to every one of them. I was wearing a casual dress for the occasion and had had my hair done professionally for the first time in my life.

The hairdresser remarked, as she stepped back to inspect her work, "You're such a spectacular advertisement for my shop, I shouldn't charge you. Why on earth have you been hiding this beautiful hair in a ponytail?"

Then I had looked in the mirror and discovered an entirely new person. The hair I had always considered drab had been transformed. And something had happened to my face, giving it a new interesting shape and nice contours.

My natural skepticism about compliments almost disappeared when she said, "Don't forget to tell everyone who styled it. With your hair and figure, you're a real knockout."

Harry Phoenix, the boy who had halfheartedly escorted me to the senior prom, drifted toward where I was sitting and struck up a conversation. I was so busy noticing the girls crowding around Bryan that I was barely aware of what he was saying as he sat down. My mind was still on the action around Bryan, so I merely smiled and nodded agreeably at Harry as he kept up a patter of small talk.

Then I realized with a shock that Harry had asked me for a date, and he'd taken my nods and smiles to mean yes. As I turned my eyes back to him, I saw that he was looking at me with lively interest. A few minutes later, we were joined by two friends of Harry and their dates. Suddenly, there were five pair of eyes looking me over with varied expressions. All of them acted as if they were seeing me for the first time.

I was feeling slightly giddy when Bryan joined us.

"You're looking prettier than usual tonight, Michele," he said with a lopsided grin, taking in the ring of admirers. "I'll be closing up soon, if you'd like me to walk you home."

I can't imagine what got into me. Maybe it was the giddiness brought about by the knowledge that I was suddenly admired and sought after, or maybe it was the aftermath of seeing Bryan surrounded by pretty girls, or maybe it was just sheer obstinacy, but I actually heard myself turn him down.

"Thanks, but Harry is walking me home," I said, almost as surprised as Bryan.

As he walked me home and we made plans to go to the movies, I reasoned with myself and came to the conclusion that I had made the right choice. He was a nice boy and ideally suited to introduce me into the dating world.

In the morning, I raced downstairs before Bryan got up, gulped down a few bites of breakfast, and headed for the beach where I walked aimlessly, completely losing track of time and place. I wasn't even conscious of leaving the beach until I suddenly found myself standing in front of Margot's, a boutique, which had just opened for the season.

I gaped at the display window. It was alive with color—brilliant print skirts and blouses, tank tops and trendy beachwear, and hot-colored jewelry. On impulse I walked in. When I came out, my arms were full of packages, including the sexiest sandals I had ever seen.

I rushed home to get my chores out of the way, almost dizzy with the thought of the stir I would create later tonight. When the last bed had been made and the last room straightened, I showered and made up carefully and, at last, slipped into a colorful new jumpsuit.

My aunt raised an astonished eyebrow on seeing me. "Just who is this ravishing creature?" she asked.

"The new me." I laughed, twirling around for her inspection.

"There was nothing really wrong with the old you,

Michele. You just learned how to package it better."

When Harry picked me up that night, I saw the surprised admiration in his eyes and my confidence soared. After the movie, we walked to Hot Dog Heaven where I made the spectacular entrance I had promised myself. I made sure I was in Bryan's line of vision as people crowded around us.

My phone rang a new tune after that. I turned down more dates than I accepted at first, waiting for Bryan to notice me. But while I waited, a strange thing happened. I discovered I liked the attention, and my confidence grew with each new boy I dated. I flaunted my popularity, making it a point to end my evenings at Hot Dog Heaven with every new conquest. If, as it sometimes happened, I was the center of attention, I gloried in it.

Bryan was always friendly with the boy I was with, stopping to buy us a cold drink and to talk for a while. But it was always with the interest of a big brother, fondly giving the new boyfriend the once-over, but careful not to scare him off.

His little stand was becoming the gathering place for young people. They liked Bryan because he was near their own age and understood them. And although he didn't tolerate outright rowdiness, he allowed them to be their high-spirited selves.

We were at the beginning of the tourist season and rooms in my aunt's house were always occupied now. Although she had hired part-time help, we were busy from early morning until evening. The tempo of Tyler Springs had picked up and the shops and beach were doing well and Hot Dog Heaven thrived.

I rarely saw Bryan at the house. He left before I

was up in the morning and came home after I had gone to bed.

There were times, hearing him come in, that I would lie in bed and listen to the sounds from his room and know that no matter how many boys I met, none of them could compare to him. If one of them kissed me, it was Bryan's kiss I imagined and yearned for. My circle of friends grew. Girls who had resented my crashing their circle at first, now accepted me as one of them. I even had the impression that they admired me. I knew they envied the opportunities I had with Bryan, and I'm sure they wondered why I failed to take advantage of them.

It was actually my aunt who kept me up-to-date on Bryan. We were preparing breakfast when she mentioned the new burger grill he was having installed that day and the beach umbrellas and tables he was adding.

"Maybe I'll stop over to see him this morning," I said.

When I got to Hot Dog Heaven, he seemed delighted to see me. He showed off his burger grill as if it were a thing of beauty and insisted I try out one of the new tables. As we sat under the brightly colored umbrella, it was impossible to listen to him, watch his eager expression, and not be caught up in his enthusiasm. Soon we were laughing and talking as we had during our walks on the beach.

"It gives me an idea for next year," he said. "You kids don't have a place to go in the evening. I thought maybe a deck with lanterns strung up around it with tables and a jukebox at first. As for the tourist trade, I wonder if your aunt would part with her seafood chowder recipe. Mrs. Kelly already agreed to supply me with home baked pies . . ." He rambled on, his eyes lighting up as he envisioned the scene.

"You're almost describing a restaurant," I said, almost awed by the scope of his ambition.

"Only in a small way . . . nothing grand or complicated." He grinned.

"You've worked very hard, Bryan," I said with sincerity. "I hope your dreams come true."

He leaned forward and took my hand. "What about your dreams, Michele?"

His touch threw me off balance momentarily. In confusion, I laughed and tossed my head carelessly so that my hair would catch the slight breeze and be shown off to its best advantage. "I'm having too much fun to have dreams or be serious about anything." I wanted to bite my tongue the minute the words came out of my mouth. Suddenly, I hated the frivolous airhead I had created with all her meaningless vanities.

"I suppose at your age you're smart to be playing the field," he said, but I heard a trace of disappointment in his voice. "They're all nice boys."

Yes, I thought, *they're all nice boys.* I wanted to shout that being with them was an empty experience and sometimes it took all my patience to keep up the pretense.

When I left, I was miserably aware that I had reinforced the image he had of me. To him, I was just another empty-headed teenager with a lot of growing up to do.

Later that week, Tad Dobbin and his red convertible careened down Main Street, alerting everyone that he was home from college and looking for action.

Tad was one of the "in" crowd who lived in beautiful, well-tended homes on the hill. They rarely came down from their lofty heights to mix with the common citizens of Tyler Springs. Most of the year, that crowd was away at college. They went to Ivy League colleges, wore designer clothes, drove flashy cars, and went to each other's house parties. Most of our adult citizens didn't take·them very seriously, but to my crowd they were a very special breed to be admired and envied. To me, they were our "beautiful people."

The day I met Tad, I was coming out of Margot's as he pushed open the door of the sporting-goods store next door. We collided, sending packages bouncing all over the walk.

He looked me up and down boldly, then grinned. "Could we go back in and start over?" he asked. We scrambled to our feet laughing.

As he handed me my parcels he continued looking at me as if he was trying to remember me. He smiled again. "Say, aren't you Adessa Lang's niece?"

"Yes, I'm Michele Reeve," I said, noticing how good looking he was up close. Until now, I'd only seen him from a distance.

I should have felt shy with the, richest, most-eligible man in town, but it's hard to be impressed by someone you've just seen sitting on his wounded dignity. We exchanged small talk, and he offered to drop me off at my house. It wasn't until I was getting out of the car that I realized he hadn't introduced himself, no doubt assuming I knew who he was. It also occurred to me that he had an overblown opinion of himself. I couldn't resist taking a jab at his ego.

"Are you somebody I should know?" I asked with the innocence of a lamb.

His eyebrows shot up in surprise as if I had dropped in from another planet. "I'm Tad Dobbin," he said almost defensively.

I put on my best blank expression.

"Judge Dobbin is my father," he said impatiently.

Of course, I was well aware of whom his father was and that he owned half the county, but I managed to appear unimpressed.

"Oh, of course," I said with a polite smile. "Well, it was nice meeting you. Thanks for the lift."

"Hey, wait," he said, climbing out of his car to stand next to me. "If you aren't doing anything tonight, suppose I pick you up and take you to Baugh's . . ." Baugh's was a roadside bar over the county line with a shady reputation. I wasn't flattered.

"Sorry, I'm busy," I said. Without another word or a backward glance, I turned away and walked up the steps of our porch and let myself in, feeling his eyes on me every step of the way. Once inside, I leaned against the door and let out the breath I had been holding.

So that was the notorious Tad Dobbin! I realized my palms were sweating and my pulse was racing.

I heard my aunt's voice from the next room. "Was that Tad Dobbin you came home with?"

"It sure was," I said. "Talk about conceited!" I told her what happened, and she looked relieved.

"Thank goodness you turned him down. A lot of girls are sorry they ever got mixed up with that one."

"I can't see what they see in him," I said, but my ears were tuned for the telephone call I knew would come.

It came just as I was leaving for a beach party with my friends Yvonne and Mia. My aunt reached the phone before I did. When she said, "Tad Dobbin?" and looked toward me, I shook my head and heard her say, "Sorry, she just left."

The girls questioned me about what had passed between us and clung feverishly to my every word. They were still talking about it when we joined the others.

"Tad Dobbin?" Bert parroted. "That creep! My folks told my kid sister that if he even so much as looked her way, they'd ship her off to my grandparents in Kentucky."

"Tad Dobbin!" Bryan exploded later when we had drifted over to Hot Dog Heaven for cold drinks. "Guys like that ought to be kept locked up."

"You don't even know him," I said, pleased with his angry reaction.

"Yes, I do. I've seen a hundred Tad Dobbins, in my life, all out for what they can get and too bad for whoever gets hurt. A decent girl is fair game to his kind."

At last—a man in my life, someone he couldn't call a nice boy! A tingle of excitement went down my spine.

The escapades of Tad Dobbin became the subject matter for the entire evening. I listened to them all—the suspensions from high school, the time he showed up at the church picnic drunk and made a crude pass at the mayor's wife, the brick he had been caught heaving through the drugstore window when he was fifteen, after the pharmacist refused to sell him certain unspecified devices, the girls he was rumored to have gotten pregnant—all allegedly hushed up by his father and his money.

Bryan's usual smile had all but disappeared. I gloated inwardly, knowing that by tomorrow the details of my encounter with Tad would be all over town, and Bryan would be hearing it again and again from anyone who came to the stand, exaggerating it until it was blown out of all proportion.

When I got home and checked the telephone stand, there were three messages for me, about an hour apart, all from Tad. The last one asked that I call back. I crumbled them up and went to bed smiling.

For the first time in weeks, I went to sleep as soon as my head touched the pillow and slept so soundly that I didn't hear the alarm in the morning. As I rushed down to breakfast, Bryan was still there, and he and my aunt had their heads together. From their expression and their sudden silence upon seeing me, it wasn't hard to figure out that they had been discussing me. I didn't let on that I had overheard her say, "Leave it alone, she's a levelheaded girl. . . ."

I felt their eyes on me as I poured a cup of coffee. Suddenly, my aunt was talking about the coming holidays and the Christmas dinner she was planning.

"Are you closing for Christmas?" she asked him.

"For two days. How about letting me help with the tree?"

My aunt smiled, obviously pleased. "That's Michele's job. I'm sure she'd like it."

WAITING FOR LOVE

"Oh, sure," I said, trying to be very casual, but my pulse rate was anything but casual.

"Maybe you could help me with my Christmas shopping," he said directly to me. "I never know what to buy my mother."

"Sure," I said agreeably as if I weren't insanely happy at the mere thought of it.

"I can take a couple of hours this morning," he offered.

The couple of hours turned out to be five hours. When we ran out of shops in Tyler Springs, he surprised me by borrowing a car and convincing the owner to mind the stand for him, so that we could drive into the next town.

"Is the bike giving you trouble again?"

"No, I thought we'd make an occasion of it. I wouldn't expect you to appreciate pulling up in front of a restaurant sitting behind me on my bike." I looked over at him quickly to see if he was teasing, but he seemed quite serious. I wished I could tell him that I'd be proud to ride behind him on his bike anywhere.

I'm sure the sky was never bluer or the sun brighter than on that day we strolled down the main street, talking companionably and stopping to look in store windows. I watched as he picked out a pipe for his father, then I helped him choose a pair of earrings for my aunt and a delicate silver pin for his mother.

Afterward, we had lunch at a well-known seafood restaurant on a pier overlooking the bay. As we lingered over a third cup of coffee, I thought it was an achievement on my part that he seemed in no hurry to get back. He rambled on comfortably about his parents and his life up north. It was only when he touched on his first year of college and how easily he had fallen into fast company that a warning bell went off in my head. He was inching toward a point where he could introduce the subject of Tad Dobbin. I wasn't ready for brotherly advice and quickly maneuvered the conversation around until the waiter let us know by polite glances that we were overstaying our welcome.

He was very quiet, driving back, and I suspected he was waiting for another opportunity. I did the only thing I knew how to prevent it—I chattered about everything I could think of until we pulled up outside my house.

He broke in finally. "Thanks for your help, Michele."

"It was fun," I said. "I really enjoyed lunch." This was his cue to say he'd like to do it again, but he didn't continue. He didn't ask me out.

"Will you be coming by tonight?" he asked as I slid out of the passenger seat.

"I'll be there with Bert," I said. We said our goodbyes, and as he pulled away from the curb, a flash of red came out of nowhere at high speed, horn blaring wildly, barely missing him. The car gave a lurch forward as Bryan applied the brake, then shuddered and stalled on the spot. The last thing I saw before going in was Bryan slamming his fist against the steering wheel, but not before he had noted Tad Dobbin was the driver of the other car.

My aunt had left a note saying she had gone out. I was in the utility room loading linens into the washer when the phone rang. By the time I had counted sixteen rings, I knew it was Tad. I stood there rooted to the spot, wondering if I should answer it, until it stopped ringing.

One part of me was happy that Bryan cared at least a little about my welfare. Another asked what had been the point of it all. Had my aunt been anxious enough about Tad's attentions to put Bryan up to it? Had she even paid the bill? My cheeks burned with the mere thought of it.

My aunt returned home, and I helped her unload groceries filling her in with the details of my morning. She beamed when I told her about lunch. By now, I was convinced she had engineered it, and I was deeply hurt at the thought of her conspiring with Bryan because of their lack of confidence in me. Most of all, I was humiliated by Bryan's rejection.

This time when the phone rang, I didn't hesitate to answer, quickly putting a smile in my voice.

It was Tad. "Hi, Michele, what does a guy have to do to get you to talk to him?"

"He has to call when I'm home." I laughed, hoping my voice sounded as breezy as my words. Inside, I was terrified by what I was doing. I was actually encouraging the town letch, the man I was least equipped to handle.

As Tad came to the point of his call, I could barely believe he was apologizing—especially to me.

"Michele, I know I was out of line when I asked you to go to Baugh's. I should have known better, but let me make it up to you. My parents are having a pool barbecue tomorrow night, and a few of my friends are coming. Let me bring you."

A gentlemanly invitation to a perfectly innocent party on the hill. Even my skeptical aunt couldn't object to my going to the Dobbins's. They were pillars of respectability, even if their son wasn't.

I went through all the motions on my date with Bert, the life of the party as always. At the end of the evening, when he suggested we stop at Bryan's, I begged off, saying I was tired. I no longer felt like playing kid games; I was about to move up into the adult world.

The next morning I was at Margot's before the doors opened, frantic with my own ignorance about what to wear to a poolside party. Margot personally waited on me, bringing one swimsuit after another. I brushed aside the bikinis and chose a more modest two-piece swimsuit with a matching wraparound skirt.

"If you're going with that Dobbin kid, you're probably better off with this," she said. "He gets enough ideas on his own without giving him any more."

By two in the afternoon, I had four phone calls asking if it were true that I was going out with Tad. Aunt Adessa looked worried.

"Good grief," I muttered under my breath, "you'd think I was going out with Jack the Ripper."

But when he called for me, he turned a full battery of charm on my aunt. Meticulously dressed in designer sportswear, freshly shaved and smelling of just the right amount of lemon-scented aftershave, and his hair at just the right conservative length, he was the very picture of the boy next door. Polite and respectful, he assured her he would get me back at a reasonable hour, even driving through town at a sedate speed.

By the time we reached his house, butterflies were doing battle in my stomach as I realized I didn't have the slightest idea of how to act. Was I dressed right? Would I know what to talk about? Would they laugh at me?

There were several cars in the driveway, and I could hear music and sounds of a party in the distance. Tad's mother came to meet me with a welcoming smile, and. Mr. Dobbin was right behind her, asking about my aunt.

It was like a stage setting—an elegant pool, gleaming deck, stylish lounge furniture, and Tad's friends grouped around laughing and sipping tall drinks, or gathered around the ribs and chicken crackling over an immense barbecue. My mind absorbed the scene in a second, and I was bewitched.

As he took me around to be introduced, someone handed me a tall frosted drink swimming with fruit slices. My throat was so dry that almost without thinking, I drank it down. Mrs. Dobbin must have been watching because she was at my side again.

"Have you ever had wine punch before, dear?" I stared down into the empty glass like a fool. "I thought not," she said, then turned to Tad and said something I wasn't able to hear above the other voices.

He looked startled, then grinned at me. "My mother just reminded me to watch over you," he whispered. "I never thought to ask if you drink. I promise the next one will be nonalcoholic."

Mrs. Dobbins reached over and patted my hand. She meant well, I knew, but I was warm with embarrassment at being treated like a child. It put even more space between me and the other side. But no one seemed to notice, and gradually I lost some of the jitters I'd come in with.

Tad's friends went out of their way to include me in their conversations, but I was painfully aware of how sophisticated they were, and, more than once, I almost panicked about being so completely out of my element.

They were the best-behaved crowd I had ever seen; a far cry from the wild kids I had been led to expect. When Mr. and Mrs. Dobbin said good night and the party went on without them, they were as well behaved as before. I wondered how so many people could be so wrong.

Tad took me home shortly after midnight, driving straight to my house. When he kissed me good night, it was pleasant and undemanding, without a word or gesture that was out of line.

From that night on, we were a twosome. I could almost hear the tongues wag as he swept me along on a wave of parties—dancing and swimming at fashionable homes and boating on slick cabin cruisers that I had always admired from a distance.

Almost miraculously, his friends accepted me as if I'd been born into their magic circle. I didn't mind that they treated me like a mascot or sometimes patronized me. I was grateful they put up with me because in their company, I could forget that I was ordinary.

The rare times I saw Bryan, one of us was rushing off somewhere, and I felt an ache in the pit of my stomach as if I had lost something precious. My aunt appeared to accept the fact that I was dating Tad with good humor, but I noticed tight, little lines around her mouth that hadn't been there a month earlier. I couldn't shake the feeling that I had failed her somehow.

One day I ran into some of the old crowd and, just for a minute, I missed their easy, uncomplicated companionship. I envied the good time they were having without me.

My relationship with Tad was changing. He was still the perfect gentleman when my aunt or his parents were around, but away from them his guard slipped. He had a quick temper that flared when things didn't go exactly as he wanted, and his rudeness in public never stopped embarrassing me. I made excuses for him; blaming his money, his parents for spoiling him, and even his friends for kowtowing to his every whim. But I was running out of excuses.

The first few times we parked in a secluded spot, he accepted my refusals to go beyond kissing, but lately his kisses were more demanding. And if I drew away, I could feel anger boil up in him. My arm still ached where he had dug his fingers into me and pushed me away roughly, his voice cold with anger.

"You're no different from all the rest . . . leading a guy on, then pulling the ice-maiden routine."

The truth was that I had never led him on as I had the other, younger boys. I was afraid to, afraid of what he might do.

I was doing a lot of serious thinking about us lately, wondering just how long I could keep him in line—and why I wanted to.

Every girl in town considered him a prize catch despite his reputation, and any one of them would trade places with me in a minute. But he was interested in me. I fit in well with his friends, even his parents liked me. Maybe I could learn to live with his faults. I certainly could get used to the Dobbin way of life.

And there it was in a nutshell—what was really bothering me. I could "get used to it"—not love it, or even like it—merely get used to it. Another truth hit home. I didn't like Tad and never had.

Tad's voice broke into my thoughts. We were driving to yet another get-together at his parents' home. I had been far away and mentally drained. In the end, I hadn't been able to bring myself to disappoint Mrs. Dobbin, who had always been kind to me.

"Why so quiet?" he asked. "Is your aunt giving you a hard time because of me?"

"No, she'd never do that," I said.

"But she doesn't approve of me." He said it as a flat statement of fact, with a smug smile. "Haven't you reported that I'm the very model of good behavior, that I don't smoke pot or do drugs, or booze a lot, and hardly ever make passes at her darling, virginal niece?"

"She knows I wouldn't be here if you did," I said, annoyed by his jeering tone, but immediately regretting my own self-righteous words.

"Tell her she has nothing to fear. The old Tad Dobbin is no more. He's a reformed character." There it was again, that jeering tone. "My parents have seen to that. On my second day home, dear, old Dad took me aside to explain some new facts of life. In short, I am to straighten out my act or he will pull me out of college and send me out into the cold, cruel world to get a job." He snorted. "He had the gall to throw that Bryan Fortson person in my face!"

Before I could ask him what Bryan had to do with

it, we were pulling into the driveway, and his mother was running out to meet us.

"Tad, I'm leaving now to meet your father. Your grandfather is in the hospital and we're driving to Ryerton. We'll call you tomorrow." Her voice dropped to a confidential level. "For heaven's sake, hold things down here." There was clear warning in her words.

Inside, I helped him set things up for the evening. There was a new energy and enthusiasm about him as we put the customary wine punch on ice.

When the first guests arrived. Tad called out, "Sorry things aren't ready yet, but my mother and father had to rush off to Ryerton." He explained about his grandfather. "Help yourself to the wine punch."

"Wine punch?" They laughed. "Your folks will be gone all night, won't they?"

Tad's face lit up with a grin. "Right on! Bring out the good stuff!" Another couple arrived and joined in. By this time, things were getting lively. They all trooped out to the bar, leaving me standing at the refrigerator with an ice bucket in my hands. I could hear the sounds of good-natured scuffling and squealing as they argued about what liquor to bring out. I didn't think it was nice that they treated the news about Tad's grandfather so lightly, as though it were a gigantic joke or a great stroke of luck.

When they came straggling back, I told them nothing had been taken out of the freezer. Someone offered to go out for steaks.

"Hot dogs would be fun for a change," I suggested. "There's mustard and relish in the fridge."

There was a sudden silence as they turned to

look at me. I had the strange sensation that they had forgotten I was here.

"Join the party, Michele," someone said. "Let's hear a toast to Grandpa . . . he set us free!" Then she giggled, and a chill went through me at the callousness of her remark. I put down the drink and walked over to the bar to pour myself a glass of plain club soda, not even bothering to dress it up with fruit so that it would pass for the real thing.

"Hey, let's get hot dogs at Hog Dog Heaven," someone said.

Tad's expression darkened. "That beach bum," he muttered.

"But a very sexy beach bum," Becky said, her face flushed as she refilled her glass. "Lucky little Michele, having that hunk living in her house."

"Confidentially, Michele," Nate said as he leaned toward me, "is he really the paragon of virtue my parents say he is or does he tiptoe down the hall and try get into your room at night after auntie is in bed?"

Tad had been staring moodily at his shoes, but now his head shot up and he glared at his friend. "You're out of line, pal."

"Just kidding, Michele," Nate said. "Hot dogs sounds good."

"Have him deliver it," Tad snapped. "One of his flunkies can tend the stand."

Tears must have filled my eyes because suddenly my vision blurred, and my "beautiful people" disintegrated in front of me. They weren't tears of disillusionment, but tears of anger because I had been so easily seduced by their glamour. They weren't only drinking heavily, but they started using drugs, too.

When Tad reached out for me, I gave him a furious shove, almost sending him backward into the pool. He started to laugh. "A girl after my own mother's heart. Did you know she thinks of you as a good influence on me?"

"Almost as saintly as Bryan," Nate said from somewhere in the darkness.

Tad's voice suddenly grew angry again, his speech slightly slurred. "Bryan . . . some bum out of nowhere comes into town with nothing in his pockets, sets up a rinky dink hot-dog stand, and overnight he's supposed to be a role model for the rest of us. Can you figure my father comparing me to him?"

I could and did. I got up, picked up my purse, and started walking. They all stared at me, suddenly quiet. Then I heard Tad come up behind me.

"You can't leave, Michele. I'm sorry the party got out of hand." Tad was following me like an anxious puppy. All his bravado and bluster were now gone. I kept walking, hardly hearing his words until I got out into the street. I should have felt some satisfaction from the half-hysterical note in his voice, but I almost felt sorry for him. "My parents will kill me if you walk out on me. I swear things will be different."

Halfway down the block, I turned around and said, "Don't worry, Tad, .I won't tell your parents about the liquor or the drugs, or the traffic in and out of the bedrooms. They'll find out fast enough without me around as a smoke screen."

I left him standing there and started walking. Halfway home I heard a motorcycle in the distance, a wonderful, familiar, honest sound. I ran into the street to meet it.

Bryan came to a stop beside me. "Where to?"

"Anywhere the real people are," I said, wondering if I looked as sheepish as I felt, or as happy.

"Sure thing. It's good to have you back." He grinned as I hopped aboard.

We went to Hot Dog Heaven, where the gang was holding down the fort. As they gathered around, I wondered how I had ever thought all the good things were up on the hill. They had been right here all along.

"You look great," Bryan said later after everyone had left, "but are you really okay?"

I told him everything. We sat drinking coffee, then closed up the stand, and walked along the water's edge in our bare feet. We talked and I was even able to laugh at the idiot I had been.

"Your aunt was right when she said you'd work things out for yourself. You don't know how my fingers itched to slug that—"

"Me, too," I said. Then we both laughed.

I found out that one thing hadn't changed. I still turned to mush when I looked at Bryan, but now I was willing to let things take their natural course.

Something happened to Bryan, too, because he stopped treating me like a kid sister. At first, there were simple gestures, like guiding me through a door ahead of him with his hand resting on my elbow, and complimenting me about my hair, or telling me that I was dressed nicely. He started leaving someone at the stand so that he could come back to the house for lunch and dinner, bringing me a magazine I enjoyed, or a special dessert, like my favorite ice cream.

WAITING FOR LOVE

One night as I got into bed, my hand slipped under my pillow and I found a box with two beautiful seashell combs that I had admired. In the morning, Bryan's eyes found them in my hair, and we smiled at each other without speaking.

As we walked home late one night, Bryan took me in his arms and told me he loved me. I fit against him as if somebody had made a mold of our bodies, and I knew I was home at last.

We announced our engagement formally at Christmas and plan to be married in June. That way we can have the beach to ourselves without stumbling over tourists at every turn, because we'll spend part of our honeymoon building that deck Bryan has his heart set on.

Rumor has it that Tad Dobbin unexpectedly dropped out of college and has taken a job with a friend of his father's who owns a big timber operation. He is starting at the bottom to learn the business, they say.

I'll never quite understand what happened to me during those weeks. Sometimes I think I turned a corner in my life too suddenly and lost my sense of direction for a while. I'm just thankful that Bryan, with his rare understanding, was willing to wait until I could sort out who I was and where I was going.

Bryan's parents came to visit him recently. Although his father tried to convince him to go back with them and enter the family business, they went home satisfied that he was making a good life for himself.

And it will be a good life. Everything we love is in Tyler Springs. Of course, nothing much changes

WAITING FOR LOVE

here, but that's part of its charm and we wouldn't
have it any other way.   THE END

ONE WEEK TO MAKE HIM MINE

Jerry Sutton certainly fit the fortune-teller's description—he was charming, witty, and unbelievably handsome. I still tingled, remembering the first words he called out to me: "Hey, good looking, wanna try your luck?"

He stood behind a low counter juggling softballs. Goofy-looking, fluffy dummies all in a row waited to be knocked over. There were huge stuffed animals stacked on shelves beside him, and his smile was even brighter than the carnival lights surrounding us. Beth and I started over to "try our luck" and I whispered, "It's him, Beth—just like the gypsy fortune-teller said."

"Oh, Lindsay Blackwell, you are so gullible. Don't you know he gives that line to all the pretty girls?"

I shushed her as we were nearly at the counter.

"How much?" I asked, although there were huge signs—THREE BALLS FOR A BUCK—everywhere.

"Three balls for a dollar, sweetheart." Then he whispered, "Fifty cents for you, because you're so cute, and it's your first time."

His smile warmed my entire body and when he handed me those balls, his fingers brushed my hand, sending an actual shock through my body. Thinking back, I believe he had me hooked at that moment, although I was strong enough to leave the carnival with Beth that first night.

The next morning I headed for the grocery store, to do some shopping for my mother, but I just happened to go about ten blocks out of my way—past the field where the Hamilton Carnival was set up for a week.   Logically, I knew I couldn't get involved with someone who would only be in town for a week, but curiosity and my wildly beating heart overrode my logic.

The carnival had a totally different look in the early morning. There were no bright lights or music, and the Ferris wheel and merry-go-round stood silent. There were no delicious smells drifting out to the street to entice passersby. Just the huge red-and-yellow sign—HAMILTON CARNIVAL—DAILY-11:00 A.M. TO MIDNIGHT.

There were some muted sounds coming from the back of the field—voices and hammering. I even thought I could smell bacon frying. I realized I'd gone off the street and was walking toward the back of the lot where rows of trailers were set back in the trees. I'd never thought much about those trailers in the years I'd been coming to the carnival. Now, I realized the workers lived there—carnies—that's what Jerry had called them the night before.

"Carnies," he'd said with pride, "are the best people in the world. We're family. Just like your family at home. Carnies take care of each other."

ONE WEEK TO MAKE HIM MINE

In between "marks," as Jerry called the people who played the games, I had asked him about his family. He told me very matter-of-factly that he'd been orphaned at the age of ten, then lived with an uncle who physically abused him. When he couldn't take it anymore, at the age of fourteen-and-a-half, he ran away and lived on the street for almost two years.

It had hurt me even to listen to his story, but I sat and listened for most of the evening.

He'd begun to hang around the carnivals, and when he was sixteen, he'd picked up enough of the jargon to try for a job. Coupled with lying about his age, he landed a job with the Hamilton Carnival.

His whole manner softened as he told me about the older couple who owned the carnival. "They started almost thirty years ago, in a small town, with four concession stands, one food tent, some kiddie rides, and three trailers."

He paused and his smile struck me again—full force. "Mom and Pop Hamilton treat me better than anyone has in my whole life, Lindsay."

And I knew he meant that. "How long have you been with them?" I asked.

"This is my third summer," he answered.

"You're not even nineteen?" I blurted it out without thinking. He looked so much older than the guys I'd graduated with last month.

"Shh—I told you I lied about my age. Everybody thinks I'm twenty. I celebrated my eighteenth birthday last month all by myself."

Shortly after that, Beth came by and pulled me off to the side. "Lindsay, I'm tired of walking around here all by myself. You've been hanging around this

211

guy all night."

"Sorry, Beth, honestly I am, but he's so fascinating."

"And so good looking," she added.

We both giggled. "You'd think we were twelve-year-olds instead of high school graduates," I said.

After I'd said good-bye to Jerry that night, with a promise to see him again, I sat on our front porch for a long time, with only the crickets for company. I'd thought about what Jerry had been through in the same eighteen years that I'd had. My family had loved, protected, and cared for me. I'd never had to do anything in the way of hard work and never wanted for food, clothes, or spending money. I'd taken it all for granted.

My dreams that night had been filled with bright colored lights and music. I dreamed of traveling across the country with the carnival—meeting new people, loving the exciting, festive atmosphere of carnival life. In my dreams, I traveled with Jerry. We had our own little trailer, and I'd fixed it up with frilly curtains at the windows and my grandmother's quilt on the bed.

I had awakened that morning with the thought of that bed in my mind, and to my surprise it made me blush. I couldn't wait to get back to see Jerry at the carnival, so I rushed over as soon as I could.

"Hi, Lindsay! Over here." Jerry's voice greeted me. "Good morning," I called back, heading for the big tent where Jerry stood waving.

"Have you had breakfast yet?" he asked as I caught up with him.

"No, I haven't," I lied. He had me under his spell already. I would've followed him into the lion's cage at that point. Instead I just ate my second breakfast of the day.

And what a marvelous breakfast it was—smoked ham slices, scrambled eggs, grits with melted butter—no food had ever tasted better to me.

Colorfully costumed carnies added to the already pleasant atmosphere. Surprisingly, as large as the tent was, it had a very homey feel to it, with everyone talking to one another, greeting even me, a stranger, with cheerful good mornings. Jerry had been right, it was like one big, happy family.

Jerry told me we were in what the carnies called a grab joint—logical, I supposed, since they were grabbing a bite to eat before the eleven o'clock opening.

Jerry showed me all around the back lot, pointing out the trailer that he shared with two other carnies. "Men, of course," he joked.

I had felt a twinge of disappointment when he told me of his shared living quarters. I surprised myself by thinking of going into a stranger's trailer. Of course, I didn't even think of Jerry as a stranger. For some reason I felt I'd known him a long time— maybe because he'd shared his life story so openly with me. I didn't know that many details about kids I'd gone to school with for four years.

When he'd taken my hand in his, to step over some rocks in our path, it felt very right to keep holding hands. He showed me everything on the midway and explained how each game or ride worked, and he introduced me to friends we met along the way. It would easily remain one of the best mornings of my life.

By the time we'd seen everything there was to

see, I could smell fresh popcorn and hear the music from the merry-go-round. Everything was being set in motion for the eleven o'clock opening.

"I have to get over to Jay's and get my cash box and stuff ready," Jerry said. "Will I see you later?"

"Sure, Jerry, and thanks for breakfast and the grand tour of the carnival. It was a lot of fun."

He kissed my cheek. "I enjoyed it too, Lindsay."

I laughed. "Like you've never eaten at Big Al's grab joint before—or shown a girl around the midway, right?"

"Never anyone like you, Lindsay, and Al's food never tasted as good as it did today."

My brain was telling me: *What a line!* But my heart said he meant every word. I listened to my heart. Our eyes met and held for a moment, then he squeezed my hand in his and turned and left. "See you tonight," he called back over his shoulder as he walked away and gave me a big smile.

By three o'clock I felt like the evening would never come. Then I decided, why wait—even though Beth and I, or any of our friends, never went to the carnival before eight o'clock. But that day I couldn't wait.

It had turned cooler that afternoon after a brief rainstorm, so I pulled on my best jeans and a sweatshirt that I knew accented my hair and brought out the color of my eyes—at least Mom said it did. I had to look my best. I brushed my hair till it shone and applied my makeup carefully, so it would be perfect—soft, not gaudy.

I called Beth about four o'clock and she thought I'd lost my mind, wanting to go to the carnival so early.

"You're crazy, Lindsay—that guy's really turned

your head," she said.

"That guy's name is Jerry Sutton and he's already given me the most exciting morning of my life," I said.

"Lindsay Blackwell, you be careful now," she said.

"You sound suspiciously like a mother, Beth," I said back. And we laughed again.

"Listen, why don't I meet you later? That way you can spend some time with Jerry and walk around with me later," she said.

"Sounds great, pal," I answered. "How about eight o'clock in front of the Ferris wheel?"

"Okay, see you later—and stay out of trouble."

I hung up the phone with her words still in my mind. Am I headed for trouble?

I brushed the thought aside when I realized I'd have three full hours to watch Jerry at work before I met Beth. I knew I'd have to spend the rest of the evening with her. I sure didn't want to lose my best friend over a new guy.

I ran the brush through my hair once more, then grabbed my purse and headed out the front door.

"Bye, Mom. Be back later."

"Lindsay, Lindsay, where are you going? Dinner's almost ready!" Mom called from the kitchen.

"I'm meeting someone at the carnival, Mom. I'll have dinner there." I thought I'd make it out the door, but before I had my tennis shoes tied, she came out of the kitchen, wiping her hands on a dishtowel, giving me "that look," with which I was sure she could see into my mind. I glanced down at Tipsy, our old cat, so she couldn't see my eyes.

"Who are you meeting, Lindsay?" she asked.

"Beth, of course," I said, thinking to myself that I wasn't actually lying. I would be meeting Beth—later.

"Don't you usually go to the carnival late?" she asked, catching my eye.

"Usually, Mom, but after all, it's our last summer before we're on our own. You know—adult responsibilities, college, jobs, so we're going to make the most of this last summer of freedom." I laughed, trying to ease her mind. "And the carnival's only in town for a week," I added.

She smiled and I knew I'd passed the test. "All right, go, enjoy your freedom. Do you have enough money?"

"Sure, Mom, thanks anyway." I kissed her on the cheek. "'Bye, I'll be late. We're going to close the midway tonight."

"Midway?" she asked. "I never heard you use that word before."

"That's what carnies call the grounds, Mom."

"Carnies?" she asked again, and I realized my mistake in using the jargon Jerry had taught me.

"Uh . . . yes, that's what they call people that work in carnivals," I answered.

"Where are you getting all these new words, Lindsay?"

"I guess you just pick it up around the carnival," I answered.

She looked a tad suspicious. "The carnival closes at midnight. You be home at twelve-thirty, promptly. That should give you plenty of time to close down the midway." Then she added, "If you see your brother, please tell him to get right home. He's been there since noon."

ONE WEEK TO MAKE HIM MINE

"Sure, Mom. See you later." I was off and running.

I must have run all the way because I was looking up into Jerry's eyes fifteen minutes later. "Hi, babe—you're here early." He smiled and my heart flipped over.

"Just a little," I answered.

"Listen, I'm glad you came early," Jerry said. "As soon as you left this morning, I realized I didn't tell you my break was from five to eight o'clock."

"Wow!" I said. "What a break—for you and me."

He laughed at my obvious delight at being able to spend some time with him. "They figure we need the time off so we're fresh for the nighttime crowd. I'm glad you're here. How about some dinner?"

"Okay, but it's my treat this time." I was suddenly very thankful that Beth wasn't coming till eight.

I'd never known three more pleasurable hours, except maybe on Christmas morning when I was five years old. That's exactly what being with Jerry those three hours felt like—Christmas, my birthday, hunting eggs on Easter, Fourth of July fireworks, and Thanksgiving all rolled into one.

I never knew you could fall in love so fast and so hard. It took all my willpower to leave Jerry at eight o'clock, explaining that if I didn't spend some time with Beth, I'd probably lose my best friend.

"You go right ahead, darling," he said. "I'm going to be busy here tonight anyway. Can I walk you home later, and Beth, too?"

"Don't you have to close up and turn in your cash box and all?" I asked.

"Sure. But you can wait, can't you?"

"I'm supposed to be home by twelve-thirty," I said, looking pretty sad, I'm sure.

217

"Then I'll rush—we'll make your curfew. I promise." He kissed me lightly on the cheek, then turned and started his spiel.

I rushed to the Ferris wheel where Beth stood looking awfully upset. "You're late," she said.

"There you go sounding like a mother again," I said. She tried not to smile, but couldn't help herself. "I'm just a teeny bit late anyway, and if you're nice, I'll tell you all about my evening with Jerry."

As we walked through the midway, I elaborated on my evening with Jerry and then told her of his idea of walking us home.

As midnight approached Beth asked me if I'd like her to go home with the other kids. "Then you'd have a few minutes alone with him on the way home," she explained. Her tone let me know she didn't approve, but, after all, we were best friends.

"Oh, Beth, you're the best. Thanks."

The soft summer breeze had never felt so cool, the pavement never felt so soft, the stars never shone so bright, as they did that night.

We talked so easily; it felt so comfortable being with Jerry. When I mentioned this to him, he told me carnies had to make friends fast since they moved around so much. I knew it had to be more than that. I felt such a special closeness with him.

That night, I wished my house was ten miles away, instead of a ten-minute walk.

"Well, here we are," I said as we stood in front of my house.

"You have a beautiful home, Lindsay," Jerry said, taking in the red brick ranch house with the tall oaks surrounding it. I watched him look over the yard with its neatly trimmed borders and saw him pause as he looked at Mom's flower beds surrounding the wooden gazebo Dad had built her.

I'd never looked at my home and yard as someone else would, but I knew from Jerry's eyes that it was beautiful.

"I like flowers," he said. I realized I had never heard a boy say that before.

"Me, too," I said. "Would you like to sit in the gazebo for a minute?" I asked, glancing at my watch. "A minute's about all I do have."

So we sat, for just a minute, and kissed for half of it. I was breathless.

"You better go in, Lindsay, or you'll miss your curfew." He walked me up to the front porch and kissed me gently on the lips. "Good night, Lindsay."

"Good night, Jerry." He turned and started down the walk. I impulsively picked a white rose that grew near the porch and called his name.

He turned and came back. I handed him the rose. "I'm glad you like flowers," I said. Another kiss and he was gone.

I didn't know if Mom had seen him or not. If she did, she never mentioned it. After breakfast she asked if Beth and I had had a good time.

"Yes, we did." Then I added, "I saw a bunch of kids from school, too." If she had seen Jerry, at least she'd think it was one of the guys I'd graduated with. I guess, deep down, I knew Beth was right—Mom wouldn't approve of Jerry's lifestyle.

Tuesday and Wednesday followed a similar pattern. I would find some excuse to go out after breakfast, then meet Jerry for coffee, and sometimes I'd help set up at whichever concession he was working.

ONE WEEK TO MAKE HIM MINE

We would spend his three-hour break together, much of it spent talking and kissing on a blanket in the woods behind the trailers. Then I'd spend some time with Beth and the other kids from school and Jerry would walk me home.

Our kisses had become much more passionate and I began to wonder how I would survive without him. On that third night in the gazebo, I asked him if he'd ever considered settling down, maybe even going to college.

"And get a real job?" he asked. "That's what you really mean, isn't it, Lindsay?" It was the first time I'd ever heard an irritable tone in his voice.

"Jerry, no. I didn't mean that," I answered.

"The carnival is my life. It's the only home I've ever known." He sighed, then seemed to get back in control of his emotions. "I'll never leave, Lindsay. Never."

"I understand how you feel, Jerry, but don't you want to have a home and family some day?" I asked.

"Of course, and I will. Just like Mom and Pop. They've raised five sons," he said.

"In the carnival?"

"That's right, Lindsay, and they turned out real well."

"What about school?" I had trouble imagining little children growing up in the carnival atmosphere.

"We only travel summers. Kids aren't in school in the summer." He was answering all my questions so patiently. It seemed important to him that I understand his life.

"We're based in Florida in the winter," he continued. "They have good schools there. Mom and Pop only ended up with two sons in the carnival. The oldest is a doctor, one's a contractor in Florida, and the youngest is an artist."

We went on to talk of other things, but all that he'd said stayed in my mind. I didn't sleep much that night. I did finally understand that no matter what happened between us, I'd never talk Jerry into settling down in some mundane job in a little town like mine. I also knew that I loved him and it was going to hurt when he left.

The next day I talked Beth into lying for me. I told Mom I would be staying at her house overnight and Beth backed me. I packed my overnight bag and hid it behind the gazebo when I left for the carnival that night. I'd get it later if my plan worked.

I was as nervous as a bride that evening and Jerry sensed it. "Lindsay, you're jumpy as a cat with a mouse running under its nose," he said.

I couldn't help laughing. "Where did you get a line like that?"

He smiled. "I think my mom used to say it when I was little and fidgeting at the dinner table—but quit changing the subject."

"Okay, I've just been trying to get up enough nerve to ask you if you'd like to spend some time alone with me tonight." There, I'd said it.

His eyes sparkled and he pulled me into his arms. "How much time? Did you get a later curfew?"

My heart beat wildly as I rubbed my hands across his broad shoulders. "How about all night?"

His mouth actually fell open. He stepped back, his large hands gripping my shoulders. "Lindsay, do you mean what I think you do?"

"I think I mean what you think I mean."

"But, but I thought . . ." he stammered.

"You thought I wasn't that kind of girl and I'm not. But I can't let you go without spending the night with you." I paused and leaned against him, not wanting to look into his eyes. It was hard enough to have said this. "I've never felt like this before, Jerry. I love you and I want my first time to be with you."

"Lindsay, you're a virgin?" he asked.

"Yes. Is that bad?"

"Oh, darling. No, no, that's not bad." He pulled back and looked into my eyes. "Are you sure you want to do this?"

"I've arranged it, haven't I?" I rattled off my plan before I could lose my nerve. "Beth's backing my alibi. My mom and dad think I'm staying at her house. My overnight bag's behind the gazebo. We just have to go by and pick it up. No one's home this evening, so it's okay. See, I've thought of everything."

"Everything?" he asked.

I felt myself redden. "Well, I was hoping you could handle that part. I'm not protected or anything since I didn't plan on."

He laughed and the tension eased a bit. "Yes, I can handle that part, but that's not what I meant." He pulled me over to a bench behind some bushes.

"This is an awfully big step for a girl. Are you sure this is what you want, Lindsay?" He was very serious again.

"It must be, because you didn't even ask, and here I am practically begging," I answered.

"Oh, darling, you don't have to beg. I'd never want to hurt you." He caressed my cheek with his fingertips and my whole body responded. *Oh, yes,* I thought, *this is what I want.*

He continued. I wondered if he was trying to talk me out of it.

"You're so special, Lindsay. I'm not going to kid you. Carnies get involved with lots of girls over the summer, but we can't take any of them seriously, because there's always a new town next week. We always have to keep that in mind. That's why it's not a very good idea to fall in love with a carny."

"Jerry, please, I know I won't be the first for you, but I can hardly bear to think of you leaving." I took his hand in mine. "If I at least have this night with you, I'll always have a very special memory to carry with me."

As I said the words I knew I wanted more than the memory. I wanted it to be so special, so perfect between us that he'd want to stay, find a job, and marry me. What a dreamer I was!

I was as jumpy as a cat with a mouse running under its nose that night. Until we'd picked up my overnight bag and gotten away from the house, I felt like I was walking a tightrope—over a river filled with crocodiles. One wrong move and zap, it would be all over.

Finally, though, we were on our way, and I began to feel an excitement at the wondrous night with Jerry that lay ahead. It would be the most adventurous night of my life.

As he opened the trailer door, he asked again, "Are you sure you don't mind the trailer?"

"Oh, no, Jerry, it's perfect." I told him about my dream and we both laughed.

"Well, Granny's quilt isn't on the bed, but it's comfy." He sat down and patted the bed beside him. "Come on, try it out."

I sat down slowly, suddenly very unsure of myself. "Please don't be scared, darling. I'd never hurt you." And I knew he wouldn't.

I suddenly remembered he shared the trailer. "Jerry, the other guys . . ."

"Don't worry. Carnies work these things out. I've bunked many a night in other trailers when one of the boys wanted some privacy."

A twinge of guilt and shame passed through me as I wondered how many other girls had been in that bed. I quickly buried those thoughts. I'd come too far, except to ask or, I should say stammer, "Did you take care of. . ."

"Got them right on the nightstand, sweetheart. I wouldn't let you take any chances." He took my hand in his and gently kissed my fingertips. "Enough of this talking," he said.

His lips touched my forehead; softly he kissed my eyelids, my cheeks, my neck. Then and only then did he cover my mouth with his. By the time he'd unbuttoned my blouse and touched me, I felt as though my flesh was on fire. The rest of the night was everything I'd ever dreamed love would be.

Jerry was patient and gentle, and later, passionate. No girl could have asked for a better initiation to lovemaking. As I lay in his arms later that night, I knew I could never let him go.

When we woke it was still dark and we made love again. I'd just begun to drift off again when Jerry got out of bed and said, "Come on, sleepyhead, get your clothes on." He was already dressing. I could hardly believe he wanted to get rid of me so early. I thought maybe I made a mistake in thinking he cared about me.

"It's not even daylight, Jerry," I said quietly. "I can't go home yet."

"Home? Don't be silly." He leaned over and kissed me. "I love to watch the sunrise, and today, I want to share this new day with you."

He tossed me my clothes and headed for the tiny kitchen at the other end of the trailer. "I'll make some coffee while you dress, but hurry."

We'd only had a couple of sips when he put his jacket around my shoulders. "Come on, we don't want to miss it."

He walked me down a path through the woods and up over an embankment, where he spread a blanket for us to sit on.

The sky was just beginning to brighten. Some fluffy clouds dotted the horizon and seemed to turn dark blue as the sky behind them began to turn orange. The contrast was spectacular.

"Jerry, it's the most beautiful sunrise I've ever seen," I said.

"It's not up yet; just watch the changes." Minute by minute there were dramatic changes. The deep orange light turned to shades of pink, the bottoms of the clouds began to lighten and then, within minutes, the first edge of the sun appeared. When it was still halfway behind a hill it was already too bright to look at. I closed my eyes and saw little sun dots inside them.

I turned to Jerry. "Thank you for the night. Thank you for your love. And thank you for sharing the sunrise with me on my first day as a woman." We kissed and soon our passion mounted till we were both lost in the moment.

ONE WEEK TO MAKE HIM MINE

Somehow we managed to get back to the trailer and get my things together.

"Lindsay, can you get away tonight?" Jerry asked.

The same thought had come to my mind, too, but I knew it would be impossible. I'd never spent two nights in a row at Beth's.

"I don't think so, but I'd sure like you to meet my parents and little brother. Could you come to dinner during your break?" I knew my family had to meet Jerry. He meant so much to me; I felt it was important that he meet my family.

"What will that prove, Lindsay? That your family can accept a carny in their house?" There was that angry tone in his voice again.

"I don't want to prove anything," I said, taking his hand in mine. "You are the most special person in my life and I want you to meet three people who are also pretty special to me."

He sighed, then said, "If it's okay with your parents just let me know. I could be there by five-fifteen."

It was all right, although Mom seemed a little hesitant at first. "How friendly are you with this carnival person, Lindsay?"

"Mom, Jerry is a nice guy. I just feel bad because they travel around all the time and he never gets a home-cooked meal." I tried not to let my true feelings show—not yet. "I think you'll like him."

They all liked him. Mom, Dad, even my little brother, Jason. "Neat!" he kept saying, every time Jerry told him something about the carnival.

"Can I join the carnival, Mom?" Jason asked after Jerry finished talking about their winters in Florida.

"No, you may not, young man—that's no life for a . . ." She caught herself just a minute too late. I noticed the stricken look in Jerry's eyes, but he just picked up his mug and finished his coffee.

Mom tried to make it up. "Jerry, uh, I didn't mean . . ."

"It's okay, Mrs. Blackwell. I understand. Most people feel that way about the carnival. When you live in such a pretty little town in a splendid house like this, it's understandable." He paused for a moment, then continued, "The carnival is a great place for a guy like me that had no home or family to speak of. As I've told Lindsay, it's my home and the people there are my family. Thanks for dinner. It was the best meal I've had in a long time."

He shook Dad's and Jason's hands, and then held Mom's hand in both of his. "Thanks so much, Mrs. Blackwell, for your hospitality."

I went to the door with him. I didn't dare kiss him with the family watching.

"How about breakfast tomorrow at Big Al's?" he asked.

"I'd love it." Neither of us had mentioned that tomorrow was his last night in town. The midway would be torn down—he'd told me it was called slough night—everything would be packed up, and they'd take off for the next town by daybreak.

As we walked out to the porch, I whispered, "Can you get the trailer tomorrow night?"

"No, Fred's already staked it out. Besides, it'll be a late night with all the packing."

My disappointment was evident. He squeezed my hand and added, "But there is a little motel in town."

I smiled and we parted with just a brush of his hand down my arm. It was enough to send chills through my body.

I went back into the living room and anxiously listened to the family's comments about Jerry. "Seems like a fine young man," Dad had said. "Very polite, well-mannered," Mom had added. Neat seemed to be Jason's only word that night.

Mom looked at me with a bit of a frown on her face, and asked, "How did Jerry get involved with the carnival?"

"Mom, you make it sound like he's with criminals or something," I answered defensively.

"I didn't mean any such thing," she shot back. "It's just such a nomadic lifestyle—I was curious."

"Jerry's parents died when he was only ten years old." I paused and they expressed genuine sympathy.

"That has to be awfully tough on a little boy," Dad said.

"It was even tougher when his uncle began to abuse him." I noticed the shock on their faces. In our little town you heard about abuse in the news, but you didn't know about it firsthand. "He ran away when he was younger."

"Wow!" said Jason, who at age thirteen was already in awe of Jerry.

I continued. "Jerry survived on the street for almost two years, then he joined the carnival. This is his third summer with them and it has been his home—the only place he feels safe, and cared for, and loved."

Suddenly I realized they were all looking at me. Had they seen the love in my eyes?

ONE WEEK TO MAKE HIM MINE

"He's only eighteen?" Dad asked.

"Seems older, doesn't he, Dad?"

"Yes, a very mature eighteen. But if he's had to survive on the streets after being orphaned and abused, he's had to grow up very quickly." I could see the concern in Dad's eyes.

"Has he any plans to go to college or settle somewhere?" Mom asked.

"He hasn't even finished high school, Mom. And like he said, the carnival is his life, his home, and his family. He'll never leave." As I spoke I knew it was true and I also knew what I wanted to do.

The next day after a call to Beth to cover for me, even after she gave me a hundred more warnings, I told Mom we would be camping out at Wheeler's Farm with a bunch of kids from school. We'd been doing it at least once a summer for several years, so it wasn't an unusual evening. Mom trusted me and had no reason to question me about it—for that I felt guilty. Mom had never had any reason not to trust me. I knew this would hurt her.

I got out my sleeping bag and Mom gave me a couple of bags of snacks to share with the gang.

I left about six and found Jerry at Big Al's, eating. I hadn't told him what I'd decided yet—I would surprise him later.

He looked at my sleeping bag and burst out in raucous laughter. "Sleeping out tonight, Lindsay?"

I smacked his arm playfully. "Stop teasing. Do we have a place, or do I have to use this sleeping bag?" I joined in his laughter then.

"Just waiting to hear from you, darling," Jerry said with a wink.

We borrowed Pop's car and drove into town

229

where Jerry rented us a motel room. We had an hour before he was due back for his shift. We made love like there was no tomorrow. Of course, Jerry thought there wouldn't be a tomorrow.

He gently stroked my cheek and said, "I have to get back to work, babe, and then help with the loading. It'll be late—you get a nap till I get back."

I held his hand against my cheek. "I love you, Jerry."

"Oh, Lindsay, you can't fall in love with a carny. Didn't I tell you that before?" He looked so sad.

"I didn't. I fell in love with a man who likes flowers and sunrises. I fell in love with Jerry Sutton and it doesn't matter what he does for a living."

He got up and started pulling on his jeans. Trying to be stern, he said, "Well, Jerry Sutton is leaving tomorrow at sunrise, baby, so don't think love's going to change that." His voice softened. "I told you I'd never deliberately hurt you—that's why I told you all about my life from day one. You know I can't leave the carnival, Lindsay. It's my life."

I rose and stood beside him. "Of course I know that, my darling, but I can leave Hillcrest. I can go with you."

His arms fell to his sides and he closed his eyes for just a moment. "Get dressed!" he barked.

"Why? I thought we were going to sleep here tonight?"

"No way. I'm taking you home to your mother right now, before you talk me into this crazy scheme."

"You mean it's possible?" I asked.

"No! Absolutely not!" But I could sense his mind clicking with the possibility.

"You said I was special," I said.

"You are." He actually had started dressing me, buttoning my blouse, pulling on my jeans.

"It's impossible, Lindsay, so skip it."

"Well, if it really is—impossible that is—I'm staying right here so we can at least end our last night together." I began undressing again. In my mind I knew he was weakening and if I had till morning, the carnival would have a new employee.

He seemed hesitant.

"All right, Jerry?"

"I don't know. You'll probably spend all night trying to talk me into this lame-brained scheme. We ought to end it now." He pulled on his boots.

"Why is it so lame-brained?" I asked. "Unless you don't love me as much as I love you and don't want me with you?"

"Oh, Lindsay, you know I do." He slumped down in a chair across the room.

"Then tell me why it's such a bad idea."

"For one thing, you don't work for the carnival and you can't just go along for the ride," he said.

"I kind of talked to Mom Hamilton yesterday. She's not adverse to hiring me if true love has come along."

He turned to me, eyes wide. "You talked to Mom?"

"Uh-huh."

"What makes you think it's true love?" he asked.

"Jerry, we wouldn't even be having this discussion if it weren't."

"But your home, your family."

"I'll call home in the morning, and I'll write a letter explaining our feelings." I would have an answer for any question he asked. I had decided that last night.

"You're my life now, Jerry. If the carnival is your life, then it's my life, too." I saw the look in his eyes. He was going to agree.

"I'm going to be late. We'll talk this out when I get back."

Our kiss was long and hard and I trembled with love for this man. There was fear in his eyes when he pulled back. "I can't believe you'd give up everything for me. No one's ever given up anything for me," he said.

"That's true love, my darling," I said, and with another quick kiss he was out the door. I ran to the window and waved. He honked the horn in return and sped off.

Having some time alone was a luxury for me. I took a long, steamy bath, watched some TV, and read a magazine. Then I began a letter to Morn and Dad to try and explain what had happened to their daughter, but I couldn't find the words to explain it.

Jerry had said he'd be late, so around eleven I decided to take a nap. I left a note on his pillow. *Wake me with a kiss, and I'll reward you,* it read.

But Jerry's lips didn't wake me. It was the harsh sunlight coming through the thin drapes that woke me. I grabbed my watch off the nightstand—it was seven-fifteen! I looked at the pillow next to mine. The note was still pinned to it.

I got dressed and hitchhiked back to Hillcrest. I knew I was taking a chance, but the buses didn't run often on Sunday and I had to try and catch him. Luckily, a little old lady picked me up, and all the way to Hillcrest she regaled me with the horrors that could befall hitchhikers.

ONE WEEK TO MAKE HIM MINE

As we approached the town I could see the Ferris wheel was gone. "Just drop me here, and thanks so much," I said, anxious to get to the field.

I walked over to the empty lot where my life had been centered for the past week. It was empty—completely empty—not a car, or a trailer, or a living person was left.   I had never asked where they were headed because I believed I would be with them.

Just then, Officer McBride walked by the corner. "Carnival's over, Lindsay."

I tried to smile and nonchalantly asked, "Where do they go next, Officer McBride?"

"Who knows?" He looked over the empty lot, then added, "Carnival people are like gypsies—they move in on one Sunday and are gone the next."

I went into the house quietly and tried to tiptoe to my room, but Mom heard me.

"You're back awfully early," she said.

"I didn't feel well, Mom. Beth drove me home." I was beginning to lie so easily.

"Can I get you something? Aspirin, or a cup of tea?" She looked worried.

"No, Mom, I just need to get into bed and sleep."

She fussed till I was settled in bed, then went out, with orders to call her if I needed anything. I just felt more guilty for deceiving her.   I   just   couldn't believe he was gone. I cried and cried until there were no more tears left to cry.

There was a soft knocking at my door a little later. I turned toward the wall so she wouldn't see my eyes. "I'm okay, Mom."

The door creaked open and there was a whispered, "It's me," from Jason.

"I'm sick, Jason. Please go away." I heard the door click shut and thought he'd gone, then realized he was tiptoeing toward my bed.

"Jason, please."

"Jerry left this letter for you," he whispered.

I sat up and grabbed the envelope from his hand, suddenly filled with hope. "Oh, Jason, when?"

"Real early this morning," he said. "I heard a tapping at my window and he told me it was real important that I give this to you first thing this morning and not tell anybody else about it. Guess he meant Mom and Dad, huh?"

I impulsively hugged and kissed my little brother, which I knew I wasn't supposed to do now that he thought he was all grown up.

"Thanks, Jason. Thanks so much."

"Hey, none of that mushy stuff," he said, wiping my kiss off his cheek. Then he turned and left me alone.

As I ripped the envelope open, I knew it would say that he would be back for me. I had realized we wouldn't have had a place to live if I'd gone with him that day, so I was sure he'd be back as soon as he got us a trailer.

Relief flooded through my body as I unfolded the pages. Then I began to read his words:

My darling Lindsay, I will never forget you, my love. You are a very special girl. I knew that days ago, but last night I realized how deep your love went.

It was one thing to give up your virginity to prove your love, but to give up your home and family and everything you owned to be with me has to be the greatest act of love I can imagine.

ONE WEEK TO MAKE HIM MINE

Please don't think I didn't consider it, because for six hours last night that's all I thought about. I even talked to Pop, and he agreed with Mom that they could hire you. He'd even see that we got our own trailer and would work out the payment arrangements for us.

So, don't think it was a totally bad idea. I clung to it—to have my carnival life and you, too would be heaven on earth.

Then I realized I love you too much to let you give up the good life you have there in Hillcrest.

You see, darling, you have everything in your life that I had to go out and find—that I did find in the carnival.

This life could never mean as much to you as it does to me. The excitement and the travel and winters in Florida would all be a wonderful new experience for you, but I realize now that eventually you would tire of it. You would miss your home, your family, your friends—your whole way of life. Then your love for me would turn to bitterness. You would begin to resent the fact that you gave up so much for me.

And I, my love, could never leave this way of life. So, maybe, just in your decision to come with me, you have proven that your love is deeper. I'm just not worthy of that much love.

Please forgive me if I've hurt you. Don't hate me. What we shared was too beautiful to end that way.

You will get over this—believe me. I've gotten over a lot of hurts. You will eventually forget me. Your whole future is in front of you—college, career, and a normal life with a husband and children who will love you and their home as much as you've loved your parents and your home.

Thank you for giving me the most precious week of my life and for so unconditionally giving me your love. I will never forget you or the love we shared.

God bless you and watch over you, darling. Love, Jerry

Silent tears streamed down my face. My love was gone and I had nothing but memories. I knew if it were physically possible, my heart would break into a million pieces. Unfortunately, hearts are sturdier than that and mine continued beating intact.

The next month, my so-called last month of freedom, seemed to drag on forever. My mother tried to get me excited about shopping for clothes for college, but I couldn't muster any enthusiasm. I was relieved that I'd decided to go to our local community college. I could never have managed a major move at that point. By the end of August, Mom insisted I go see Dr. Rider. He talked to me awhile, then he ran some tests.

When I was dressed again, I went into his office. "Lindsay, could this malady you are afflicted with have anything to do with the young man from the carnival?" he asked.

I was startled at his question. "What do you mean? How?"

"I suppose I shouldn't have said anything, but your mother believes this all began when that fellow left town."

I slumped back in my chair and smiled. "I guess moms aren't dumb, huh?"

He smiled in return. "Sometimes, Lindsay, falling in love is tough."

"Falling out of love is even tougher, Dr. Rider," I said with a sigh.

The next afternoon Beth and I were sitting on the front porch.

"Lindsay," she said, "college will turn this all around. New experiences, new people—you'll forget Jerry."

"Never!" I practically shouted at her. "I'll never forget him. I don't want to."

"I give up. See you tomorrow." Then she was gone. The phone rang, but I knew Jason would get it, so I stayed on the porch swing.

"Lindsay," Jason called from the house. "Lindsay, it's for you."

"Who is it?" I asked as we passed in the hall.

"I don't know," he muttered.

"Hello," I said softly.

"Lindsay, this is Dr. Rider."

"Dr. Rider, is something wrong?" I asked, thinking to myself: *My God, maybe a heart can break.*

"Lindsay, I want you to come down to the office this afternoon—alone," he answered.

I sat in front of his huge oak desk, waiting, and wondering. He came in, looking more serious than usual. He opened a folder on his desk and said, "Lindsay, you're pregnant."

"Oh, my God, it can't be. We used contraceptives."

"What did you use, Lindsay?" he asked.

"Jerry . . . he had condoms." I couldn't believe I was talking to our old family doctor like this.

"Well, they are a fairly effective means of birth control, Lindsay, but there's always a possibility—if they're not used properly or forgotten just once. . . ."

ONE WEEK TO MAKE HIM MINE

"Oh, no!" I suddenly remembered the sunrise. Jerry and I on the blanket—we had been overwhelmed by our passion. The condoms had been left in the trailer. "What is it, Lindsay?" he asked.

"You're right, there was once. We got . . ."

"Carried away?" he finished.

"Yes," I answered softly.

"I think you should talk to your parents about this, but it's your decision. They could be the support you need at this time. If you'd like, we could talk to them together."

"Yes, Dr. Rider, but not yet," I said. "I have to figure out what to do first. Please, just give me a few days."

Oddly, after the initial shock, I was happier than I'd been in a long time. I had something of Jerry's, more than just my memories. I had his child. I knew I didn't want to have an abortion or put the baby up for adoption.

I tried again through the police department to find out where the carnival had gone. "Lindsay," Officer McBride explained, "of course they come in and get a license for the week they're here, but—"

I interrupted. "Then they must have to put an address on it."

"Yes, there's an address. But it's just a post office box in Florida. It's not where they are now. They probably have the mail forwarded or someone there just checks through it for important mail."

I finally convinced him to give me the address and I wrote Jerry in care of the post office box. Although I was very hopeful, I also knew I'd have to speak to Mom and Dad.

That night after dinner Jason went out to play,

and Mom started in again about us going shopping for clothing. I hadn't planned on telling them just then, but it just seemed to come out. "I'm not going to college—I'm pregnant!"

The silence was like a huge black cloud that engulfed the room.

"Who?" Mom finally asked.

"Who's the father?" I asked defensively. "Is that what you want to know? That's at the top of your list? Don't you want to know if I love him or if I want the baby?" The tears had begun to build, but I continued. "It doesn't make any difference who the father is. I'm not going to marry him and I'm not going to have an abortion."

I barely paused for breath. "If you can't accept this baby, I'll go to one of those homes for unwed mothers." The tears came then.

Mom got out of her chair and came and put her arms around me, with Dad just a step behind.

"Lindsay, we love you and of course we would accept your baby, but a baby is a big responsibility and you're so young."

I got up and held on to both of them and we all cried. Finally Dad got himself under control and suggested we go into the living room and discuss the situation.

"Lindsay," Dad began, "the father should know, even if you don't love him or want to marry him."

"Oh, I love him, Dad. And I'd marry him in a minute."

"He doesn't love you?"

"Yes, he loves me. That's why he left without me."

"It was Jerry, wasn't it?" Mom asked.

"Yes," I answered simply, suddenly so tired of all

the lies.

They listened to the whole story and held me while I cried. I let them read his letter so they'd understand our love.

"Oh, Lindsay, whether he loved you or not, he's probably right. You might have grown to hate him for pulling you into that life," she said.

"Mom, I thought you understood. I love him so much, I'd live in a tent with him." I ran to my room and slammed the door.

She came in and sat on the bed beside me. "I didn't mean to upset you, honey. But I'm very concerned about you and I'm on edge. As far as Jerry is concerned, I guess all you can do now is wait for the letter to catch up with him." She rubbed my back.

"I don't want him to give up the carnival, Mom," I said. "That's not why I wrote. I told him I wanted to go to him. They'll still be in Florida in April. I just want to be with him when the baby's born. I need to be with him."

But there was no reply to my letter—no phone call—nothing. I sent two more letters before my pride made me stop.

The months went by slowly. The holidays were particularly difficult. I tried to keep busy during the winter months fixing up a room for the baby and working on some correspondence courses. I knew that if I was forced to raise my baby on my own, I would have to continue my education, so I could get a good job and my baby could have a comfortable, good life.

Spring arrived, with warm sunshine and flowers everywhere. Mom's daffodils and hyacinths filled the yard with color and lovely fragrance. I often sat in the gazebo, remembering how happy Jerry and I had been.

Then one sunny and bright April day, my son was born. Mom and Beth were both willing and able baby-sitters and tried to get me to go out. But I was content to be at home with the baby.

My only wish was that Jerry could have known the joy of holding our child in his arms. I never did accept the fact that he hadn't replied to my letters. I had honestly believed that even if he didn't want me, he would at least want to know his child.

I was able to explain away one letter getting lost in the mail. But three? *Maybe I'm wrong about him,* I thought. *Maybe I am just another notch in his belt—one more girl in one more town. Can I be so wrong?* I held little Will and cried, saddened by the fact that he would never know his father.

I even thought I could learn to hate Jerry. That it would make it easier then. But each day with his baby only made me love and miss him more.

The spring flowers died and were replaced by even more colorful summer ones. Mom certainly had a green thumb. The days had grown quite warm, and on the Fourth of July we celebrated Will's three-month birthday with a picnic. I celebrated every month—Mom told me we'd be out of candles before his first birthday.

I was fully aware of the fact that the carnival was in town, and although Mom suggested I might want to speak to Jerry before he left town again, I stayed away. I did, after all, have some pride.

I made Mom, Dad, and Beth all swear to stay away from the carnival and not to talk to Jerry.

On Friday of that week I had resigned myself to

the fact that Jerry didn't want to see me, either. After all, they'd been in town five nights and he hadn't even called.

I was sitting in the living room in my grandmother's old, wooden rocking chair with Will sleeping peacefully in my arms, while I daydreamed again of how my life would be if I'd been with Jerry. I heard the front screen door bang shut.

"Lindsay?" Jason called out.

"Shh—Jason, be quiet. I just got the baby to sleep."

"Someone's here to see you," he said.

I turned, my heart beating frantically. He was even more handsome than I remembered. "How? Who?" I stammered.

"Jason told me." His voice sent tremors through my body. I was grateful to be sitting.

"You didn't make me swear not to talk to him, Lindsay." With those words, Jason left the room.

Jerry came and stood beside us. He gently touched his sleeping child's cheek. Then he looked at me with tear-filled eyes. "Why didn't you want me to know?"

"Didn't want you to know! I wrote you three letters letting you know. Are you trying to tell me you didn't even get one of them? I know the mail doesn't always get through. But three?"

"Oh, my God, Lindsay." He was on his knees, tears streaming down his cheeks, his hands grasping mine. "I tore them up without opening them. Oh, darling, forgive me. I was afraid I'd weaken if I read your letters, so I just never opened them. When you stopped writing, I figured you were on your way to forgetting me—that's why I didn't try to see you this week. If Jason hadn't come . . . I never imagined you could be pregnant. We were always so careful. . . ."

"You forgot about the sunrise," I said softly.

It took just a second for him to comprehend what I meant, then his face softened and he leaned forward and kissed me, with our sleeping child between us. He kissed the baby's head and nose, then looked into my eyes and said, "What a perfect time and place to conceive our child, Lindsay."

I handed him the baby then, and his face could have lit up the whole carnival at that moment. "He's beautiful, my love," he said. "What's his name?"

"William Jerome Sutton," I answered, adding, "William for my dad and Jerome for his."

That bright and beautiful July day over six years ago was the beginning of a new life for me.

William Jerome started school today and when he gets home, the three of us will probably walk to the beach for a swim. Will loves the ocean—almost as much as I do. And when school closes at the end of May, we will be back on the road again.

I have never tired of the carnival life and have never regretted my decision. Each day is exciting and I am totally happy with my husband and child. As for Will, he's already decided he wants to be a clown when he grows up—his grandmother insists he already is one.

Mom and Dad visit us in Florida for a whole month every winter and Jason usually gets down for at least a week during his summer break from school. We stay at their house for the week we're in Hillcrest, and Will loves the gazebo and his grandmother's flowers.

On that July day when Jerry discovered his son,

he tried to convince me that he wanted a house and yard and a real job, but I knew my husband. If he had tried to put down roots, they would have eventually strangled us. So Jerry's carnival life is now my life—and I love it!   THE END

I NEVER KNEW
A TOUCH LIKE HIS

I had saved for over six months to buy my motor-cycle, and as I sped up the driveway and parked behind the house, I was feeling pretty satisfied. Why drive a big old gas-guzzler when all I needed was something to get me where I was going? And there were lots of places I wanted to go! That morning, I had already driven around the lake and cruised on the interstate, yet my gas tank still registered full. That sure beat the seven-year-old crate I'd been driving!

I eased off my blue crash helmet and set it on the cycle seat. Then, giving my hair a shake, I headed for the house. It felt good to let my hair hang free. My job at the bakery required that I wear a hair net, and that was about as confining as the crash helmet.

It wasn't the greatest job, but it wasn't the worst, either. The hours were terrible, but the money was good. And money was important to me because I was, basically, on my own. My mother had been killed in a boating accident two years before. That left just my stepfather and me, and the way he showed his concern for me was by vanishing with all the insurance money. I hadn't heard from him since.

I had blown my chance to go to college. In high school, I was voted "the girl most likely to become a professor." I was interested in teaching as a career, but after graduation I decided to forego the scholarship I was awarded and go to work for a year. I soon learned that college-educated people didn't necessarily earn more money than anyone else, so I kept working. I liked having my own money, and I enjoyed living free, traveling, and not having to answer to anyone.

As I had explained to Jack Benson, my steady boyfriend, I was in no hurry to make commitments. Jack was great for commitments. He was totally committed to college and being a dentist. I couldn't stand him sometimes, with his answers to everything. Being around Jack made me feel very incompetent. But he'd do until someone better came along.

The bakery job filled my nights. I didn't like to plan my days too far in advance, and it was the kind of job I could leave without feeling any remorse. There were hazards to it, though. My hands were scarred from lifting hot trays of bread, and I had a new burn on my arm from just last night.

Since my family disintegrated, I'd been living with my mother's brother, Mack, and his second wife, Barbara. Mack drove a truck and didn't give me any unwanted advice. Barbara worked in the local bank, and the only thing she expected from me was a little work around the house when I felt like it. We'd only had a few problems about that, and they had been resolved quickly. I liked to clutter my room a bit, so she never touched any of it—just as I never invaded their bedroom. They had been married about two years now and seemed very happy with each other.

Barbara was about ten years older than Mack, and a super person, too. She had a couple of grown kids somewhere—a boy and a girl. The daughter was married and lived on the West Coast, and the son was in the Air Force.

My head was down as I slid the patio door open. I couldn't wait to get to sleep. I still wasn't used to working nights. I knew Barbara was at work and Mack was on the road, so no one was home. At least I didn't think so, until I stumbled clumsily over two big combat boots, tripped, and fell on the living room couch. And there was a person—a man—lying on it!

He didn't seem to mind having a strange girl fall on him. "This is nice," he murmured. "Should I go back to sleep, or did you have something else in mind?"

I blinked, rolled off onto the carpet, and bounced up quickly. "What are you doing here?" I glared at him. "How did you get in? Who are you anyway?"

He looked amused. "You must be Julia," he said. "Mother told me about you. You're Mack's niece, right?"

"I know who I am!" I blurted. "That doesn't tell me who you are."

"Perry Thorpe." He sat up and buttoned his shirt. He was wearing a military uniform.

"Oh." I looked him over quickly. *Barbara's son,* I thought. He looked like her, except he was so tall, and had such wide shoulders. "You're in the Air Force," I stammered.

"Airborne," he corrected. "There's quite a difference. I'm Army." His voice was deep as thunder.

"You do have something to do with planes, though," I argued.

"I jump out of them," he said, smiling. His teeth were nice.

"Gross!" I blurted. "How do you psych yourself up to do that?"

"We went through a lot of advance training first. But actually we just get into a line, hook up our rip cords, and jump in sequence. There's no special preparation," he said.

"What made you decide to do it in the first place? A death wish, maybe?" This whole subject interested me in a curious way.

"It's a part of being an effective soldier." He stood up and shrugged his shoulders. "Facing a situation like that makes a man more positive, more alive. It's just part of being a man. . . ." His voice trailed off and he narrowed his eyes when I smiled.

"What's so funny?" he snapped.

"Nothing." I tried not to laugh out loud. "I always wanted to meet a genuine, certified, honest-to-goodness total man."

I walked into the kitchen and searched the fridge for some orange juice. Maybe I should have chosen my words more carefully, I thought. I shouldn't poke fun at Barbara's only son, at least not to his face.

I measured coffee into the automatic machine and filled the top with water. I looked out the window as I sipped my juice. The leaves were falling fast, I noticed. The maple tree in the corner of the yard was almost bare.

"You got any coffee?" Perry was leaning in the doorway.

"In a minute." I gave him a wide smile. "You can have some juice, though. The glasses are in the disher."

"Disher?" He looked confused. I liked that.

"Dishwasher." I kept smiling. Mack had bought us one last Christmas. Before that, we left dishes all over. "The coffee won't be ready for a few minutes."

Perry turned back into the living room without answering. He hadn't returned my smile, but so what? I wouldn't waste another minute on him. I shook my head in an attempt to clear it of my rude thoughts. What was the matter with me? He was Barbara's son, after all, and I was being a brat. I had to shape up.

I finished my juice and glanced out the window again. The red maple leaves were rolling across the lawn like birds flying south. . . .

"Are you going to sleep?" Perry barked from the doorway, disturbing my reverie. "If you are, you ought to go to bed."

"I'll bet you're great at raking leaves," I mumbled, easing myself off the window seat and crossing to the sink. I rinsed the juice glass and read a note from Barbara on the bulletin board. She wanted me to wipe out the fridge, vacuum the rec room, and wash two loads of clothes.

I stuffed the note into the back pocket of my jeans and ran some soapy water into the sink. I poured Perry's coffee and set it on the table. Then I began to clean the refrigerator shelves.

As Perry sat at the table, I could feel his eyes following me across the room. I tried not to look at him. I would probably say something better left unsaid. There was something about his pride, his unbelievable arrogance.

"You shouldn't leave eggs in those trays on the door," he said as he stirred his coffee. "When you open the door, the eggs crack. They don't stay fresh as long."

I leveled a stare at him. "Why do you suppose they manufacture these beauties with egg trays in the door?" I retorted. "I mean, nothing else fits there, does it?"

"Well, people who make refrigerators don't know everything." He stared back at me.

"No, but I'll bet you do." I smiled evilly.

He gave a low whistle, his eyes watching me closely. "You don't like me, do you?" he asked.

"Of course I like you," I assured him. "What's not to like? You're confident, bossy, arrogant, and so manly—"

"Look." He stood up suddenly. "I think I've had enough." He glanced at his watch and walked briskly from the room.

"Listen!" I raced him to the door and stood blocking his exit. "If I don't see you again, I know when you grow up you're going to be a very nice person."

"When I grow up?" he repeated. His eyes were impatient. "Who do you think you are?"

"I know who I am," I breathed.

His eyes raked my face. "You're nothing," he whispered. "Nothing and nobody."

It was a low blow. I almost felt as if he'd hit me.

His words made a strange sinking thud in the pit of my stomach, and my head hurt with a sudden loss of energy. I looked at the shine on his boots for a second. Then I raised my glance to his. "Like I said before," I muttered, "I know who I am."

After he'd gone, I pulled Barbara's list from my pocket. I still had to wash the clothes and vacuum. I could let the first load wash while I vacuumed the rec room, and put the second load in before I went to sleep.

It was almost noon when I returned from the basement with the laundry. Perry was still nowhere in sight. I showered and blow-dried my hair before lying down. I also tacked a note on the kitchen bulletin board, so Barbara wouldn't wake me for work. I was off tonight and wanted to catch up on my sleep. *What a day,* I thought as I rubbed cream on my burned arm. I stared at the ugly blister. Perry was right! I was nothing and nobody. On that depressing thought, I drifted off to sleep.

Later, Barbara shook me awake, asking me what I'd eaten. I squinted into the overhead light and rolled over. With one eye open, I saw it was dark outside. The digital clock beside my bed read 7:21.

"I drank some juice," I mumbled. "I'm not hungry. I'm tired." *Go away,* I thought, but I liked Barbara too much to say it aloud.

"My son Perry is here. Don't you feel like getting up?"

"We've met." I closed my eyes. "He's nice," I lied. "I know you're really proud of him."

"He said he quarreled with you." Her voice was quiet. "I know Perry can be tactless at times, and not the easiest person to get to know."

"Well—" I took a deep breath and exhaled. "I'm not exactly up for the Nobel Peace Prize, either," I admitted. "Tell him I'm not angry, and I don't blame him for being honest."

"You have a new burn." She looked at my arm. "Did you put anything on it?"

I said I had, and then I asked her if she'd seen my motorcycle and what she thought of it. I already knew what she thought of my job. I commented quickly on the gas mileage—much better than my old car—and how beautiful the lake was in the morning with the fog lifting. "You and Mack ought to go up to the cottage before it gets any colder," I said. "The leaves are fantastic right now."

"It's going to be cold riding the motorcycle this winter." She shook her head. "Julia, I don't understand you sometimes. You criticize Perry for jumping out of airplanes, yet you struggle with that horrid job at the bakery and zip around on a motorcycle without a thought for your safety."

I narrowed my eyes. So he'd gone to his mother with our conversation. He needed support for his ideas, no doubt. It only proved that I was right in my original assessment. "It's different for him," I murmured. "He's got you to worry about him."

"I worry about you too, Julia. You know that." Her voice was soft. "I wish you and Perry could at least be friends."

I shrugged. "I shouldn't have ridiculed him. He knows who he is and what he wants to do. That's more than most of us know. People like that always bring out the worst in me." I laughed shakily. "What happened was my own fault. I never know when to keep my mouth shut. But I really don't have anything else to say to him, Barbara. I just want to go back to sleep."

"All right." She stood up and crossed to the door. "I'll go now. You do what pleases you." I took that to mean that I always did.

"Wait a minute," I blurted. "Barbara, I'll talk to him. Just give me a second to—"

"Wear something nice." She smiled and left before I could object.

"You look nice," he offered. "I hope we can be friends. Mother thinks a great deal of you."

"I guess so," I stared anxiously toward the hallway, wondering where Barbara was and how long she would be. "Barbara likes everybody. She's a terrific person."

"And I'm not," he countered smoothly.

"I didn't say that."

"But it's true," he muttered. "I'm not. I had no right to say what I did. I didn't know you really believe you're nothing and nobody. It was a foul thing to say. But how could I know you feel so sorry for yourself?"

"I do not!" I jumped up and stared at him. "You're amazing!" I completely forgot my plan to be patronizing. "You don't even know me!"

"I know you at least as well as you know me," he argued, his eyes flashing. "You act like a rude brat, and if you can say I'm a little boy, I can say you're a little girl."

"I didn't say you're a little boy," I snapped. "I merely pointed out that you aren't as much of a man as you think. Jumping out of airplanes won't make you a man, and insulting me won't either."

"Why don't you tell me what will?" he demanded.

"That is not my concern." I looked toward the hallway. "Where's Barbara?" I asked hotly. She could hear the noise we were making. Why didn't she come and referee?

"She isn't here," he answered evenly. "She met Mack at the truck garage and they went out to eat."

"But—" I whirled on him. "You mean I got dressed to stand here and argue with you? Good grief!" I stomped out, kicking my shoes off and slamming the door to my room. I was reaching for the back zipper of my dress with my left hand as my door opened and Perry stepped across the threshold.

"To answer your question," he muttered, "I believe it was Mother's intention that we meet them later."

"I never go out with creeps," I snapped, turning quickly. As I did, I brushed my arm against the bureau drawer handle and ripped the bandage off my burn. "Ow!" I screamed.

He gently pushed me onto the bed. "Just lie there and try to be quiet. I'm going to take care of that arm of yours."

Perry came back soon and sat beside me. "You're a bundle of laughs," he said softly. "Some guy is going to have a great time taking care of you someday."

"I don't need any guy to take care of me," I replied weakly.

I noticed the first-aid cream in his hand. He studied the burn on my arm.

"Don't touch it!" I squealed.

"How'd it happen?" he demanded.

"I burned it at work and now I've made it worse,"

I gasped. "It's your fault."

"It is not!" he insisted. "I'm just an innocent bystander. You're a very destructive person."

I stared at him angrily.

"I'll go scramble some eggs. How would that be?"

"Sounds fine." I tried to smile.

A little later, I munched on toast and eggs and seemed to get my strength back. Then Perry talked me into going out, and we went to a seafood place. Perry ate fish, drank beer, and flirted with the waitress. His eyes twinkled mischievously across the table.

He told me offhandedly that he was divorced. He liked Army life—and moving about on his own.

"What happened to your marriage?" I was suddenly interested.

Perry considered the question for a long moment and shrugged. "I guess I just didn't love her," he admitted finally.

"Did you ever?" I demanded. "I mean, isn't real love forever? Or is that just an illusion?"

"I don't think I ever did love her. I didn't know her well enough. But yes, I think real love is forever. I hope so," he added thoughtfully.

"But can you be sure what you feel is love?" I blurted.

"Can you be sure it isn't?" he asked.

"It's all very uncertain, isn't it?" I asked.

"I'll know next time," he said, laughing nervously.

"Well, you figured that out, at least." I nodded and sipped my iced tea.

"What?" Perry stared at me in a fixed way.

"You know what love is. I've never been able to

define it. I see it as one of life's great mysteries."

"When you want somebody so much you're ready to die, that's love," he answered.

"Wanting somebody?" I was doubtful. "I've known a lot of guys who wanted me, but it wasn't love. It was something physical. I don't think of love as just wanting someone. You should want to do something for the person you love without asking anything in return. You're an awful flirt," I said quickly. "You should be ashamed."

"I'm shameless, too." He laughed, and left a huge tip for the waitress.

We never did find Barbara and Mack. We thought they must be waiting for us at home, so Perry bought a bottle on the way back. When we got back, he laced my soda with something that didn't smell or taste. I sipped it and snuggled comfortably on the couch. I began to relax.

Perry found a note from Barbara. She and Mack had driven up to the lake cottage for the night and they wouldn't be back until morning. She expected Perry to stay until Monday and asked him to be there when they returned. They hoped we had a good time.

The lights were low and Perry played some heavy rock music on the stereo—not too loudly, though. He explained it was a new tape he wanted to listen to. It was full of shrill screams, pounding drums, and zinging guitar. I sipped my drink and drifted into a soft, embracing mood. Since there was no one else to embrace, it just seemed logical to allow Perry to lead me around the room in a dance that ended with me on his lap in the armchair.

His hand was on my shoulder as he kissed me,

and the caress warmed me with a kind of pleasant hunger. I felt drawn to him like a magnet. His other hand was pressing my hip gently.

"I never knew anyone who kissed like you," I gasped.

"Is that right?" he whispered against my ear, and traced my neck with kisses. His lips moved back to mine and we kissed hungrily. When he tried to pull away I wouldn't let him. Once he said we should stop, but I pressed closer. He gave a moan and his body seemed to take me everywhere at once. We couldn't have stopped for a bomb alert. Then we made love, and I gave myself to him with wild satisfaction.

When I awoke it was near dawn, and I was in my bed under the sheet. Perry was nowhere to be seen. I couldn't believe what had happened. It's my fault, I thought. I couldn't blame Perry; he had tried to put the brakes on. But I had raced into his arms at ninety miles an hour.

I went into the shower and let the warm water run over my body. Not that I felt dirty. I felt touched, useful in a way I didn't know I could.

I patted myself dry with a towel and thought about the day and what to do. I would have to act normally, of course. Barbara and Mack couldn't know what had happened. They wouldn't, unless I told them. I didn't think that Perry would say anything.

From my room, I heard voices and the clatter of dishes in the kitchen. Perry's rich voice cut across his mother's laughter. A little later, Mack poked his head into my room and summoned me for breakfast. I hesitated. I didn't want Perry to see me. He would probably think I was cheap for losing control last night.

I managed to walk into the kitchen and pour myself a cup of coffee without looking at anyone. *So far, so good,* I thought. My hands trembled, and I set the cup down quickly to avoid spilling coffee. I glanced across the room and saw the three of them watching me.

"I'm so glad you and Perry went out last night," Barbara said. "Did you have a good time?"

"Of course." I managed an awkward smile.

"He brought you home too early," she teased. "I think you should have gone dancing."

"He did everything I asked," I said softly. "It was fine, really." I looked across at Perry. He seemed to be studying me. I felt embarrassment wash over me in a hot wave.

"Perry is going to leave you his car to drive," Barbara said. "He doesn't really need it at the base, and he has to park it somewhere."

"I don't need a car," I answered carefully. "I have my motorcycle."

"Don't be silly, Julia." She laughed nervously. "I'm sure you'd rather drive Perry's car. After all, it's practically new."

"I'm sure Jack is going to just love my driving another guy's car." I shook my head. "Barbara, you have to be kidding."

Mack laughed and almost choked on his ham and eggs. "She has you there, Barbara," he said. "Jack is a jealous nut. Where is he today? It's Saturday—he's usually here."

"He'll be coming over later." I wasn't very hungry. In fact, my throat felt like it had a block of wood stuck in it. I wished Perry would stop staring at me. I could feel his eyes burning against my skin.

"What have you planned for today, Julia?" Barbara asked.

"I'm going to rake the yard and just visit with Perry. Unless there's somewhere you want to go, Perry?"

"No." He straightened his shoulders. "That sounds fine."

The phone rang and I jumped. It was Jack. He wanted to drive over and pick me up in about twenty minutes. I hung up and turned back to the table. "I have to get ready," I stammered and started to my room.

"Julia, you've hardly touched your food," Barbara scolded. "Come back and eat."

"Mother!" Perry shook his head. "You're treating her like she's five years old. She's a grown woman."

Mack laughed. "I guess it takes a man to spot that, Barbara. Perry has a good eye." He winked and stood up, saying he had a truck to get out. He pulled on his coat, kissed Barbara, and left.

Jack arrived soon after. He stayed in his car and leaned on the horn. I grabbed my blue jacket and started out. Perry was watching a ball game on TV. He stood up as I crossed the room. "Doesn't he ever come in?" he asked. "Or do you run curb service all the time?"

I glared at him. All my friends did the same thing. The guy arrived, and the woman went out to the car when the horn sounded. "I'm a grown woman, remember?" I snapped.

"If you are, then you need a man. And a man comes to the door." His eyes were determined.

"You aren't going out."

I could hear Barbara rattling the dishes in the kitchen. I was not going to have an argument. I turned around and headed for the sliding door, but Perry cut off my exit in two quick strides. "You have no right!" I gasped.

"After last night, I have a right." He took a step toward me. "A lot more right than that turkey outside, I think."

"Last night was no example of what to expect from me." I backed away. "I had a buzz on. But, thanks, it was a real education."

"Is that what it was?" He seemed puzzled. "Is that all?"

"Of course." I shrugged. "I just felt free—no commitment."

Outside, Jack leaned on his horn again and Perry looked at me strangely. "You're a very cool customer," he said evenly. "You used me, didn't you? You wanted an experience and you picked me. I thought you were carried away—that you didn't know what you were doing."

"I always know what I'm doing." I gave him a serious look. "I knew you were safe to be with. You've been married. You know the score. There was no danger of your being indiscreet, or that I might become pregnant."

His face drained of color and he sat down suddenly. Jack's horn sounded loud and long.

Barbara walked in, drying her hands on her apron. "Is that boy completely without manners?" she asked. "He just keeps blowing the horn louder and louder. I'm glad to see you aren't going out, Julia. I think that's terrible."

"There are worse things," I muttered, going back into my room and slamming the door.

Jack finally gave up and came to the door. Barbara called me, and I went out through the living room without a word and slid inside Jack's car.

"What's the matter with you?" Jack demanded. "Why didn't you come out to the car? Who's that guy inside? He tried to tell me off for honking the horn! Who does he think he is? Who—"

"Shut up!" I exploded. "He isn't any worse than you are. He's just as stupid. Both of you are stupid, chauvinistic pigs!"

"Wait a minute—" Jack said. "What's the matter with you?"

"What's the matter?" I screamed. "If you say that one more time, Jack Benson, you can just stop the car!"

He screeched to a stop. I jumped out and stormed down the street. Jack drove along beside me for a few blocks, but I cut across a couple of lawns and lost him in the park.

I sat down and leaned back against a tall oak and closed my eyes. I thought for a long time about what I had said to Perry. It hadn't been true. I didn't plan to make love with him. I only said that because I didn't want him to know I'd been under his control completely. I had wanted him so much. I hardly knew him, but I went all to pieces at the thought of him. What had happened between us seemed like a soft, velvet dream.

I walked back home slowly. Barbara and Perry were in the front yard raking leaves into neat piles and stuffing them into plastic bags. I slipped inside and changed into my jeans and boots. Zipping my jacket up under my chin, I went out to the motorcycle and sped off.

The interstate was three blocks south and I cruised toward it, loving the feeling of the wind racing past and the traffic moving in and out around me. I was watching the red car in front of me, trying to keep a safe distance between us. I looked away for just a split second, and when I looked back the car had stopped short. Its rear bumper was coming at me fast! To avoid it, I let the cycle jump over the curb and I was thrown from it onto the pavement.

A searing pain tore through my left knee and I could feel warm blood trickling down into my boot. I was already light-headed and I knew if I could get back home, I could somehow take care of myself. I didn't seem to be badly hurt anywhere else. Anything except the hospital—I couldn't afford that.

I went up the driveway and noticed that Perry's car was gone, and Barbara's green sedan was not in the garage. I moved away from the cycle after I put the kickstand in place. My knee was stiff with pain.

As soon as I felt able, I took off my gloves, helmet, and jacket. But I had trouble with my left boot.

I heard a car door slam and I hobbled to the hallway. Perry was coming in the front door, munching an apple.

Quickly brushing away my tears, I hopped out into the living room.

"You're back," Perry observed from the doorway. "Did you forget something?"

"Not exactly. I had a little accident."

"Accident?" The word burst from him like a curse, and he dropped to his knees in front of me. "Where are you hurt?"

"Just my knee," I mumbled.

He looked and grimaced. "It's a nasty cut." He ran his hands down my leg to my boot and tugged gently until it came off. I clenched my fists and gritted my teeth, but I couldn't hold back the tears. I knew I shouldn't be crying in front of Perry, but everything was going so wrong!

"You'd better get this looked at," he said, touching both sides of my knee. "How did you do it, or should I ask?"

"I lost my balance on the cycle. It was just a little accident—nothing to tell Barbara about." His hands soothed the pain and stopped my trembling. His touch was almost magic.

"Of course she'll never guess," he replied sarcastically, but his eyes were worried. "You'll be unable to work, but you can just tell her anything and she'll believe it."

"I can't miss work," I insisted. "You have to fix it."

"If you're putting me in charge of this detail, then I'm taking you to the hospital."

"No hospital," I protested. "I can't afford it."

"Forget money!" he growled. "I'll pay." He carried me out to his car. His chest was wide and hard, and the roughness of his sweater reminded me of the bark on the oak tree in the park. As I pressed my face against his shoulder I noticed he smelled comfortingly, of leaves, sunshine, and fresh air.

He eased me into the car and kept his face close to mine. "Julia, I know you say you don't need anyone, and you want to be independent," he said softly. "I understand that. But there are times when you will need someone." His hand turned my face to meet his eyes. "You needed someone last night, and I was there. You need someone now, and I'm still here. Julia, please take what I offer and hold on. I need you in a way I can't explain." His lips brushed my cheek, and he stood and closed the car door.

He drove to the emergency entrance of the hospital without saying anything else. I was too startled by the sudden burst of tenderness he had shown— and what I was feeling for him.

Perry quickly and efficiently explained to a nurse what had happened. I was taken to an examining room and he stood beside the table waiting impatiently for the doctor.

"You're something else, you know!" I laughed. "My knee is cut and I'm in pain, and here you are—"

"Making you feel better, and you know it," he finished. "First you're going to get your knee patched, and later—well, later we'll find something else to do." His eyes told me what that would be and his lips were against my ear.

"I never knew a touch like yours," I whispered. "I didn't plan last night, Perry. I just told you that because I couldn't believe I would ever want anyone so much. You make me feel like I'm caught in a whirlwind."

"You are—and so am I," Perry murmured as he kissed me. "Think you can stand being caught in one for the rest of your life, babe?"

So right there in the hospital, while a doctor patched my knee, my whole future got put together, too! Because neither Perry nor I was the type to play it cautious, once we'd made up our minds. And, as far as we were concerned, loving and needing and wanting equaled marriage. It was as simple—and as exciting—as that!

THE END

OUR GREAT LOVE

Everything looked good to me, that first day. It was a warm summer day, just to start me right. I put my two heavy suitcases outside the entrance marked, "Hotel Employment Office." I was going to work as a busboy in the restaurant of a big Atlantic City hotel and live right there. Away from home for the first time.

Well, this is it, I said to myself. My first big crack at the mean old world.

The girl at the employment desk gave me a key to a room in the men's rooming house, and a meal pass for the employee cafeteria. I lugged my bags to the warehouse building and took the elevator to the men's rooming house, where I found my key fitted the door of a nice single room. Inside the room I threw myself on the bed and began to bounce up and down because I was feeling so happy. Kid stuff maybe, but nobody was there but me.

Why shouldn't I feel good? I was eighteen, not too hard to look at, and—finally on my own. I didn't have much time to think about it then. There was a knock on my door, and a tall, lanky young fellow came in.

"You Dan Barnes?" he asked, looking me over as I stood there waiting.

He turned out to be the captain busboy. His name was Kerry. And he told me I was to start work that afternoon. He gave me a starched blue and white busboy jacket to put on, and we walked over to the employees' cafeteria together to eat lunch.

The cafeteria was large, and the thing that impressed me most was all the pretty waitresses eating there. A lot of the girls nodded to Kerry as we walked to an empty table. I could feel dozens of eyes watching me, and I tried not to let the new-comer attention make me nervous.

While we were eating, a bunch of girls stopped by our table on their way out of the room. I heard some of them asking Kerry who the cute new busboy was. I couldn't picture myself as cute, with a pushed-in football nose. But I was glad to know that the men situation was so bad that they thought I was cute.

After lunch, Kerry took me up to the dining room where I was to work. He was telling me about how we had to fill up water buckets with ice cubes and place two of these small silver buckets on each waitress's serving table. He filled two buckets and handed them to me.

And then—I stood with the buckets hanging by my sides, and stared at the loveliest girl I had ever seen. She seemed to have been soaked in beauty because every square inch of her was lovely.

I walked up to her and looked into her face. There was a darkness beneath her eyes—not eye makeup, but the stain beauty leaves when there is too much in any one place. Her hair permed, somersaulted, back-flipped and twisted into all sorts of attractive designs. Her skin was soft. For some reason she reminded me of a beautiful bird.

"Hello there," I whispered, almost drooling.

"Hello, I'm Lisa Jennings," she said. Her voice was low, a little husky.

"I'm Dan Kratonitch, grandson of the famous Russian General Kratonitch," I told her in my best solemn, deadpan manner.

"I'm not sure I believe all that," she answered, smiling.

"Well, it will take some time to prove it to you. How about if I start tonight after work?" I was trying to sound matter-of-fact but my insides were jumping up and down.

"I think that's a fine idea," she said. "Dan Kra— Dan what?"

"Kratonitch, princess," I told her. I smiled and floated away with my water buckets.

When I got out of her hearing distance, I heaved a great sigh. I felt like yelling yippee! It didn't seem possible that such a luscious girl would encourage me. Maybe the manpower situation really was bad there. I grinned at myself in a large mirror on the dining room wall. "Hello, Kratonitch," I said. Now where in the world did I dream up that name?

That night as I readied myself for my date with Lisa, I tried to decide which line I should use on her. I thought about walking up to her and kissing her full on the lips and whispering, "This is the only fitting way for our romance to start." It would take a lot of nerve to do it and I got a thrill just thinking about it.

OUR GREAT LOVE

Finally, I decided to play a little hard to get. I reasoned that a lovely girl like Lisa was used to having fellows chase her. Whatever a woman is used to, do the opposite. That was the first rule I'd learned when I'd been a lifeguard the previous summer.

I began to remember pretty love poems from high school English, to get in the mood before I went to see Lisa. On my way over to the girls' rooming house, I found myself saying aloud, "Hello, princess, you're not a bit beautiful tonight, for compared to you, beauty is ugliness." Too flowery, I said to myself, not in keeping with the hard-to-get type at all.

Waiting in the lobby of the girls' rooming house, my mind was still searching for a good opening remark. I could have saved my mind the effort, for when Lisa approached I was speechless.

Her perfume seemed to be the natural aroma of her freshly washed hair. I gazed at her fingers to divert the thoughts that were soaring in my mind, but it was no use, for even her pinkie aroused me. She must have thought I was crazed when all I did was take her hand, shake it, saying, "You look lovely, princess. How much do you cost in the four-inch size?"

She thought for a minute, and retorted, "What could you do with the small size that you couldn't do with the life-sized model?"

"I could keep you with me all the time then," I replied.

"Well?" she queried, invitingly.

By the time we got to the boardwalk, I began to feel intoxicated. It was a warm night and the breezes from the ocean were cool. Moon rays slid across the water and melted into the lights of the boardwalk. The sand stretched in shifting patterns. The shuffling feet on the boardwalk, the surf breaking, combined to make a special tune just for Lisa and me. I found myself picking up the rhythm as we walked along.

"You and the night and the music—" I said to her. "Mostly you—"

She looked up at me, smiling, and I almost forgot my "hard-to-get" approach. The way I was leaning toward her, well, she might get ideas. I got hold of myself, fast, straightened up, and looked away from her.

"Today in the dining room, I thought you would ask me for a date," Lisa remarked.

Oh, she did? I thought. That was bad. That was no way to make a real dent on her.

I stared at a couple of girls who were walking slowly toward us. They were looking at me, too. They were nothing to me at all, not when I was with Lisa, but I got the idea I'd better show Lisa she wasn't dealing the cards.

"There's a babe, the one on the right," I said to Lisa.

"Oh?" she said, barely noticing the girls.

I leaned back against the railing, very casual. "Nice view around here," I said to Lisa, watching both girls, who'd stopped walking.

Lisa got the point, all right. She looked a little bothered, I thought. I figured I was doing all right, running the show.

"Getting crowded around here, isn't it?" one of the two girls said to her pal. Since there was nobody around but the four of us, I knew she was tossing the ball back to me.

I turned straight around toward the two of them. "Why don't we all team up, look the place over?" I said to them. Not that I would have done it, you understand—all I was interested in was the impression I made on Lisa.

Something slipped in the technique, though. Lisa was walking away from me. I guess my approach backfired.

"I think you lost somebody," one of the two girls said, and they both started giggling.

I didn't pay them any mind. I went after Lisa, fast. "Hey—" I said. "Hey, Lisa!"

I was beside her, but she didn't look at me. "Why don't you go and talk to—your friends?" she said.

"I was just kidding," I said. "It was just a joke, Lisa."

"I'm laughing," she said, not laughing at all.

"Well, come on, let's go someplace," I told her. "I'm sure we'll here some music on the beach so that we could dance."

"I'm going home," she said. Not mad, just very firm.

She meant it, too. Right back to the girls' rooming house she went, with me alongside, talking fast and getting nowhere.

By the time we got there, I stopped talking. *Let her simmer for a while,* I reasoned. *Stay away from her, and maybe that will work.*

"Well, good night," I said. "Thanks for the short walk."

"Good night, Dan," she said. And just for a minute there, her face looked funny, almost as if she wanted to cry, and I felt bad. But before I could say anything, she was gone.

"Now how do you figure that?" I asked myself, going back to my room. If she felt bad because the evening ended on us—she liked me, didn't she? Maybe I hadn't made such a bad start, after all. Maybe things would work out, if I stayed away from her awhile, if I managed not to fall flat on my face next time I saw her.

For several days, Lisa and I didn't speak. I couldn't be near her without being tempted to go crawling back to her, so I avoided her.

One day, however, I found her looking helplessly at a tray of dinners, which she had to carry into the dining room. She seemed to be debating whether she could carry it or not. I hurriedly placed the tray on my shoulder, and said, "Allow me." I carried the tray to her serving table, and as I was walking away I hard her warm, low voice say, "Thank you. Thank you, Dan."

And there we were again, where we'd been the first day—smiling at each other.

That afternoon Lisa and I went to the beach. We found a secluded place in the sand, and I told Lisa the qualities I liked and disliked in her. There wasn't much I disliked, except the way she'd walked off the other evening, the way she'd wasted all that time. I made it clear that I wanted to see plenty of her, but I was telling her. I figured that the way I felt about her, if I didn't keep a good grip on things, I'd be rolled in the surf for sure.

She liked me; she didn't hide it. The way we felt, it was as plain as the heat shimmering across the sand. And suddenly, she gave me a look that almost melted me. Her lips were trembling. And whatever had been holding us apart let go, the way a stretched rubber band snaps together. We were holding each other, and I was kissing her. Lisa kept her lips tightly closed, and I could feel something from her body coming into mine through our lips, like a current passing from her to me.

After that—it was all wonderful. I was near Lisa practically all the time. We ate together, worked together, and sometimes sat on the beach all night together watching the sea and stars and waiting for the dawn. We would walk barefooted, hand in hand along the shore, and I'd carry her over the sharp rocks. The way she clung to me made me feel stronger than I'd ever felt before.

"It's nice—having you take care of me," she told me, and there was a strange look, almost a wistful look in her eyes. Why would she look wistful, I wondered. I was going right on looking after her, wasn't I?

Once in a while like that, I wouldn't understand the way she looked, or the things she said. Like the time, once, we were saying good night.

"I keep thinking—maybe it won't be the same tomorrow," she whispered, looking frightened. "Nothing good ever lasts—for me."

I kissed her eyes and mouth, till she relaxed against me. "Tomorrow will be better," I told her. "What are you worrying about, honey?"

"We're different, aren't we, Dan?" she asked me then, her eyes wide with a reaching look in them. "Nobody else is like us, nobody feels the way we feel about each other, do they?"

All that talk was sort of over my head. Besides, why waste time thinking? I kissed her till she couldn't speak anymore.

"This is the way I feel about you," I said, and kissed her so she would remember it till next morning. "Don't go asking stupid questions!"

For weeks, we wouldn't go to a movie, club, or anything like that. We were happy just being together. And I noticed something that gave me a warm feeling even across a room from her—the way she took my part, when anybody said anything against me, even jokingly.

It was like that with us. And then one night, when we were walking along the beach and wishing all the other people would go home, Lisa asked me a sudden question.

"Dan—" she said, "wouldn't it be wonderful if we had a place of our own?"

"You've got something there," I said. "It wouldn't be so bad, would it, being alone?"

She changed the subject then, but I kept on thinking about it. The next day I rented a room.

That night when I steered Lisa off the boardwalk, she wanted to know where we were going. I shook my head.

"It's a surprise," I said.

When we reached the house I took Lisa's arm and steered her to a second-floor room. It was a cozy little room with blue wallpaper. Lisa looked at me funny for a minute and I thought she was going to tell me off and leave. But then she grinned and sat on the bed and bounced.

"Soft," she said, smiling at me. Her eyes were full of excitement like a little girl's.

"Well, stop bouncing, or you'll break a spring," I kidded her.

"Who's going to make me stop?" She put up her small fists.

"I am," I said, and pounced upon her. We rolled and tossed on the bed till we heard a rip.

"Oh—" she exclaimed, "my dress!"

She jumped to her feet and looked at the tear in her dress. She thought for a minute and then began taking her dress off. She got the dress halfway over her head, and asked, "Please help me."

I pulled the dress over her head and looked at her soft bare shoulders and at the breasts under her slip. I dropped the dress to the floor and grabbed her. I rubbed her soft body against mine and I kissed her eyes, ears, neck, and shoulders. I looked into her eyes and saw a frightened expression there.

"Are you—are you sure?" she said. And then she said in a strange voice, "I am not going to deny you anything. I know you want me, and I want you, Dan."

About midnight, I got up to close the window. Lisa came with me. We stood watching the ocean in the distance. The night was so quiet that there was a sort of electric buzzing in the air. Lisa blinked sleepily at the moon, and even in the moonlight I could see the dark beauty beneath her eyes.

I looked at her reverently and said, "Little sleepy-head, you give me more happiness in one night than most men have in a lifetime."

"That's the nicest thing that anyone has ever said to me," Lisa replied drowsily. And then she held me tighter and added, "You're the nicest thing that ever happened to me, Dan."

"That goes double," I told her.

"Maybe everything will be all right now," she said

in that half-asleep voice. "It's got to be! I love you so—I love you so!"

She sounded like a little kid wanting reassurance about the dark. I told myself that it was strange for her, the first time being so close with me. I took her back to lie down and held her and loved her.

In a few minutes she was asleep in my arms. Had anyone ever been so happy before? I lay for hours watching her, and all that time she never let go of my hand.

Away from Lisa, working that next day, I went around in a happy daze for a while. It was amazing that so much could happen to me, and nobody knew about it. I wonder what Kerry, the captain bus-boy, would say if I told him. I remembered how Kerry had looked at Lisa once, and said, "That gal knows her way around."

Thinking about Kerry and the other fellows, and things they said about the girls—I suddenly began wondering about Lisa. She hadn't acted shy or surprised or scared the night before. She hadn't even held back. I hadn't exactly been doing any heavy thinking at the time, but now—I remembered things.

It wasn't the first time for her, I told myself then. And for a little while that made everything seem different.

Then I asked myself what I was stewing about. She hadn't tried to put on any shy act, and that was fine. She hadn't tried to pretend she was any different from what she was. We felt something terrific together—that was what counted. I pushed my thoughts away and forgot them, and all I cared about was Lisa.

For two months then, Lisa and I were blissfully

happy. Sometimes we argued, but it was always so wonderful to make up again. Once in a while I would start wondering about Lisa again—how many men had she been with before me, that kind of thing. She acted as if she loved me, but she must have had enough experience so she could fool me about that. I didn't like to think about what happened before I knew her.

And then she would look at me with her whole heart in those little-girl clear eyes and I would feel awful doubting her.

Lisa kept talking about some modeling job she had a chance to get in New York. She went to New York three times, to see about it. Then she would come back, and talk about it to me. I couldn't see why she wanted that job, because if she took it, she'd have to leave me.

"Lisa—do you want to take that job—when we couldn't be together then?" I asked her one time. "You keep on talking about it."

She looked at me with the wistful look back in her eyes. "You don't want me to take it, then, Dan?"

"Hell, no. And have you way off there, where I couldn't reach out—like this—and touch you?"

She moved closer at the touch, and settled down against me. But she didn't speak.

"Don't you want to be with me, Lisa?"

"Yes—yes," she said, with a swift urgency in her voice.

"Well, then, quit thinking about that old job in New York," I told her.

She looked at me—as if she was waiting for me to say something more. She looked ready to cry. *Funny girl, wonderful girl,* I thought, and I pulled her over to me and quit talking.

"I thought you loved me," I said to her another time. "More than any old job!"

She turned to me swiftly, the wind alive in her hair. She had the flying look as if something beat to be free in her.

"You're everything I want," she said, low. "Everything I want forever. I thought I'd never have it, and then I found you. Don't you know how I love you?"

"Then why don't you forget that stupid New York job?" I asked her.

"I don't want it—I don't want it," she answered me swiftly. "Danny, Danny—I don't want to have to take it."

"Nobody's forcing you to," I told her. "So that's that!"

For an instant she looked at me, and then she turned, and was running away down the shore. I was after her, catching her and swinging her back into my arms.

"Think you can get away like that?" I asked her, laughing.

She put her face down against me so I couldn't see it. "Don't let me get away from you," she said.

"Not a chance," I told her. "I found you—I'm keeping you!"

She was my girl all right; when I was with her everything was great. I wanted to go on like that with her and never stop. If we went on like that, would we get married someday? But I shrugged that off as something dim and far away. Now was what mattered, every day and night now. . . .

And the time went on, like sand sliding through our fingers, till suddenly one day Lisa told me she was going to New York again, overnight. She told me, just like that, and looked at me.

"That modeling job again?" I asked her. "They're still holding it open for you?"

"I've got to see," she said in a vague, queer way. "I'll be gone just one night. Dan. Miss me a lot, Dan."

"Miss you, when you go racing off like this?" I teased her.

But it was fierce when she was gone, every time it was like that. I went around, lost, not enjoying anything without her. When she was gone, I began to know how much I wanted her.

I wondered with a quick stabbing jealousy if she was with a man, now, in New York. How could I marry her, and never be sure? How could I be sure even if she loved me?

But I want her, I thought, and then I was going around in circles again, loving her and doubting her.

Then she returned. I ran across to her. I was so glad to see her I felt I'd burst.

Then I saw her face, the forced smile she gave me. And I knew something was wrong.

"What's up?" I asked her.

"Let's go somewhere we can talk," she said unsteadily.

We sat down by ourselves on the sand, where the rocks made a shelter. I saw the tears in her eyes. "What is it, honey?" I asked, holding her hands.

"Dan—" she said. "Dan, I took the job."

"The New York job?" I said stupidly. "You mean that?"

"Yes," she said. She pulled her hands away and dug them into the sand.

"I guess you always were crazy for that modeling work," I said slowly, trying to tell myself it had to be this way. And then I turned to her sharply. "It's got to be more than that. Aren't you happy with me, anymore?"

She stared at the water, as if she wouldn't let herself look at me. "You know I'm happy with you," she answered me. "But it can't go on this way forever, Dan."

I wanted to tell her I wouldn't let her go. I wanted to ask her to marry me and stay with me. But all my doubts dragged at me.

"You don't have to go," was all I said.

"I've been stalling them about the job, these weeks and now they say I've got to take it or lose the chance. I've been waiting, hoping that, never mind."

She was crying then as if she couldn't stop, she was crying on my chest, and I was holding her hard.

"I don't know what you're talking about; you don't make sense," I said, bewildered.

"You big, stupid lug," she said, and with her fingers pushed back a lock of hair on my forehead.

I didn't understand why she was going. She was leaving me—she had decided it.

"When are you leaving?" I asked.

"Tomorrow," she answered with her cheek pressed tightly against mine.

That night we went to a quiet harbor bar. We sat at a table near the fireplace. I looked at her, and couldn't believe she was going.

We danced a few times, and then slipped outside and stood by the edge of the water. The harbor water looked like black gelatin, it was so calm. The sky was thickly freckled with fat stars and the half moon looked a little sad. We just stood in one another's arms for a long time.

"Lisa," I whispered, "I feel so sorry for every man who hasn't loved you. Why am I so lucky? Why was I lucky enough to be loved by you?"

"Stop—please stop," Lisa begged me, and then she was talking and crying all mixed up so I could hardly get the words.

"I thought it could be like this," she was saying. "I thought I'd go to a safe place—where I could be like other people—only loving you more than anybody else could love you. But it's no use, nothing's any use. When you fool yourself it hurts worse afterward." She sighed.

"What do you mean, you fooled yourself?" I asked. "You said you were happy, all those weeks. Weren't you?"

"Oh, yes!" she cried. "I mustn't spoil that. I'll remember it forever. Never mind me, Dan. Let's go back inside."

We went back into the bar and sat at our table. I stared at the fire, and almost said aloud, *Why? Why does it have to end?*

Soon it was closing time and Lisa looked at me. I took her hand and we walked out to the dance floor. The jukebox was just beginning to play a love song, one of our favorite songs. We poured out our hearts in that dance. Every moment meant something to us. My fingers dug into Lisa's back. The tears were streaming down from her eyes—I could feel her stomach sobbing, it was so close to mine. The music stopped and we kissed not just with our lips, but with every part of our bodies which touched.

OUR GREAT LOVE

What took place that night belongs to Lisa and me alone and I can't describe it. In the morning, I took my picture from the bureau and wrote on it, "Although we may never meet again, what if we had never met?" I wrapped the picture in an old newspaper and slipped it into her suitcase when I picked her up.

The train pulled into the station just as we got there. I looked at Lisa. She, too, was breathing heavily. *No, this can't be,* I said to myself. *She can't be leaving me.*

Lisa looked at me and sobbed. "Good-bye, Dan." She threw her arms around me and kissed me.

"Lisa, you're not leaving me," I said in a voice choked with emotion.

All she could do was nod weakly. "Yes."

"You're not leaving me."

"I have to go."

"No!"

I grabbed her roughly and held her tight against my body. She clung to me hard.

I need you," I said to her. "I need you like a baby needs his mother. Don't leave me, Lisa. I need you."

I squeezed her with all my strength. I was hurting her terribly but I held her harder.

"Then—then marry me," she said in a tormented, pain-ridden voice.

I released her, and if I hadn't grabbed her, she would have fallen.

"Then marry me, Dan," she repeated.

"Marry you now? I'm not sure," I said, before I realized I'd said more than I wanted to say.

"You're not sure of what, Dan?" she asked me.

She didn't say another word. She picked up her

281

bag and hurried on the train.

My first impulse was to run after her, but I was frozen to the spot with grief. The train started to pull away, and Lisa's face was pressed against the window.

I ran over to the window, and all I could think of to do was say through my tears by motioning lips, "I love you, Lisa." I caught her eyes for an instant, and I'm not sure if I saw love or hate in them. I watched the train till it was out of sight.

I walked through the crowded streets trying to hold back my tears, but my grief squeezed them out. I walked and walked and was not aware of anything going on around me. Where was I to go? What was I to do? I could still see Lisa's face smiling at me. I could hear her voice, her laughter. She was so vivid in my imagination that if she were to cut herself, I was sure I'd bleed, too.

I finally looked around me. I saw a green coat, the kind Lisa wore. I passed a movie, and wondered if Lisa would like to see that picture. She had been my world, and now I was lost in a strange new world. I listened to people talking, but my mind was so on Lisa that their speech sounded like so much static. I went home and cried like a baby. I tried to make a go of my work after that, but it was no use with Lisa gone. Everything reminded me of her.

I began to see her standing in the dining room where she used to stand. I saw her among the crowds on the boardwalk. Sometimes I would turn around abruptly when I thought I heard her voice. I went to our room, and stared so long at the dressing table that I began to see her sitting there, brushing her beautiful hair and wrinkling up her nose at me in the mirror. It went on like that. It got so bad I had to quit work and go home.

Going home made it easier. Just being away from all the places I'd known with Lisa, that helped. And being back with my folks and the friends I knew well made the time with Lisa seem sometimes like a far-off, special dream.

But other times I'd remember her sharp and close, as if she stood in the room with me. I missed her—I wanted her.

I looked at the other girls I knew, girls I'd gone to school with. Nobody in town could point at one of them and say, "She belonged to a lot of men." If a guy married one of those girls, he'd know that he was the first. In a little town, you know that sort of thing about a girl. A few girls were easy in our town, but not many. *You have to think about things like that when you marry a girl,* I kept telling myself.

I got a job in a factory, making machine tools, and after that time went faster. After a while I dated one girl and another—and they weren't Lisa, but I liked one of them—Betty Wayne—a lot.

Two years went by. It was all of two years later when it happened. I'd been promoted, and they were trying me out on the buying end of the business. I was engaged to Betty—we had everything planned and set and happy. Then one of the men above me got sick, and I was sent to New York to see one of the firms we bought from. You know how it is on a trip like that—you get taken out to dinner and around town. I was feeling really excited, hoping I'd do everything right, and get sent on more trips like that.

The man who was taking me to dinner wangled

us in on a big party. They were really playing up the out-of-town buyers, on that party. We went to a nightclub, but we didn't stay out in the big room, we went upstairs to a private room. And when we walked in—thee was a flock of girls waiting for us.

Well, I didn't mix in with the girls, what with being engaged to Betty. But I watched what went on, and nobody wasted any time getting acquainted. There was a redhead sitting in one guy's lap while he poured her a drink, and the other girls were moving right in. They were used to entertaining the visiting men, all right.

I didn't believe it when I saw her. Lisa—poured into a green dress, snuggling up to a fat old guy who kept feeling up and down her arm. I couldn't believe it, Lisa there, like that.

But suddenly time switched back on me, and it didn't matter who was in the room and why Lisa was there. All that mattered was that she was there. She looked as lovely as I remembered her, and that was plenty. And something reached right out and pulled me to her, the same as always.

I was beside her, not knowing how I got there. I tried twice before I spoke.

"Lisa," I said. "It's you again, Lisa."

She turned fast, and her face went white. She caught my hand tight and stared at me as if she didn't believe it was really me.

"Come along," I told her.

We left the old guy staring after us, and went to a little table in the corner. We sat there, bending across and looking at each other. And we said foolish things, like how have you been, and all that. But what it did to me, seeing her—well, she was on my wavelength, and when she moved her head my heart jerked.

"I'm engaged to a girl back home," I told her fast, before I made any mistakes.

"Some girl is lucky," she said. She smiled at me across the table, the same old wistful smile.

I thought of Betty, and I loved Betty. The fact that Lisa always could have that pull for me—well, that was one of those things.

"Why are you here?" I heard myself blurting out. "Do you—do you have to entertain these guys?"

Her mouth twisted, but she kept on smiling. "That job, it wasn't so much," she said. "Modeling in a cheap house dress. Most of the money comes from this—this kind of work, tonight."

"Why did you take the job then?" I demanded.

She leaned a little nearer across the table. All I could see was her eyes looking at me, clear and desperately honest.

"I hoped to the end you wouldn't let me go, Dan," she said slowly. "The way I loved you—it was clean, no matter what I'd done before. I kept on telling myself that was my chance to be married right and have everything with you. I couldn't stand it, being with you, when I knew you didn't want me enough." She sounded like she might cry.

I stared back at her with a queer sharp loss. I couldn't go back to that other time. But I saw it then—that maybe she was right, maybe she could have been a good wife to me. And I had loved her so much. Maybe I had been wrong.

"I didn't know you felt like that," I told her. "I didn't—"

She said with sudden bitterness, "Do you know

what you did to me, Dan? You pushed me back into this! You were my chance to go right, but you wouldn't let me have it."

I couldn't answer her. I saw it then, how I'd turned her loose with nothing sure to hold onto. We'd been so happy together, and then I'd as much as told her she wasn't good enough for me to marry. Now I was going to marry Betty, and Lisa was here. I was the guy who could have saved her. But I hadn't been able to.

"What can I say?" I asked her miserably. "I was a mixed-up kid back then. I loved you more than I knew."

"I loved you more than you knew," she answered me.

She stood up quickly then. She looked at me, and touched my hand.

"It's no good talking, Dan," she said. "I hope you'll be happy. I want you to be happy."

"What can I do?" I asked her, standing beside her. I was so sorry for her it was an ache in me.

"Go away now, and don't stay here watching me," she answered. "Go away, and just remember me once in a while."

I held both her hands tight and then I went away like she asked me to. That was all I could do. All except wonder what might have been if things had been different. If we'd been able to hang onto ourselves before the fire in us flamed so high it burned us—and made us weak forever. Maybe if we'd only taken time to know each other. . . .

Well, it was too late now.

The next day I would be going back to Betty and all my life I would be Betty's. But that night I walked the streets alone and remembered Lisa the way she wanted me to remember her—Lisa walking along the sand with me, with love in her eyes.   THE END

IN LOVE
WITH A PRIEST

I went to the christening with Daphne, because I knew she thought there was no other baby in the world like her niece. Also, it gave me something to do on a Saturday. Since Hal had gone into the military, I hadn't done much except mope around.

Daphne thought I was wasting time. "It isn't as though you and Hal were ever engaged or anything," she said. "You should get around more and meet people."

Daphne was engaged. She wore George's ring like a beacon on her finger. As soon as they had a thousand dollars in the bank, they were going to be married. Meanwhile, Daphne worried over me, sure I was destined to be an old maid.

She and I met at the small plant where we both were working typing and doing other office work. That first day I wasn't sure I'd stick to the job—it was tedious work—but Daphne enthused over it so much, I began to see it in a different light. Daphne was like that. She could get excited over a hamburger.

As time went by, I got to know most of Daphne's family. She lived with her married sister, but it was a two-family house, and she and her mother had the upstairs apartment.

I took Daphne home, too, to meet my mother. My father had died the year before of Parkinson's disease, and Mom looked ten years older than she was. Dad had been in a veterans' hospital for almost five years before he died. Mom worked in a factory making out shipping orders, but her job was right in our neighborhood so she could come home at lunchtime to check on my younger brother, Pete.

I knew it wasn't easy for Mom during those five years, and I helped out as much as most teenagers would, I guess. But I was young and all involved in my own affairs. Sometimes when Mom would ask me to go with her to the hospital on a Sunday afternoon, I'd turn her down because I had a bowling date or wanted to meet a girlfriend and go to a movie. And then I'd be remorseful and take a bus out to the hospital the next Wednesday afternoon after school and visit with Dad.

I loved my father, but I couldn't stand to see him suffering. That's why I kind of avoided visiting him as often as I could have. Then I'd feel guilty, and I'd give him money to buy cigarettes—money I'd earned baby-sitting and had planned to spend on a new sweater or blouse.

Mom would ask us to pray for Dad every Sunday in church, but I found myself praying that he would die and find rest. When he did die, I fell apart and grieved until I went to confession and told the priest how I'd prayed for my father's death. Of course the priest told me as long as I hadn't questioned God's wisdom, I hadn't really committed any sin, and I felt better after that.

Then, all in that next year, I started dating Hal and I graduated and I got my job and met Matt!

Meeting Matt came the day I went to the christening with Daphne. Matt was standing in for the godfather, who was in the Army and stationed overseas. I remember how terribly intense I thought Matt was as he made his responses to the priest, and when the baby let out a howl he looked startled, as though he had caused it.

Later, at the family's home, Matt was teased about scaring the daylights out of the baby. He smiled, a slow, wide grin, and—well, I felt that smile right down to my toes. There was a buffet luncheon, and afterward I helped serve the coffee. Father Meeghan was there, and I saw him talking quietly with Matt in a corner of the room. As a matter of fact, it was Father Meeghan who was doing all the talking.

"Go and rescue Matt," Daphne whispered to me. "As soon as we get these dishes out of the way, let's you and Matt and George and me go bowling."

"I can't ask him," I told her.

"Then I'll ask him for you," she said, walking boldly up to Matt.

"Father, we want to steal Matt and take him bowling with us," she announced.

"You're not inviting me?" Father Meeghan kidded. "Afraid I'll show the lot of you up, eh?"

Everyone laughed, and Matt got up and said good-bye to Father Meeghan. I got my coat and said my good-byes, too.

Matt was a big man, and he bowled like a champion. When I told him it wasn't fair, he laughed and admitted he'd been bowling with a league the past year. And when he was with the National Guard, he'd made extra money fixing up bowling matches between himself and some other expert.

That night the four of us ate pizza and danced to jukebox music in an old Italian place on Shore Road. Later, with the top down on George's old car, we went for a drive. Matt put an arm around me and pulled me close to him. I stayed in his arms and found I liked it. But he didn't even try to kiss me good night when he took me to my door. He just stood a moment, smiling down at me.

"I had a good time," he said.

"I did, too. Thanks, even though you kind of got roped into it."

"I would have asked you anyway," he said. "Daphne just beat me to it."

"I'll believe that, because I want to," I said. "Good night, Matt."

"Good night, Kathie."

I went inside. After I got ready for bed, I talked to Mom a few minutes—and I waited for Daphne to call. I knew she'd be on the phone the minute she got into the house. And I was right. In no time, the phone rang.

"Did you like him? Isn't he terrific? He likes you, too. I asked him," Daphne gushed.

"Daphne!" I gasped. "I won't be able to look him in the eye when I meet him again, if I ever do!"

"Oh, you will," she said. "The way he talked, he'll be ringing your doorbell tomorrow morning!"

She was wrong about one thing anyway. I did see

him, but not on my doorstep. I slept so late that I barely made twelve-thirty Mass. But after I got to church and sat down in the back, I saw Matt sitting up front next to a gray-haired woman. I wondered if she was his mother.

When the Mass ended, I slipped out and then slowed down, hoping Matt would catch up with me. I saw him leave by the side door, his hand on the woman's arm. I walked home, feeling kind of let down because Matt hadn't seen me.

I stayed home all afternoon, telling myself I had clothes to rinse out and my hair to set. Actually, though, I was hoping to hear from Matt. But he didn't call, and I felt more and more depressed. I suppose that's why I was so happy to see him the next day. When Daphne and I went across the street to the diner for lunch, Matt was there. Daphne headed right for him, unhesitatingly.

"Hi," she said. "Where were you yesterday?"

He looked beyond her at me, and his color deepened. "I had to see someone," he said. "Hi, Kathie."

I nodded, wondering whether Daphne had told him we would be there. I felt annoyed with her suddenly. After all, I didn't want Matt to think I was chasing after him!

"George said you're thinking of leaving town for a while," Daphne said to him. "Why?"

"You ask too many questions," he said, laughing to take the sting out of his words.

"I don't discourage easily," she said. "I have an idea. Why don't the four of us make a date for Friday night? We can go to a movie or something."

"That's a good idea," Matt said. "You make a date with George, and I'll make a date with Kathie.

But not together, okay?"

Daphne giggled. "You don't believe in wasting time, do you?" she said. "No long engagements for you, I bet! Careful, Kathie! This guy acts serious—"

I saw his face freeze, literally freeze, and he looked down into his coffee cup. I nearly died of embarrassment, and I didn't know what to say. Luckily, the girl brought our order, and we started to eat.

When we got back to work, I chewed Daphne out. "Why do you go around matchmaking?" I scolded. "Now he thinks he has to date me!"

"Stop being so touchy," she came back at me. "A girl has to chase a man till he catches her—haven't you heard? So I'm helping you because you're too backward to help yourself. George needed help, too! If he'd had his way, we wouldn't even have got engaged until we could afford to get married. But I've got news for him. I'm tired of working, and we're getting married as soon as I pick a date. My mind's made up!"

"Sometimes I don't understand you," I told her.

"What's to understand? I want to be married and start having kids, four of them."

She smiled, and I couldn't stay angry with her. Daphne was so honest. To her, life was very simple: You found a man and lived happily ever after.

When I got home that night, I found Matt waiting outside my house in his car. He beeped twice as I came up the street, and I turned to see who it was. When I saw Matt, my heart kind of jumped and I walked over to him.

"I wanted to talk to you without your shadow," he said. "I don't want you to think I'm not anxious to take you out or anything like that. I want to, but I guess I'd like to do it on my own terms."

"Oh, Daphne doesn't really mean anything by her talk," I said. "She's engaged, she loves George, and she thinks the whole world should feel the same."

"I know," Matt said. "Some people just know what it is they want, don't they? I mean, for themselves and for other people, too."

"Well, I guess so." I didn't understand what he was getting at.

"Will you go out with me Friday night?" he asked. I nodded. "I'd like that."

"Fine. I'll pick you up around seven," he said.

I didn't tell Daphne about my date. When Friday rolled around, she kept badgering me about going bowling or letting George find someone for me, and I kept putting her off. I think she suspected, but finally she gave up when I refused to take her into my confidence. I don't exactly know why I didn't, except that I felt Matt preferred that she not know.

That night Matt met Mom and talked to her for a few minutes before we went out. We didn't go bowling. We saw a bad movie and walked out halfway through it. Then we went to a restaurant and spent two hours talking and eating.

Matt told me he lived with his mother. She was a widow, and his brother was away in the Army. Matt had finished his time in the National Guard only a month before.

"What are you going to do?" I asked.

"You mean work, a job?" He looked at me and then away. "Well, I've been thinking over a few things—like going back to school, you know."

"I'm going back to school in the fall," I said. "I've

decided to take a business course and get a better job."

"That's great, Kathie," Matt said. "Are you serious about anybody?"

"No," I said. I didn't mention Hal, because I was pretty sure by then that he didn't mean anything to me. But I did tell Matt about Dad and about things being a little rough at home.

"You wonder why things like that happen, don't you?" he said, and I found myself feeling terribly happy that he'd said that, that he understood.

"Do you feel that way, too?" I asked. I told him then about praying for Dad to die so he could be released from pain. "Then when he did die, I felt awful, like I had caused him to die. There are so many things I just don't understand—"

"Me, either!" he said, and the words seemed to be torn out of him.

We left the restaurant then. But before we got into the car, Matt turned me to him fiercely and kissed me. It was as though he had been wanting to kiss me for a long time.

"Kathie, why did you have to happen now?" he whispered, and his voice held such agony I felt chilled.

"Oh, Matt, don't be sorry we met!" I cried.

"Oh, Kathie, honey!" He kissed me again, a sad, sweet kiss. We clung that way until headlights from a car picked us out and we sprang apart. After that, Matt drove me home in complete silence.

When he dropped me off, I turned to him. "Matt, is something wrong? Did I do something wrong?" I begged.

"No, Kathie, you're sweet and wonderful and—" I

thought he was going to say he loved me, but all he added was, "I've got some thinking to do."

"Will you call me? Will I hear from you tomorrow?" I asked.

"I'll come by around two," he said. "Maybe we can go for a ride up the coast."

I was so happy to know I'd see him soon that I went into the house and to bed with a light heart. I felt as though I were on the edge of some great adventure. When I awoke, I was smiling—because I knew I'd see Matt that day.

From that day on, Matt and I spent every free moment together. Daphne began to grumble about me not confiding in her, but what he and I were finding was too wonderful to share with anyone. But I began to understand Daphne better—to sympathize with her singlemindedness in wanting to get married and have babies and a home with the man she loved. That was all I wanted out of life, too. To me, just the thought of belonging to Matt was unbearably thrilling.

Mom suspected how I felt about Matt. "He's the special one, isn't he?" she asked one night as I was getting ready for a date with him.

"Oh, Mom, you don't know!" I said, and then I caught myself up. "Was it like this with you and Dad?"

She got misty-eyed. "He was in the Army then, so handsome in his uniform. I thought that all the girls in the world must be in love with him, and then I wondered how he could have picked me. When we got married, it seemed the whole world shared our happiness. While he was overseas, I just counted time. I was so crazy in love with him."

IN LOVE WITH A PRIEST

I wanted to cry for her. How terrible to have had that kind of love and lose it! I began to feel a closeness with my mother that I never had before. And I made secret little vows about how Matt and I would insist she live with us or near us, and we'd try to share some of our happiness with her.

And yet in all the times I'd been with Matt, the times he pulled me close, and kissed me as though we'd both die if we didn't kiss, something kept bothering me—Matt never once talked about the future, *our* future.

I knew there was nothing to stop our being married. We shared so much besides our love. We were both Catholics, our families were no real obstacle, we didn't crave a lot of material things, we wanted only to love and possess one another for eternity. At least that's what I thought.

I was terribly sure that Matt would give me an engagement ring on my birthday. I asked him to come to dinner with Mom and my brother and me. Mom was all excited about it, and she stayed up half the night before baking me a beautiful birthday cake.

Matt brought me a small gift and a bouquet of roses. After our coffee and cake, Mom said she'd promised a neighbor she'd baby-sit, and she dragged Pete off with her. I knew she was just making an excuse to leave Matt and me alone. She thought, as I did, that Matt would propose.

We cleared the dishes and stacked them and went into the living room. Matt fiddled with some records and put one on, then held out his arms so we could dance.

I felt like crying, I was so happy. "Oh, Matt, this is

the happiest birthday of my life!" I said.

His hands gripped me so hard I gasped. Then he let me go abruptly. "You have a long line of birthdays yet, Kathie," he said, his voice suddenly as impersonal as a stranger's.

"Matt, what is it? Did I say something wrong?" I asked. "Is it wrong to love you so much I want to burst with it?"

"Oh, Kathie—darling Kathie!" he groaned, and then he was kissing me so violently that my head began to swim.

But as I clung to him, every instinct in me wanting to be closer, closer, he sprang away from me. "Forgive me, Kathie," he muttered roughly. "Please forgive me! Now I'd better go."

"Matt, why?" I cried. "What's there to forgive? Why are you acting like this?"

"I can't tell you! I've got to find out myself," he said, and he almost ran out of the house.

I stood at the window a long time staring out into the dark street, sure that he would come back. He didn't want to commit himself yet. He didn't have a good job. He wanted to wait till he had more to offer me. . . .

A million thoughts ran through my mind. Inevitably, though, the feeling of having lost him forever washed over me, and I began to cry.

He didn't come back that night. The next morning I received a special-delivery letter from him.

"I have to do some thinking," he had written. "When I come to a decision, you'll be the first to know."

I wondered, then, whether he had another girl somewhere. Or if he didn't love me enough to marry me. I knew Daphne wouldn't know the reason even if I asked her. . . .

For two weeks I waited. Mom asked questions, wanted to know what in the world had happened on my birthday that had caused us to break up. I couldn't answer her, because I didn't know.

Finally I swallowed my pride and asked Daphne her opinion, but she wasn't any help. All she did was call Matt a beast for treating me that way.

"It's better to find out now than later," she said one afternoon as we waited for our bus to go home. "I can't understand it. I asked George, but he says he doesn't know where Matt is."

"Maybe he's sick," I cried out. "Maybe he needs me."

"Why don't you call his mother?"

"I've never met her," I said.

"Call her, anyway. Say you're a friend of Matt's and haven't heard from him and wondered if he was okay. No law against asking about a friend, is there?"

One noontime when we were in the diner having lunch, I did make the call. Matt's mother answered the phone.

"I'm a friend of Matt's," I said, my voice shaky with nervousness. "I wanted to ask him to a party, but I haven't seen him lately. Will you give him a message when he comes home?"

"Matthew is away," she said. "He won't be back for another few days. Is this Kathie?"

My heart jumped. "Yes," I said, glad that Matt thought enough of me to discuss me with his mother.

"Kathie, he'll be in touch with you, I'm sure," she

said.

That was all. I had no idea where Matt had gone or why, but evidently his mother did know and she wasn't telling me.

You have to be away from someone to know how much you love him. I had never loved Matt more. I'd keep hearing his voice or his laugh. In my dreams, he would kiss me. I'd wake up in the morning and my first thought would be: *I'll see him today! I must!*

Then one afternoon he came back. He was waiting for me when I came out from work. He looked thinner, drawn, but when he saw me his face lighted up and he walked toward me briskly.

"You don't need me anymore," Daphne said, nodding to Matt and walking away fast.

"Matt," I said his name as if it were music.

"Hello, Kathie," he said.

There was a catch in my throat. I felt sad and yet wonderful. I put out a hand, and he caught it. Together we walked toward his car. When we got in, I turned to him eagerly, wanting to feel his lips on mine, wanting to feel the warmth of his embrace again.

"Kathie, before you say a word," he told me, "let me explain. I had to do it this way. I had to have these two weeks. I was on retreat."

"Why didn't you tell me?" I cried out in relief. Retreat! I knew all about that. There was a home nearby where men of Catholic faith could go when they wanted to spend time in meditation and prayer.

"You don't understand, Kathie," Matt insisted. "I needed to go to be sure of my own mind. Now I know. Kathie, I'm going to be a priest. I enter a seminary on Monday."

I gasped. I just couldn't believe I had heard right. "What?" I cried. "A priest?"

He nodded and took my hand. "I'd planned to go into the seminary when I got out of the National Guard. I delayed, and then I met you. You don't know what it did to me to know you, to love you. I fought a thousand demons, Kathie, not because I didn't want to love you, but because it wasn't what I set out to do. All my life, every since I was an altar boy, I knew I was going to be a priest someday.

"I served seven o'clock Mass for an old priest for nine years. He used to talk to me, tell me to look in my heart and be sure. But I knew. My mother was pleased, too. It was all set—until I met you. Then I was confused.

"I talked to Father Meeghan, and he suggested I go on retreat. I did—and now I know, Kathie. I want to dedicate my life to God. I have to do it."

"What about me?" I wailed. I refused to believe he would do this, leave me. I could understand if there had been another girl, if another love claimed him before me. But to leave me for the Church! Why? Why?

"Don't you want to lead a normal life, Matt?" I pleaded. "Don't you want to he married and have children? Think, Matt—it'll be forever!"

"Don't you think I've spent these two weeks going over it?" he said. "Kathie, I even spoke to a priest about you. About loving you as I do."

"But you can leave me? How? What am I supposed to do now, Matt? I love you!"

"Listen to me, Kathie. Maybe this was meant to be my final test. I don't want to sound stupid, but I had to take this hurdle, too—to be free. Kathie, help me, please. Don't try to stop me from doing what I have to do. And I have to be priest! I know this in my heart as well as I know God."

"Then go!" I cried out in anger. "Go and live with God and be happy! Only you have no right to love me, no right at all! I hate you, and I even hate God for doing this to us. It's wrong! And you'll never be happy after having made me so unhappy."

"Please, Kathie, don't go away mad," he pleaded, but I was already out of the car and running for the bus around the corner. When it came, I jumped in. I looked back once.

Did I hope he would come after me? Did I pray in those few minutes that seeing me going away from him would make him change his mind, and he'd come for me and we'd cry in each other's arms and forget the nightmare? Yes, I hoped and I prayed, even when I reached home and went inside, even as I went about my usual routine.

Mom knew something had happened. "Did you hear from Matt?" she asked.

"No," I started to say, and then a flood of tears overcame me. "Oh, Mom, he's gone! I've lost him forever! He's going to be a priest!"

"A priest!" Mom gasped. She stared at me, and her eyes were wide. "Matt? A priest? Why, I'd never have guessed."

"He has no right!" I raged. "He loved me, Mom, and I loved him. What right has the Church to separate us?"

"Honey, the Church isn't separating you," she tried to soothe me. "Don't you see? Matt has to do this. Some men have the calling, just as some women enter a convent and become nuns. What would happen if no one felt that way? Where would our priests come from? Our sisters—"

"But not Matt!" I cried out. "I know him! He loved me, Mom. He kissed me like a man, not a priest. How can he forsake all that now? How can he pretend he's not a man?"

"God help him," Mom said so quietly I barely heard her.

It's all a bad dream, I told myself. *Tomorrow or the next day Matt will call, and he'll tell me he's changed his mind—that it was just a notion, a promise to his mother perhaps, but he can't go through with it. We won't even talk about it too much.*

I didn't tell Daphne a thing, but I didn't have to. Two days later she was waiting for me when I got to work, her eyes wide.

"Listen, I just heard," she said. "George told me. He saw Matt last night to say good-bye. Did you know he was going to be a priest?"

"No," I said. "I'd rather not talk about it, Daphne."

"I'm sorry," she said. "I mean, I thought you and he were really in love. And he's so young and good looking—what I mean is, being a priest is so final!"

Being a priest is so final. All morning I tried not to think of Matt, and yet his face kept pushing itself in front of me. *Matt,* my heart cried, *don't go, don't do this! Matt, come back. You can serve God in other ways. You needn't stop living a life of your own. Come back, Matt. Don't I count, too?*

But Matt was gone. When days passed and there was no word from him, I knew that he had left me. The pain was so pure and clean that it froze my heart in aching agony. I even refused to go to Mass for two Sundays in a row. Then Father Meeghan came to see me. I knew Mom had talked to him.

"Why are you so bitter, Kathie?" he asked me. "Because you're jealous of God? Because you blame God for taking Matt from you?"

"Didn't He?" I burst out.

"Did He?" Father Meeghan said. "Do you think Matt could be happy living an ordinary life when in his heart he always felt the need to serve God?"

"I don't believe he has a vocation. I think he just talked himself into it."

"He'll know soon enough," Father Meeghan said. "The seminary will help him find out if he is suited to being a priest. Rest assured, Kathie, no man is ordained a priest until all doubts are gone. For when a man lies prostrate before the altar for ordination, he hears the words: 'You are a priest forever.' Kathie, pray for Matt—he'll need prayers now. He'll need strength. And let him go, Kathie. He *is* a man of God."

"I don't believe it! He loved me!" I sobbed.

"And it was good that he loved you," Father Meeghan told me. "For a priest is capable of anything that a man is capable of, and that's as it should be. How else can he serve the people if he is not one of them?"

I didn't listen to Father Meeghan anymore. I knew he had to say these things. My heart was so cold and bitter that I looked anywhere to place the blame. And the Church became my rival for a long, long time. I would attend Mass and kneel; I would say my responses and then stare at the crucifix over the altar and ask: "Why? Of all the men in the world, why, God, did I have to love a man who gave his life to You? What is there for me now?"

For a long time I asked that question, but it wasn't until winter had gone and spring had come that I was able to put away Matt from my conscious mind and accept that he was irrevocably lost to me.

That spring Mom came down sick. She hemorrhaged a few times, and the doctor finally put her in the hospital for a hysterectomy. But evidently Mom had let things go too long. When the doctors operated, they found out she had cancer of the uterus. They thought the operation had been performed soon enough, but before summer was ended we knew she had gone into the hospital too late. The cancer cells had spread through her body, and she lived only until fall. My brother, Pete, had enlisted in the Navy just a few months before, but he got an emergency leave and we were both with her the night she died.

It was midnight, and I had been sitting beside her bed as I had done the past two weeks. I held her hand and felt it close convulsively around mine. She seemed to want to say something to me.

"Oh, Mom, I love you," I cried, bending over her. Pete bent over her on the other side, and if we could have poured our strength into her we would have.

I don't know whether she heard me. The nurse came in and felt for a pulse, then shook her head at us. Mom was dead. Pete and I walked out of the hospital room feeling more terribly alone than ever before in our lives.

In the weeks that followed, I seemed to have lost all sense of reality. I was young, and yet I was old inside. I would pass children on the street, and their laughter wouldn't penetrate. Pete went back to his base, and I stayed on alone in the apartment, as nearly dead as I could be and still be alive. Daphne became frantic about me, urging me to move in with her and her mother, trying to help me. But I refused. I just wasn't up to adjusting to living with anyone.

"How can I get married if you're going to be so unhappy?" she cried out.

"Have you and George set a date?" I asked.

"We want to be married at Christmas," she said. "And I want you to be my maid of honor, unless you think it's too soon— Oh, Kathie, what can we do for you?"

I realized then how selfish I was in retreating into my own sorrows. I had no right to inflict my unhappiness on people who loved me and whom I loved. I told Daphne to go ahead and plan her wedding. Mom would be the first to say the living must be served. Meanwhile, I decided I didn't want to go back to my job. I hadn't liked it much, and only being there with Daphne had helped me. I knew what I wanted to do. I had watched the nurses at the hospital working their heads off, and I had seen what a need there was for good help. I had no urge to become an RN, but I liked the idea of being a nurse's aide.

I spoke to the supervisor at the hospital, and she agreed to let me enter my name for training. When I told Daphne, she was genuinely pleased.

"I'm glad you're doing something different," she said. "I didn't like leaving you all alone at work—"

"Me and twenty-three other women!" I said. "I'm fine, Daphne, really. I can't go around feeling sorry for myself all my life."

In a way, I was glad Daphne picked Christmas for her wedding. It gave me something to do. I had never been alone before at Christmas. Being in on the plans for her wedding kept me busy and with people, whether I liked it or not. Only once did I get a sick feeling of depression. That was at Daphne's wedding as I stood at her side near the altar. The priest came forward to bless Daphne and George, and for a second I thought it was Matt coming toward me, Matt in clerical robes, his eyes upon me, his smile wide and welcoming.

I closed my eyes, feeling an almost physical stab of pain. Someday Matt would be taking his vows. Someday he would face a couple like Daphne and George. And when he did, would he remember me? And would he feel any regret, any pain at the memory?

In May I finished my training and took a job in the hospital. Because there was a greater need for nurse's aides in the hours between three-thirty and eleven-thirty at night, I took that shift. I also moved to a one-room efficiency apartment near the hospital. That meant breaking my ties with Father Meeghan and the old neighborhood. It also meant that I didn't see Matt's mother anymore in church, although I'd only seen her a half-dozen times since I lost Matt.

A clean break is the best break, I told myself. With my new job and in my new surroundings, I began to come alive once more. I think an elderly man named Louis helped me as much as anyone.

Louis was brought into the hospital after a severe heart attack. He was desperately sick, but he was courageous—a real fighter. I got so I'd sneak into the ward to see him almost as soon as I came on duty.

"Don't you worry about me," Louis told me one afternoon when he was feeling better. "I'm a tough old bird. I was gassed and was out for seven days; then I got pneumonia and pulled through. When my son was away in the Army, I got a stroke that twisted my face up like a pretzel. My daughter was sitting in a chair crying, Mama was in the other chair, and I heard the nurse tell them I was dying. That made me mad, so I sat up and said, 'Mama, I am going to live!'"

I laughed with Louis, and I pulled for him to get well. As he improved, I felt personally pleased, and the day he sat up for the first time, I realized what it means to serve others unselfishly. I had served Louis and pulled for him because I wanted him to live—not for personal reasons, but for himself. It gave me an odd kind of feeling, knowing I was becoming a different person from the self-centered Kathie Matt had once known.

The months passed so quickly that I hardly noticed. I shied away from any personal involvements, and that wasn't too hard to do. My working hours kept me from dating much. Once in a while I'd double-date with a nurse and a couple of interns, but it was just for laughs—nothing serious.

Daphne and George asked me over constantly, and if I didn't see them at least once a month Daphne was on the phone wanting to know if I was forgetting old friends. When she announced she was pregnant, nothing would do except me promising to be godmother to the baby.

Once in a while during that first year after Mom's death, I'd ask myself what I was going to do with my future. What I would do about the days and nights on end that I had to live through. If I must live them alone. But there were no answers.

My brother, Pete, wrote me he had met a girl and wanted to marry her. I wrote back giving my blessing—and feeling old and sad that I couldn't be with him to share his happiness.

Two years passed, years of work and some fun. There were moments when I'd pass a church and think of Matt, times when I'd see someone in a crowd and my heart would leap. And one day I heard my name called and I turned eagerly because it sounded like Matt, but it was only a guy who'd been in high school with me.

One spring another nurse and I went on a vacation in Mexico. We stayed five days in Mexico City and then took the tour to Acapulco. On our way, we stopped in city famous for its handcrafted silver items. We spent the night in a hotel built on a cliff overlooking the small town.

Lily and I had dinner in the hotel and then walked around the town and visited the shops. On our way back to our hotel, we passed a tavern at the foot of the cliff. Here we saw dark-haired, dark-eyed girls in native costume acting as waitresses.

Later, unable to sleep and not wishing to disturb Lily, I got up and stood on the small balcony overlooking the town. The roses' aroma was heavy, and the oleanders grew over the balcony. The moon shone bright on the tiled roofs below. I heard the music from the tavern and felt unaccountably sad.

Then I saw a man and woman embracing in the shadow of the wall leading to the steep steps to the hotel. I watched them unashamedly, and it was then I knew that I could never love another man the way

IN LOVE WITH A PRIEST

I had loved Matt. *I love a priest*—I said the words softly. I couldn't love anyone else. *So I must live in the shadows of life, peering as I was now at flesh-and-blood people in morbid jealousy and need.*

In Acapulco, Lily had a brief but shattering love affair with one of the band players at our hotel, and we returned to our jobs two days earlier than we had anticipated.

A month or so later I was in a restaurant one night with a group from the hospital. Someone was having a birthday, and we had pooled our money to have a feast. I enjoyed myself at these parties. I could be myself and not have to look for a man or pretend that I didn't care that I was alone. Since we all knew one another, it was like one big family.

That night Luigi, the owner of the restaurant, brought a slim, handsome man to our table.

"Here is Renaldo," he said to us with a flourish. "He is the son of a nephew, and he will be an American doctor someday. Renaldo, sit down and learn everyone's name so you can work in the hospital with them."

Renaldo was obviously embarrassed, but he sat down and let us recite our names—for him to forget instantly, I was sure. Much later, when someone put money in the jukebox and pushed tables back to dance, I found myself next to Renaldo.

"Are you really going to be a doctor?" I asked.

"Uncle Luigi thinks so," he said, grinning. "What I am is a pharmacist. In Italy I studied for that, but here I have to take tests all over again to get a license. But Uncle Luigi likes to brag a little bit."

"It's a healthy thing to do," I said, smiling back at him.

"You're a nurse, too?" he asked me.

"No, not really," I said, and explained about being a nurse's aide.

"Like me," he said. "We match up."

"We match up, that's it." I picked up my wineglass. "To a couple of matchups," I said, and we drank.

A few days later I had a call from Renaldo. He had tickets to the opera and wanted me to go with him. The opera in our town was the biggest thing that happened in the month of August. You had to reserve tickets weeks ahead of time. I admired Renaldo's resourcefulness and told him I'd be pleased to go.

Renaldo, I soon found out, was an opera buff—a real expert. I spent the evening being awed by him and later insisted he go to my kind of opera, a little joint out in the sticks where a small combo played the wildest jazz going.

I remember how excited Renaldo got over the music. "It is real America, this music," he told me. "Not opera, but good."

"Not opera, for sure!" I agreed.

I didn't realize until Renaldo had taken me home and kissed me politely on the cheek that I had had a perfectly marvelous time. I even looked forward to seeing him again, something that hadn't happened to me in a long time.

What I enjoyed most about Renaldo was "Americanizing" him, teaching him all there was to know, or at least all that I knew, about being an American.

"You don't have to bow to a woman when you are introduced," I would tease him. "Renaldo, I adore your kissing my hand, but it isn't done here," I would remind him.

One night Renaldo didn't let me go into my apartment immediately. He pressed me close to the wall of the building, and his hands held me so I couldn't move.

"Kathie, you are so lovely," he whispered. "You know what I want, don't you?"

"Yes, Renaldo." I sighed and pushed him away. "But we American girls have some funny ideas about marriage and such."

"Then I will marry you," he said.

I laughed. How wonderful he was, how blunt and beautiful.

"Slow down, Renaldo," I told him.

"Are you afraid of me, *carissima*?"

"No, darling, only afraid for you," I said, knowing that as much as I liked being with Renaldo, I didn't feel for him what I had felt for Matt.

Renaldo pursued me diligently. He called me at all hours, and he showered me with gifts—perfume, candy, flowers. One day when I was in Luigi's with two nurses, Luigi came to our table with a small bottle of wine.

"To taste," he said, pouring some in a glass for me. "Renaldo is a very warm blooded boy, no?"

"Yes," I said. "A nice boy, Luigi. I like him."

"He likes you, too. That is good," he said, smiling.

I felt uncomfortable. It was as though Luigi was putting his stamp of approval on me and Renaldo, and I didn't want to be pushed into anything.

At the time I had lost Matt to the Church, I had been deeply wounded. I had promised myself that I'd never love anyone again as I had loved Matt. I still wasn't sure of myself, even though so much time has passed. Only now and then I did catch myself thinking of Matt, where he was, what he was doing, how he looked in his clerical robes. I'd think of him wearing a surplice and facing a congregation—and then I'd remember a man whose lips were tender on mine, and all the old rebellion and heartache would return to me.

What a waste! I'd cry out in the night. *What a pity!*

Once I even thought of going to Father Meeghan and asking about Matt, but I knew I didn't dare. Matt was beyond my reach now.

One evening I came on duty at the hospital feeling particularly amused with Renaldo. He'd bought me two dozen towels, because I had complained about not finding time to shop for them. *He's dear,* I was thinking, *and I'm a lucky girl to know him.*

I went on duty and was told to spend as much time as I could with a cancer patient in the ward, seeing that he received all the attention he wanted. The nurse had given him an injection to ease his pain, and his family had just gone. I pretended to fluff up his pillow and told him he looked mighty chipper.

"Is it spring yet?" he asked me. I remember that so well.

"Yes, just today it turned spring," I said. "The wind suddenly became balmy and the sky was the most beautiful blue."

He nodded. "We have an old saying in my country, Greece. I don't know who first said it, but it goes like this: 'Just see the time that death has come to overtake me, now that the trees are beginning to bud and the grass begins to turn. . . .'" He closed his eyes and sighed. "I will die now, too. In the spring, the old die—"

"Nonsense," I said. "In the spring, there's new life, you'll see. You'll feel stronger tomorrow morning—I guarantee it."

He didn't contradict me, but somehow I felt he didn't even hear me. I started toward the nurses' station to tell Miss Feeny about the patient's distress, but just then an orderly wheeled a new patient in.

"Bed three," he said to me. "Want to give me a hand? He's out like a light."

I took the foot of the stretcher and pulled it along to the bed. As I did so, I saw the man's face, beaten purple or bruised in an accident, the lips swollen out of proportion, the eyes closed as in death. But it wasn't that that made me gasp. The man on the stretcher was Matt!

I couldn't be mistaken! I glanced down at him again, went close to him and touched his face. "Matt! Oh, Matt! What happened?"

The orderly heard me and thought I was talking to him. "They picked him up outside of town. Someone had beaten the hell out of him, that's for sure. Doctors said it was a concussion, maybe brain damage—the poor jerk is going to hurt when he wakes up. Hey, mind swinging his feet over?"

I picked up Matt's lifeless legs and swung them over toward the bed. My heart was pounding so hard I thought the orderly would hear it. What was Matt doing in this ward? Who had beat him up? And why would anyone beat up a priest?

I don't know why I didn't say something then. I was just so upset about seeing Matt, so shocked at his condition, that I wanted only to make sure he would live. That night I spent every spare moment beside his bed.

His chart gave the name Charles Madison, age twenty-five to thirty. But I knew he wasn't Charles Madison; I knew it was Matt. Before I went off duty, I tried to speak to him, to make him hear me, but he didn't respond. He was still sleeping, thanks to the pain-killing drug the doctor had given him. Still, I just couldn't leave him alone in the ward. I had to do something. Then I thought of Father Meeghan. He'd know what to do!

Late as it was, I called Father as soon as I was off duty.

"Are you sure it's Matt?" he asked me over and over. "You're not mistaken, are you?"

"No, I'm sure," I cried out. "I'd know Matt anywhere. But why is he there like that? Didn't he become a priest?"

There was a long silence, and then Father Meeghan told me that Matt had taken his vows but had not been able to live up to them. Sure as he was when he had gone into the seminary and up to the day he was ordained, his doubts ate at him so that in six months he collapsed completely. He just left his parish one day and no one knew his whereabouts.

Dear God, what Matt must have suffered all this time! I cried silently.

"Father, he's here under an assumed name," I said. "He's listed as Charles Madison."

"I'll get right over there," Father Meeghan said. "Have you told anyone about this?"

"No," I said.

"Good. Now you're not to mention this to anyone,

certainly no one at the hospital," he warned me. "Kathleen, you must obey me in this matter. I cannot tell you how important it is to do exactly as I say."

"Yes, Father," I said, then added, "but I intend to see Matt in the morning. You can't stop me from doing that, Father."

"No, I can't stop you. Only please be careful. Remember what Matt has been through."

Matt was back! That was all I could think of that night as I tried to sleep. Matt had come back. He had not been able to remain a priest, but he had been too ashamed to come to me and admit it. As if I cared! I longed only to hold him close, to comfort him and make him forget all the years we'd been apart.

Father Meeghan was as good as his word. He was with Matt when he woke up, I found out later. The moment Matt recognized his old parish priest, he almost panicked.

"Go away!" he begged Father Meeghan. "Pretend you've never seen me! I don't deserve to talk to you! I am the worst of sinners. Do you know what I've done? Do you?"

Father Meeghan told me some of it—I suppose because he was trying to enlist my aid in helping Matt. All I knew was that he was back, he was no longer a priest, and he needed help. I would give it to him.

I went to the hospital early the next afternoon, my heart hammering because I wasn't sure if Matt would accept me. I went to the ward. The curtain around his bed was drawn. For one awful moment I thought he might have died. I hurried toward his bed and looked around the curtain. Matt was lying in bed, his eyes closed, the picture of dejection.

"Matt," I said. "Matt, it's Kathie."

His whole body stiffened, and for a moment, I thought he would turn his face away. But he opened his eyes, and they were black with suffering, deep suffering.

"Oh, Matt!" I cried, kneeling beside his bed and taking his hand. "Matt, get well. Please, be well again!"

I was crying, my tears falling on his hand. He withdrew his hand and touched the top of my head. I looked at him, and he was crying, too—slow tears that broke my heart.

"I don't care, Matt! Whatever happened, I don't care," I sobbed. "I don't even want to know. I still love you. Let me help you—just let me be here with you!"

"Kathie, my poor Kathie," he said. "I've sinned against you, too!"

"No, Matt! Don't talk like that," I begged.

"I couldn't make it, Kathie," he said bitterly. "In the seminary, I made myself obey. I even exulted in the hardship—no privacy, no quarter given, discipline and study. I took it all. I realized that deep inside my doubts still lingered, but I fought them like St. Michael, the archangel, fought Lucifer and sent him to hell. I thought I had won, too. The day I was ordained, I felt sure I had sent my dark angels to hell."

"You never wrote. I never where you were," I said.

"I was sent to a small parish in Oregon," he told me. "There was a saintly old priest there. I followed him around like a puppy dog, hoping that his faith and dedication would rub off on me. But I couldn't live that life, Kathie. I couldn't cope with my problems, let alone the problems brought to me by our parishioners.

"One night I even got in my car and drove a hundred miles to a strange town. I didn't wear my collar. I went into a bar and ordered a drink. I stood next to a girl and smelled her perfume and thought about you. I started to shake, and I had another drink. When I finished, I was dead drunk. Later I found myself in my car, all my money gone. I didn't know what I had done.

"I went back to my parish, but I felt filthy. I couldn't say Mass—it would have been sacrilege—and yet I couldn't bring myself to confess my guilt to the pastor, my superior. And so I ran away with just the clothes on my back.

"That night I slept in the car. The next day I worked five hours washing dishes in a diner for a meal and five bucks. I kept on going. For three months I wandered. On Sunday, I'd find myself standing outside a church trembling, because I couldn't go in—because I couldn't receive the sacraments!"

His voice broke. He turned his face away, and the bed shuddered with his sobs.

I put my arms around him and held him close. He reached for me, not in passion or in love, but as a child reached for his mother to comfort him.

Father Meeghan found us like that, tearful and shaken. He patted my shoulder and asked me to give him a few moments with Matt. I had to get to work, so I told him I'd be by later.

I felt absolutely drained when I left Matt. It was as

though I had come through a long siege of illness and finally I was being forced to start living again. I had Matt back now. It didn't matter that he was ill and broken in spirit. I would nurse him hack to health. I would stand by, offering my understanding and my love. It had been wrong for him to be a priest, and now it was over.

Father Meeghan found me before he left. He said he was going to take Matt to the rectory with him and see that he was taken care of. He didn't want him in the hospital too long, and since his illness was more of the soul than the body he could probably leave the next day.

"Did he tell you how he got here?" I asked.

"He couldn't stay away from home," the priest said. "He came here two weeks ago. He has seen his mother, but without her knowing it. He watched you, too. He wanted to come to me, but he was ashamed. Poor Matt! What devils must have tormented him as he walked these streets!

"He took a jab digging a trench for that new sewer on the edge of town. It was a temporary job. When he got paid night before last, someone followed him and mugged him. He's been abusing himself so much that he was too weak to resist. He got badly beaten and was left on the street. A passerby called an ambulance."

It was incredible that so much that was bad could have happened to Matt. I remembered him as young and handsome and proud. To think of him wandering the streets was almost as impossible for me to believe as to think of him as a priest at the altar saying Mass.

"I am going to see Matt, Father," I told the priest.

"Let him rest, child," Father Meeghan said. "He has gone through the fires of hell. Let him be for a while."

"Not this time, Father," I said. "Matt has come back to me. This time he belongs to me—and no one will separate us again!"

The next day Matt went to the rectory with Father Meeghan. I said I would visit him the next day, my day off. Matt seemed listless, glad to be taken care of, and almost pathetic in his trust in Father Meeghan.

We'll be married, I told myself. *I'll take care of Matt. Slowly he'll get over this nightmare, and we'll make a life for ourselves. We might even move away. That would be wisest, to move somewhere new and build our life together.*

When I visited Matt the following day, I found him up and about. He looked terribly thin, but at least the bruises on his face had faded almost completely. He seemed happy to see me, and we drank coffee and talked. Mrs. Porter, the housekeeper, had nodded politely at me when she brought our coffee into the parlor, and I'd wondered just how much she knew about Matt.

"How long have you been a nurse?" he asked me.

"I'm not really a nurse," I told him. "I'm a nurse's aide. I like the work."

"In all this time, Kathie, haven't you found someone to love?" he asked.

"I have loved someone all this time," I said. "I have loved you."

"Don't, Kathie—don't!" he cried out. "Don't make me feel worse than I do! I've ruined your life, too!"

"No, Matt, no," I said. "Can't you see? I couldn't

love anyone but you. When you left, I just stopped looking."

"I hurt you," he said, his eyes holding mine.

"Yes," I told him. "I didn't understand any of it— why you felt you had to be a priest."

"I was so sure." He pounded one hand into the other. "I was positive it was my calling.'

"Have you seen your mother?" I asked.

"God help me, I haven't the courage."

"What are you going to do?" I asked.

"I don't know." He spread out his hands. "I feel lost—confused. I wake up in the morning, and I tell myself I have to live just that one day and no more. I don't dare look ahead."

"Try!" I leaned toward him. "Matt, try looking ahead with me! We can build a life for ourselves now. I love you. My love is strong enough to see us through this. Believe in that!"

"How good you are, Kathie," he said. "What bad fate set me on your path?"

"Don't talk like that," I pleaded with him. "Fate sent you back to me, and that's all that matters."

A few minutes after that I left, promising to come back soon.

That night at supper one of the nurses asked me to stop in at Luigi's with her after work. She was depressed because her boyfriend was in Iraq and she hadn't heard from him in more than two weeks. I felt sorry for her. I knew how she must have been feeling.

When we got off duty, we walked over to Luigi's. We ordered some food, and Luigi brought us each a glass of wine. I hadn't told anyone about Matt, of course.

Suddenly Renaldo walked into the restaurant. He was all dressed up, as though he had been somewhere.

"Kathie!" He grabbed both my hands and sat down next to me. "I tried to call you. I had tickets to the last opera. It was magnificent!"

I smiled at Renaldo. How like a child he was, untouched by the world, happy as only someone who has not suffered can be happy.

"An old friend of mine is in town, and I've been busy," I said.

"Stop being so busy then and say you will go with me Sunday to the festival."

The Mexican festival was a yearly event in our town, and I had gone a couple of times. There was lots of food and music, and the people were generous and friendly.

"I'll let you know," I told Renaldo.

I didn't want to hurt him, and yet I wanted to be with Matt every moment that I could. Renaldo chattered away with us for the next hour or so, and finally Luigi said he was going home and we could close up. Renaldo took my friend home first, and then he drove me back to my apartment near the hospital. At the entrance, he took my hands in his and pressed them to his chest.

"Hear how my heart beats," he said. "Do you know what it is saying?"

"Yes." I tried to withdraw my hands. "It is late, and I have to go inside."

"Kathie, Kathie," he whispered, and his mouth closed over mine in a sudden, passionate kiss. I pushed him away and turned to go inside. I was angry. I didn't want Renaldo or any other man to kiss me. Now that Matt was back, I could wait a little while longer for a woman's kind of love.

Two days later, however, when I called the rectory to ask about Matt, I was told he had gone away. "Gone where?" I asked the housekeeper.

"I don't know, miss," she said.

"Let me speak to Father Meeghan," I said.

"He's hearing confessions now," she told me.

I had an hour before I had to go to work. I took a taxi and went to wait for Father Meeghan. Finally he came out of the confessional booth, and I hurried out of the church to wait for him.

"Where's Matt?" I asked as he came out the side door.

"He's gone home, Kathie," he told me.

"Home?"

"To his mother," he said. "He had to start somewhere. He can't go on hiding."

"No, no!" I was confused. I hadn't thought that he would want to go home to his mother. I had hoped he'd come to me.

Father Meeghan urged me to talk a moment.

"Kathie, it isn't the same with Matt," he said to me. "He's not the same man. Don't ask him to be. He's a priest. He has fallen. Now he is lost and sick, truly sick. Let him heal—let him decide what he will do now."

"What's there to decide?" I cried out. "When he begins to feel less guilty about what he has done, we can be married. We can go away somewhere so no one will ever know. Father, Matt needs me. I can make him happy!"

"Are you so sure?" he asked.

"I am sure," I told him.

"Then wait," he advised me. "Give his soul a chance to heal."

But I was afraid. All that evening at work I was afraid of something I couldn't define. I had found Matt, I had taken him to Father Meeghan, I had helped him to look up again. He was mine now!

The next day I came to a decision. I needed to be strong for both of us now, for both myself and Matt. I would take what money I had saved, and we would go away and be married. Later, Matt could find a job or learn a trade. Meanwhile I could always work. Nurse's aides, like nurses, were always in demand.

I went to Matt's mother's house the next day. When she opened the door, she looked at me blankly.

"I came to see Matt," I told her. "I'm Kathie."

"Oh." She wrung her hands together frantically, but she let me pass. He was sitting in the small living room reading a book. He jumped up when he saw me.

"Kathie! Did Father Meeghan tell you I was here? I'd have got in touch as soon as—as soon—" He let the sentence hang.

His mother looked pale, and her face was the face of someone in pain. I didn't know what to say or do. I wished she'd go away so I could talk to Matt.

"I'll bring some fresh coffee," she said. She acted as though she was in mourning and unable to comprehend what was going on about her.

When she was out of the room, Matt said, "She's been hit hard by this. She just can't believe it." He went to stand at the window and look out on the street. "If a heart can be broken, hers has been. Oh,

IN LOVE WITH A PRIEST

Kathie, why do I bring nothing but unhappiness to everyone? What is it in me? Is the devil so strong that he leads me by the nose?"

"Don't say that," I cried out. "Matt, please—think about us!"

"Us?" He looked at me bleakly. "Kathie, I'm nothing! Don't you realize that? I can't go to church, I can't take communion."

"We'll ask Father Meeghan—he'll know," I pleaded. "He'll find out how you can get back into the Church! You didn't kill, Matt, or commit such a terrible crime!"

"I did, I did!" he shouted. "Understand that! I broke my vow to God!"

He had spoken so loudly that I jumped up from my chair. I'd never before seen such violence in him. And then there was a terrible crash in the kitchen and a thud.

I think both of were suspended in space a second. Then Matt was racing toward the kitchen, with me at his side. His mother was on the floor, her face terribly twisted, her body twitching, and she was choking on her own tongue. I knew enough to realize she had had a bad stroke.

Matt bent over and tried to raise her head where blood from a cut on her forehead was dripping.

"Mother! Mother!" he cried.

I ran for a spoon and got down beside Matt and fought to insert the spoon in her mouth as a tongue depressor so she could breathe. Her eyes rolled backward, and she fell limp against Matt's arms.

"Call a doctor, an ambulance," I said, but he just held his mother.

"Forgive me, Mother. Forgive me, Mother," he

cried.

I ran into the hallway and picked up the phone. I dialed the hospital and asked for an ambulance right away. Then I ran back into the kitchen. I will never forget what I saw there.

Matt had laid his mother on the floor again, and he was kneeling beside her. I watched as he slowly made the sign of the cross, passed his hands over his mother's eyes and closed them, and then began to recite the prayer of absolution.

"Hail Mary, full of grace!" The prayer came unbidden to my lips, but I couldn't finish it—I was crying too hard. My tears were flowing for Matt—dear, shattered, soul-sick Matt who, in that terrible moment, had become a priest again.

I don't know how long we were there—Matt kneeling by his mother's side, me standing in the doorway with the tears streaming down my face—before the ambulance came. But finally the doorbell rang, and I hurried to let in the doctor. When he came into the kitchen, Matt got slowly to his feet and stumbled away. I spoke to the doctor, telling him what had happened, and he told the attendants to put Matt's mother on the stretcher. I went to get Matt and I found him standing by the living-room window, his hands clasped in prayer, his head bent. In that moment I approached him almost reverently.

"Matt, I'll go with you to the hospital," I said.

He turned to me as though seeing me for the first time. "She's dead, Kathie. She's been ill, she told me. Dear God, am I to blame for this, too?"

"No, Matt, no!" I cried out. "It would have happened anyway."

He turned and walked out of the house. I didn't

follow him. I felt that he needed to be alone. I picked up in the kitchen, and then I locked up the house and went to the hospital. When I got there, I found out Matt's mother had died, had probably been dead when she was taken out of the house. I had no idea where he had gone. I called Father Meeghan, but he didn't know. He asked me just to be patient.

"Matt will come back," he said to me.

But I wasn't so sure. I should have followed him, I told myself. I should never have left him alone. He needed me beside him to help fight the devils that were tormenting him. Later, I found out Matt called Father Meeghan and asked him to make all the arrangements for his mother's funeral.

I have no idea what went on in Matt's mind the next three days. He spent a great deal of that time kneeling and praying beside his mother's coffin. At the wake, he sat beside me, his head bent, his lips moving in prayer. And later, at the cemetery, I heard him sob only once as his mother was lowered into the grave.

The agony of Matt's sorrow tore at me, and I cried quietly. It seemed as though all this was too much for one person to bear. *Is there a reason?* I wanted to cry out. *Oh, God, why must Your children be torn and crushed like this?*

Once the funeral was over, I wanted only to be with Matt, to shield him and to stand by his side. I took time off from my job so I could be with him. But in the days that followed his mother's death, Matt was unusually withdrawn. Each time that I went over to help sort out his mother's things—as he'd asked me to do—I'd find him in deep thought. He'd look at me as though seeing me for the first time.

IN LOVE WITH A PRIEST

Once I threw myself in his arms and tried to give him some of my strength.

"Matt, let's go away now," I said. "There's nothing but unhappiness here. Let's go far away and start fresh. I love you. I'll make you forget—I'll make you happy. Love me, Matt!"

He held me close, and he kissed me tenderly. "Poor Kathie," he said.

I began to feel that now he would find his way back to me. It might be hard, but one day he'd be the Matt I had known—one day we'd put all this behind us.

But he began to spend more and more time at the rectory. Nights when I'd take time off to call him from work, he wouldn't be home. When I asked him, he'd tell me he had been with Father Meeghan.

"Why, Matt? Why do you keep torturing yourself?" I pleaded with him.

"I need time," he told me. "I need to think this through."

I went to Father Meeghan.

"Help us," I said. "At least tell Matt that we belong together."

"Kathie, do you want half a man?" Father Meeghan asked. "Because that's what Matt is. He's suspended between two worlds. He can't be a full man in either one. But I have been making inquiries, and I have made a suggestion to him. I want you to help him do what he must do."

I felt a chill, the first premonition of what was to come.

"There is a place for people like Matt to go, men who have fallen from the priesthood," he explained slowly. "There they are helped to return to their vocation. They are rehabilitated, not treated as outcasts. They are given a second chance to serve God. Most of them make it. I have urged Matt to go there. Help him to go, Kathie!"

"No!" I cried out. "I will not let him go back again! I will not lose him another time! You mustn't ask me to!"

"But you don't really have him, do you?" Father Meeghan said gently.

"Yes, yes," I said. "When he talks to you, you confuse him. I want to hear him say he will go away again! I want to talk to Matt!"

"He's in the church," Father Meeghan said.

I ran out of the rectory and into the church. I saw Matt immediately.

"Matt, Matt!" I touched him, and he shuddered. "Please come with me!"

He looked at me, and his eyes were no longer tormented and dark. He looked at me, and it was a compassionate look, as though he were feeling sorry for me and would help me if he could.

Slowly he got to his feet and helped me to mine. We went outside, and I turned to him.

"Don't go, Matt," I pleaded with him. "Stay with me. Please—I love you. Somehow we can make things work out! God can't be cruel!"

"No, He's not cruel, Kathie. He's forgiving," Matt told me. "You can't know the demons that have tormented me for so many days. Hating my weakness was the worst of it. I can't go through life being weak, Kathie. I want to be strong. I want to be a priest. Now I know. I knew it the very moment my mother died in my arms. Kathie, wherever I go from now on, whatever I do, I will always be a priest.

IN LOVE WITH A PRIEST

Don't you see? It's marked on my soul! I want to be a priest! I want to go back to serve God!"

"And me? What about me?" The wail was familiar. Once before I had cried the same cry.

"I could never be a husband to you, Kathie."

He was lost to me already. I could see it in his eyes, in the way he turned away from me and looked back into the dim church. He had never really belonged to me, not even before I lost him the first time, not now when he had chosen to go back.

I turned and ran. I looked back once, and Matt was still standing by the church door looking in.

I didn't see Matt again after that I didn't want to— I didn't dare. But losing him the second time was even harder than the first. I was so much older, and I'd had such hopes, such dreams, when he came back to me.

It was my brother, Pete, who rescued me from despair. He'd just got out of the Navy, and he and his wife and baby decided to settle in a city about two hundred miles from where I lived so he could attend school and learn a trade. He wrote and asked me to come visit them, and I accepted gratefully.

After I'd been there two weeks, I decided to stay. At first I lived with Pete and his family, but the apartment was small and I knew I had no right to intrude upon their lives. By then I'd taken a job in a hospital, so it was just a matter of finding a place of my own.

The owner of my small apartment house is a widower named Eric. One day when I went down to give him a check for my rent, he invited me in for coffee. We talked for a little while, and found that we liked each other. Since then, we see each other occasionally—for movie dates, for walks, for more quiet conversations over coffee.

What does it mean—my friendship with Eric? I honestly don't know. He will never take Matt's place in my heart—no man could ever do that. But perhaps he will make a place of his own. I hope he will, because I am lonely and tired of living such a barren life. I want to love again and be loved.

And so, secretly, I pray that Eric will be the one. . . .

THE END

WE LOST IT ALL!

The door to the shelter opened, and we lined up along with over a hundred other people. "Mom, I'm cold," Jenna said. She looked up at me with those big eyes of hers and hung on to my coat.

"We'll go in soon," I told my youngest daughter. Her sister, Macy, stood and watched the other people waiting to get in. She was quiet, her eyes betraying her fear. Macy was the oldest—old enough to know something was really wrong.

I knew I was afraid. I hated coming to the homeless shelter but felt we had no choice. After weeks of living in our car, I had decided to bring my kids to the shelter at night.

When our turn came, we registered with a woman at the desk. She looked as though she had seen it all at some point in life. Her eyes betrayed a deep hostility.

The three of us made our way to our assigned beds—due to the number of people, we had to double up. Jenna and I would sleep together.

Actually, the beds were cots. But there were two warm blankets on each, even if there were no pillows. Our section was roped off for women and children only. Still, we had no privacy in our area, and we all slept together in one big room.

The shelter was set up in what had once been a furniture store. The carpeting had been removed long ago and the concrete floor was cold. But it was warmer there than in the car, and I was thankful for that.

Jenna had a hard time settling down. She went to the bathroom several times. When she returned, she sat down and bounced on the cot.

The nasty woman at the desk came around to tell us we would be woken up at five in the morning and would have to be out of the shelter by six. She reminded me of a snarling cat when she made her little announcement. Why did she have to treat us so meanly, anyway? Did she think any of us wanted to be there?

As I lay back on the cot, exhausted physically from working all day as a waitress at the local diner, and exhausted emotionally from the recent events in my life, sleep was slow in coming. I thought about my life and how I got to this humble situation in the first place.

Gus and I had met in high school and dated for a year. It was a small school, and we all knew each other. His family had moved to town right before his senior year. He was a good athlete and had resented moving to a small town after playing football in the large high school he had attended.

But Gus managed to adjust and was an imme-

WE LOST IT ALL!

diate hit with all the seniors, especially the girls. One day he said, "Beth, how about getting a hamburger after school today?" We started dating after that.

Why he picked me as his girlfriend I never knew, but I was sure glad he did. He had the broadest shoulders and biggest smile I had ever seen. For me, it was love at first sight. He always said it was for him, too, and he made my heart glow.

We were married right out of school. I worked as a waitress for a while, and he got a job as a concrete laborer. Macy was born a year later, and I became pregnant with Jenna soon after.

When the company that Gus worked for folded, we moved to a larger city. We both found jobs and worked there for almost five years. It was a good time in our lives, I realized later. We only had a small apartment, but we managed to pay the bills, eat out once in awhile, and see movies. I even took Macy ice-skating and brought Jenna to dancing school.

Macy, my beautiful oldest daughter, was such a good student. She was happy and outgoing and always surrounded by friends.

Jenna was full of energy that never seemed to dissipate. She was a tomboy, and she loved playing baseball with her father. I loved them so much. . . .

But, once again, the demand for concrete workers dried up. Although I was working, I couldn't support the four of us. Both of our families were having hard times, and we couldn't ask them for help. We decided to move west, where we heard the economy was booming and the housing industry was in full swing.

We loaded our few belongings in our old car and headed west. We had never been in that part of the United States and, although it was pretty country, we were all homesick. Still, we felt we had no choice.

We had just enough money for gas and food. We slept at rest stops along the way. There were other couples with their kids at the stops, too, all heading away from the depressed economy that we were leaving. We talked with some of them. Their dreams were the same as ours—steady jobs, roofs over their heads, and good schools for the children.

One couple we talked with had three children and had stayed with her parents for six months. The five of them lived in one bedroom. Neither was able to find steady work. Finally, her mother had kicked them out. They were as worried as we were.

We spent a week in one city, but were unable to find jobs. Our car battery died, and it took the last of our money to get a new one. We had slept in the car overnight on the outskirts of the city; we couldn't even afford one of the cheap hotels. Then it was time to move on. My husband decided to drive farther west.

Finally, in one small city, out of gas and money, we pulled up to a restaurant that had a sign advertising for a waitress. I walked in and, in spite of the fact I had now slept in the car for several weeks, had washed up in gas-station bathrooms, and had clothes that were wrinkled, the manager hired me.

My kids were both crying from hunger—it had been two days without food, and I asked the manager if we could eat first, taking what I owed him out of my wages. He agreed to it, and we all had a big meal for the first time in many days.

"Mom, when will we move to our new house?" Macy asked as we ate our dinner. Gus and I just looked at each other.

"The manager says we can park our car out back in the parking lot," I said. "I'm sorry, honey, but we will have to sleep in the car for a while longer."

Macy started to cry. I put my arm around her little shoulders, but she shrugged it away. As hungry as she was, I couldn't coax her to finish her meal, and it was a hot turkey sandwich, one of her favorites.

Jenna was so excited to be eating in a restaurant that she even had trouble sitting long enough to eat. "She's going to need special help in school, I think," I told Gus. "She's so active! I hope we can find a good school when we get settled, and that she will have a patient teacher."

We were surprised at the cool weather at night in the west. We had thought the weather was always warm, even at night. But we had plenty of blankets, and we felt lucky compared to the people we saw sleeping on the streets. Gus started looking for work early the next morning. He said he would be back before my shift started at noon.

"Come on, you two, the restaurant manager said we could use the rest rooms to clean up."

WE LOST IT ALL!

They hadn't slept well—none of us had, since we started sleeping in the car. It was big, but still not meant for a family to sleep in.

"Mom, can we go to the zoo today?" Jenna asked. "I heard they have a real good one near here."

"No, we don't have enough money, honey. But maybe we can walk to a park I saw a few miles away."

My little girl pouted. Not what she wanted, I knew. She bounced up and down on the car seat. "Look, Mom! Who is that guy anyway?"

A grubby man walked up to the car. His filthy hair was long and matted. He wore an old, torn coat over a jacket that looked even worse. And all over that were what looked like layers of clothes—stained shirts and several pairs of pants. And he was barefoot.

He started shouting at us. Macy screamed and hid under a blanket and I yelled at him. "Get out of here! Leave us alone! We have no money."

He banged on the front window of the car with his fist. I was scared, angry, and humiliated that my children had to see this. A car stopped and I thanked God that it was a police car. The man ran, but the cops easily caught up to him, and took him to the squad car.

One of the policemen walked over to our car after a few minutes. I opened the window, sure we'd probably be arrested or something for parking where we were.

"Hi. I'm Officer Tate. Sorry about that guy bothering you. We've had trouble with him for a long time. We'll take him to the local rehab center where he'll dry out for a few days. I'm afraid he'll be back after that, though. You folks need any help?"

I looked up at the man. He had a nice smile, and he seemed to genuinely want to help. For some reason, I just started to cry. So did both my kids, and that made me cry even more.

"I'm sorry," I said. "We've been living in this car for weeks now, and we're exhausted. I work in the restaurant over there. My husband is out looking for work."

"Maybe I can help you. Have you heard about the homeless shelter the city has on Main Street?"

Well, I hadn't. But I couldn't see us in some shelter with a bunch of men, a lot of them alcoholics like the one who had banged on our car window. He could see the doubt in my eyes.

"The shelter has a special section for families, or single women with children. You would be safe there," the policeman said. "There are food banks in town, too."

"I hate for us to take welfare," I said. "We have always taken care of ourselves until a few months ago."

"But you have your kids to think of, and there are many people in the same boat you are in. This shelter is a temporary home, until you can get back on your feet," he said.

He wrote down the address and phone number. Then he reached behind me and tickled Jenna's chin. "Take care," he said. "I'll check on you tomorrow."

I sat there after the squad car left. I knew Gus

was dead set against taking handouts. But my kids were showing the results of our wandering. Macy was becoming more withdrawn every day. She no longer read or colored. She just sat and stared out the car window. And being cooped up was taking its toll on Jenna, who needed to run and play and get rid of her excess energy.

Jenna woke me from my thoughts. "Mommy, I have to go to the bathroom."

"Okay, honey. We'll use the one in the restaurant. And be quiet in there. Don't go bouncing around. I don't want to lose my job. My boss has been good to me, but I'm sure there's a limit to even his patience."

After leaving the restaurant, where I had to tell Jenna that she couldn't have a hamburger because there was no money for one, I told the kids we were going for a walk. We walked five blocks to one of the food banks on the list, and went inside.

Boxes and sacks were lined up against one wall. Men and women were writing on forms while the employees filled containers with food. I just stood and stared. I had never, ever thought I would be in such a situation.

"May I help you?" I turned and looked at an elderly woman with a smile on her face. "Do you want to sign up for food?" she asked.

"Well, yes, I guess I do," I said. "My husband doesn't have a job, and I work as a waitress and . . ."

"You don't need to tell me the details now," she said. "Here's a form for you to fill out. Only takes a minute. Then a minute for us to review it, and we'll have a box of food ready for you."

True to her word, there was a box filled with food ready for us in about twenty minutes. It wasn't filled with hamburgers, such as Jenna wanted, but it did contain cereals, canned goods, fruit, and juices. One of the workers even volunteered to drive us back to our car.

On the way, he told us about the food bank and about himself. "I've been working there a year now. When I moved here, I couldn't find a job. I've seen a lot of people come in for help, many of them like you—women with children." He was an elderly gentleman, dressed in old— but clean—slacks and a shirt, and he explained he was driving the car that belonged to the agency's director. The director paid for the gas herself, to drive people like us wherever we had to go.

Jenna was excited—I had to turn around a few times with a stare that she knew meant "sit still"—but Macy sat quietly. She worried me. My vibrant little girl, with the bright personality and infectious grin, had become so quiet and withdrawn. . . .

When we arrived back at the parking lot, Gus was there. He had the same expression as Macy—withdrawn.

We thanked the man again for the food and for driving us back. The kids and I put the box of food in our car.

Gus just sat and watched us. He didn't even get out to thank the man or to help. I got in the front seat of our car and looked at him. Neither of us said anything for about five minutes. My husband looked, well, beat, I guess. He needed a haircut—we had no money for it—and his shirt, even though clean, had hung on a hanger in the car and needed to be ironed. He leaned back against the car seat and closed his eyes.

My heart went out to him. I loved him. We had been through so much together in the last few months. And I knew he was a good man.

Finally, he told me about his morning. "I've been to every place I can think of. A few places let me fill out an application, but most places weren't even hiring. When I did get to fill out an application, I didn't even have an address to write down! Once they saw that line blank, they weren't interested in talking to me."

He had tears in the corners of his eyes. I had never seen Gus so down, so depressed.

"A couple of policemen came by today," I said. "They told us where we can spend the night in a shelter. We've got to go there tonight, honey."

"No! My family isn't going to one of those places," he shouted. "I've read about them. They're dangerous places to be. I won't have my wife and kids there."

"We have to go. We can't live in the car any longer. The food bank gave us some supplies, but we have to sleep someplace else. I'm really worried about our kids," I insisted.

We argued—it was something the kids didn't need to hear, but I guess the stress had finally just come out for both of us. Our words were bitter. My husband accused me of not trusting him, not believing in him.

"We're going to the shelter as soon as I get off

work," I told him.

Later, loud snoring from the woman in the cot next to us brought me back to the shelter and away from my troubled thoughts. I was thankful that my daughters had fallen asleep.

At five, I dragged the kids to the bathroom and onto the street. We walked the few blocks back to our car. Gus was waiting for us. He helped the kids bundle up in the car before he left to job hunt. There were no words between us—we didn't even meet each other's eyes.

Jenna's hyperactivity was increasing. After several days, she just couldn't sit still, and I took her to a park a few blocks away so she could run and play. But then, who could blame a healthy little girl who spent mornings cooped up in a car?

Gus had had no luck in finding a job. He was a good worker, and an honest man. I wanted to shout it to the world! His depression was taking its toll on us all. I had to force myself to be cheerful at work.

I hadn't seen the policeman since the day he arrested the dirty man who banged on our car window. I made pretty good tips at the restaurant, and the manager let us continue to park in the back of the lot. "But it's not for forever, Beth," he'd warned.

We still couldn't move into an apartment because we didn't have the money for the deposit and first and last month's rent. Each night, the kids and I returned to the shelter. Gus and I argued, but he refused to go. After four nights there, I was still lying awake most of the night.

I guess I must have fallen asleep one night, though, because the next thing I knew, the nasty woman who handled the family section was shaking me and telling me it was five—time to get up.

It was cold out and a wind was blowing, and it was still dark. We walked back to the car. My husband was gone. He left early every morning and looked for work, but he had always waited for us, to make sure we got back okay. Although we had said little to each other recently, he had always waited.

"Where's Daddy?" Jenna asked. "I want my daddy."

"I don't know, Jenna. Climb in the backseat and go back to sleep for a few hours now."

As usual, Macy said nothing. Jenna, after being woken up at five and pushed out on the street on a cold, dark, windy morning, was not ready to sleep. She started bouncing up and down, crying that she was hungry.

I turned around and slapped her. I couldn't believe I had done that. "I'm sorry, honey. I'm sorry," I told her. "Please, just lie back and sleep for a while. We'll eat when the sun comes up."

Where was Gus? Why hadn't he waited until we got back from the shelter? Unable to sleep, I sat and watched the life going on around me. A man hurried by, his briefcase in one hand. *How lucky,* I thought, *to have a job to go to.*

The waitresses who worked the morning shift arrived and parked their cars close to mine. Sadie, an older woman, came over to say good morning and smile. She was a good waitress, and she had been friendly to me. I waved back.

A newspaper boy rode by on his bicycle. He turned around and came back to the car. "Want a paper?" he asked kindly. "I've got an extra today."

"Sure," I told him. I hadn't read a paper in a month.

As I started to open the front page, I saw a squad car drive up. The same big cop got out and walked over to our car. "How are you folks doing today?" he asked. "I couldn't get back here before now."

"We're hanging in there," I said. "I guess that's about it. But thanks for telling us about the shelter. They aren't real friendly over there, but at least it's a place to sleep for the night."

"My captain told me about another place," he said. "A few blocks away, but it's run by a group trying to help families." He wrote down the address. "I think you'll find they are friendly and helpful. You can even leave the kids there during the day. And they help people find work. Give them a try."

He wrote down his name and phone number, too. "You need any more help, you give me a call, okay? I'll drive by every day or so and see how you're doing."

He reached over again and patted Jenna on the shoulder. But when he reached for Macy, she shrank away from him, and turned her head. He took his hand away and watched her for a minute, and gave me a questioning look. I just shook my head sadly.

WE LOST IT ALL!

I thanked him. After he left, the kids and I went into the restaurant rest room and washed up. I made them hurry, since I didn't want the manager to see us. I knew I was pushing my luck in that department already.

We went back to the car and ate cereal and drank juice. Macy wasn't hungry, and she ate very little. I looked at her pale face. Her little arms were thinner than only a week ago. She had lost weight, and I hadn't seen a smile on her pretty face in weeks. I couldn't even seem to get much of a response of any kind out of her.

We walked to the park—Macy didn't want to go, but I insisted—and Jenna got a chance to run around, plus go on the swings and the slide. "This is super, Mommy," she said.

"I hope I never have to go back to school."

But I knew my children belonged in school. And I knew both my kids needed help—help I couldn't afford to get them. I thought my problems would overwhelm me then. I hid my tears, since Jenna and Macy had enough problems without seeing their mom crying.

Where was Gus? I prayed he would be at the car when we returned.

But when we got back a few hours later, he wasn't there. I made the kids sandwiches. Since it was my day off, I told them we would walk to the new shelter and sign up. Neither of them wanted to go for another long walk, but I insisted.

As we walked to the shelter, we passed a bike shop. Jenna looked in the window.

"Mommy, that's the one I want! See,

Mommy?" Oh, God—would I ever be able to buy things for my children? I only wanted to give both my children the things most kids had—bicycles, nice clothes, and camp in the summer.

The new shelter was farther than I thought. We were all tired when we got there. The building was sure different than the other place we had been staying in. The floors were swept clean, there were comfortable chairs to sit on, and a drinking fountain—the first thing we all headed for.

But more importantly, we were greeted with a smile. "May I help you?" a kindly woman asked. She was about my age. She must have been burned or something, because scars covered the right side of her face and went down onto her shoulder. In spite of this, her smile was warm and sincere.

"How about a bowl of soup for the children? And could you use a cup of coffee?" She took a hand of each of the kids and led them to a table in another room. She looked back at me. "Come on. You look like you could use some coffee or tea. My name is Katie, and I'm a volunteer here."

We sat down and were served three bowls of soup. The kids got milk, and I drank coffee. Katie sat down with us, making small talk with the kids, asking where they went to school.

"We don't have to go to school now," Jenna said. "We live in our car."

But Katie's attention was on Macy, who ate little and said nothing. I admired this woman—she was certainly friendly, but did she really understand what we were going through? I pushed resentment out of my mind as best I could, because I knew I had to do this for my children.

I didn't say much as we sat there. I was tired, physically and emotionally. The coffee and corn chowder were good. When we were done, Katie went back into the little kitchen and came out with three pieces of chocolate-fudge cake. She even talked Macy into eating hers.

For the first time in many days, I noticed the hint of a smile on Macy's face. Katie kept talking to her, telling her that she had some books Macy could have, that there was a school nearby, and perhaps she could enroll there. As I quietly watched the two of them, I saw Macy's interest spark, and I was grateful to this new friend.

When we were done, Katie asked another worker to take the girls to the playground out back. She brought more coffee and asked me what it was we needed.

I explained our journey across the United States, and about our problems in surviving.

"Our center is run by private funding," Katie said. "We have twenty families at a time here, and our goal is to help people build a small nest egg—enough for a deposit and month's rent on an apartment. We help people find jobs if need-ed, and we provide child supervision."

"I . . . well, I'm not sure about my husband, Gus. I haven't been able to get him to come to a shelter at night. Today he wasn't there when we got back to the car." I just couldn't help it—I started crying again.

"When I first came here, I came alone, too," Katie said.

WE LOST IT ALL!

"You came for help?" I asked. "I thought you were a volunteer."

"I am now. But two years ago, we were among the homeless. We'd moved here hoping for work. My husband is a building contractor, and he had a good business up north. We owned our home and lived in a nice neighborhood. But one of my husband's employees had a traffic accident, and he was driving the company truck. The lawsuit wiped us out."

She explained that they had come to the shelter, or rather she had come alone. Her husband was too embarrassed and refused to join her. She finally threatened that she would leave him if he didn't at least visit the shelter. Eventually she had won him over, and they had stayed the maximum ten weeks and gotten a start again.

Katie touched the scar on her face. "I'm due for more surgery. My husband says we'll have enough money for it in six months. He worked for another contractor for a year, and then started his own business again—this time with liability insurance. I volunteer here because I am so grateful. And because I know anyone can get caught in this situation."

"Thank you for sharing that," I said. "I will get Gus here, one way or another." As we walked back, I thought of how much I wanted to come to the shelter. I was determined to get my husband to agree.

But he still wasn't at the car. I was worried, but it was time to get to the shelter on Main Street. Macy didn't want to go, and said she would sleep in the car. But with Gus gone, there was no way we would sleep in there.

The nasty woman greeted us in her usual sour mood as we walked in. I knew the routine by heart now. When she opened her mouth, I said, "Yes, I know. Out by six."

The room smelled of urine—someone had had an accident. We shared the uncomfortable cots again and heard a record number of snores that night. But at least we were safe and warm—miserable, but safe and warm. I didn't sleep at all, so I had the kids up and on the street by the time the miserable woman came around to wake people up.

Again, Gus wasn't there when we got back to the car. I didn't know what I would do when it came time for me to go to work. I couldn't leave the kids alone in the car. The shelter on Main Street wouldn't be open, and besides, kids couldn't go there alone.

As we sat and ate dry cereal and drank juice, a squad car drove up. "Look, Mommy," Jenna shouted. "There's Daddy!"

My friend, the kind police officer, was walking to the car with Gus. My husband looked beat— he hadn't shaved in several days, and it looked as if he hadn't bathed or changed clothes. His hair was a mess. I guessed he hadn't combed it, either, and it hung down in his face. His eyes were red and swollen.

"Hi," my policeman friend said. "Your husband told me where he was living, and I remembered you. So I told the other officers I would bring him here. Did you get to the shelter I told you about?"

I told him we had, but that we needed Gus to

WE LOST IT ALL!

go with us in order to stay there. They had room for one family now, and would hold it for us for only twenty-four hours.

Gus lowered his head and told me he had become so upset, he had started a fight in a bar. He had taken his last few dollars and spent it on beer. The police had come, and so here he was. He slumped into the front seat and hung his head.

"I'm going to leave you now," Officer Tate said. "You go to that shelter tonight, hear me? Those are good people. They'll help you back on your feet again." He patted Gus on the shoulder. "You hear me, old buddy?" My husband nodded.

I wrapped my arms around Gus, my love, and hugged him tight. All four of us were crying.

That was six weeks ago. Gus had agreed to go to the shelter and meet Katie. We moved in there that night. They gave us money for gas so I could drive to work.

It hasn't been an easy six weeks. With Katie's help, Gus found work with a furniture-installation company. Katie's husband said that if his business continues to grow, he will hire Gus. In the meantime, my husband is working at minimum wage.

The restaurant gave me more hours when another waitress quit. I get pretty good tips—I work hard for them—but I know now I want to go back to school, maybe a junior college, someday. I would like to study nursing and be sure I will never get caught in this situation again.

We're building a little nest egg. We will have enough money for a small apartment by the time

WE LOST IT ALL!

our ten weeks are up. Macy smiles more now that she is in school. She and Katie have become close friends. When I get the money, I want to get tutoring for Jenna and help for her hyperactivity.

We have each other and that is what is important. The future doesn't look exactly rosy right now, but it looks as if we will make it. And that's all we ask.   THE END